Patsy Cline

Patsy Cline:
The Making of an Icon

D OUGLAS G OMERY
University of Maryland

Order this book online at www.trafford.com
or email orders@trafford.com

Most Trafford titles are also available at major online book retailers.

All photographs courtesy of Celebrating Patsy Cline, Inc.

Printed in the United States of America.

ISBN: 978-1-4269-5988-2 (sc)
ISBN: 978-1-4269-6012-3 (e)

Library of Congress Control Number: 2011903451

Trafford rev. 03/10/2011

www.trafford.com

North America & International
toll-free: 1 888 232 4444 (USA & Canada)
phone: 250 383 6864 ♦ fax: 812 355 4082

CONTENTS

INTRODUCTION

Patsy Cline remains a much beloved singer, even though she died in 1963. Unlike most singers from the past, she has not faded into obscurity; this book seeks to explain her rise to stardom and continued popularity.

By 1996, Patsy Cline had become such an icon that the *New York Times* magazine positioned her among a pantheon of women celebrities who transcended any single cultural genre. A series of essays on "Heroine Worship" included Patsy Cline with such "feminine icons" as Eleanor Roosevelt, Martha Graham, Indira Gandhi, Aretha Franklin, and Jackie Onassis.

The making of an icon is a cultural process that transcends traditional biographical analysis. One does not need to know the whole life story of the subject to understand how the subject became an icon. How was Patsy Cline able to rise above class and poverty to become *the* country music singer that non–country music fans embraced?

Thus far, everything written about Patsy Cline has been based on unverified interviews. This book uses data from archives, letters, and court records—and gives complete endnotes. Since it is about Patsy Cline's long-term popularity, it does not end with her death in 1963. Indeed, the rise of her popularity—as Chapter 1 explains—commenced in 1980.

This book also includes a chapter that analyzes Patsy Cline recordings, such as "Crazy," as complex popular music. I argue that these recordings represent great popular singing, able to appeal across genres and generations.

By the end of the 20th century, few could be considered true icons. This historical analysis of how Patsy Cline rose to iconic status divides into two halves: the first part on how Patsy Cline came to create only 102 songs she recorded in a studio, then an analysis of the complexity of her considerable musical abilities, and then a final section on her increase in popularity. Thus, this book begins not with the birth of Virginia Patterson Hensley (later Patsy Cline) but with the "birth" of her iconography and then explains how she crafted a body of recorded music, then examines why such music is so universal in its appeal, and then ends with an analysis of why Patsy Cline has archived iconic status.

———————————

I thank Marilyn Moon and Judy Sue Huyett-Kempf for making this book possible.

Chapter 1

Patsy Cline Becomes an Icon

In 1980, Hollywood launched the worldwide rediscovery of Patsy Cline. That year an unexpectedly popular film, *Coal Miner's Daughter*, began the elevation of Patsy Cline from the status of just another dead country singing star to that of an icon. New fans embraced her character on screen as the sympathetic friend helping Loretta Lynn. Although actress Beverly D'Angelo, who played Patsy Cline, did her own singing, fans by the millions went out to purchase the recordings of the real Patsy Cline. At the time, major country star Dolly Parton noted, "I think people who may have not liked country music before [the movie] began to like that sound because she had this voice that was just heavenly! [Patsy Cline seemed to say:] 'Hey, I'm a girl and I'm tough, don't mess with me—just let me sing and do my thing.'" [1]

Coal Miner's Daughter is the film biography of Loretta Lynn, released by Hollywood's Universal Studios in March 1980. Blockbusters are not usually released in the spring; so its success was unexpected. The movie told the rags-to-riches tale of a poor country girl struggling to become a singing star, helped by her best friend and mentor, Patsy Cline. Actually the Cline character was not part of the original script, which instead identified the Wilburn Brothers, country music stars of the 1960s, as Lynn's mentors. But the Wilburn brothers and MCA-Universal executives could not come to terms, so the "best friend" angle was added. This change prompted Lew Wasserman, head of Universal, to sell *Coal Miner's Daughter* as a feel-good movie for women, or in Hollywood terms, a "chick flick."[2]

Wasserman was also pleased because his corporation owned the musical rights to half of Patsy Cline's songs. Profit-conscious Wasserman made a great deal of money on the new sales of Patsy Cline recordings. Wasserman's record company (MCA Records) released, publicized, and sold Patsy Cline as a pop singer, one who had taken country music into the mainstream of popular music.[3]

The film industry trade paper *Variety* praised *Coal Miner's Daughter* as a thoughtful, endearing film. *Variety* noted that the film avoided the "sudsy atmosphere common to many showbiz tales," and offered a realistic portrayal of a woman's life as a professional singer, also noting, "Beverly D'Angelo turns in a stellar performance as country singer Patsy Cline." *Variety* proved prophetic. Three weeks into its release, on March 27, 1980, the *Hollywood Reporter* front-page headlines read, "'Coal Miner' Film Strikes Heavy Vein; $16 million in 17 days."[4]

Coal Miner's Daughter relied on features of Loretta Lynn's best-selling autobiography. Patsy Cline came off as tough woman who became a professional singer because of her inner strength and work ethic. But nowhere in *Coal Miner's Daughter* did the filmmakers visualize such traditional "female" tasks as fetching water, cooking on a wood stove, or scrubbing floors, chores Patsy did as she grew up in the Shenandoah Valley of Virginia.

The central tenet of the film rests with Patsy Cline rising above the circumstances of birth and lack of formal musical training to become a star. The movie's narrative ignored the forces of history—the Great Depression, World War II, the suburbanization of the United States, and the coming of television. The filmmakers also passed over any notion that poor, uneducated people suffered most during changing historical conditions, as they had no control over these changes, save to adapt as best they could.[5]

Another boost to Patsy Cline's rediscovery came when Universal hired Owen Bradley to produce the soundtrack for *Coal Miner's Daughter*. Bradley had originally produced the hits of Patsy Cline. Yet he did not merit a role in the movie; he was not part of the narrative myth. He was a critical piece of the story, however, as I will discuss later.

Noted film critic Roger Ebert gave *Coal Miner's Daughter* "two thumbs up," and correctly predicted that it would turn into an "evergreen." In fact, the film appeared constantly on cable TV, then on home video, and in 2005, as a rerelease in a twenty-fifth-anniversary DVD edition. Thus, the movie-going public has continually discovered *Coal Miner's Daughter* since its March 1980 premiered, when first it introduced Patsy Cline to a new generation.[6]

On September 2, 1984, the producer of *Coal Miner's Daughter,* Bernard Schwartz, announced that he had signed Jessica Lange to play Patsy Cline in a movie, *Sweet Dreams.* Production started in November 1984, at a cost of thirteen million. Schwartz proclaimed that the star power of Academy Award–winning actress Jessica Lange would trump the tragic tale that would end with the death of the star. He did not mention that Universal's head, Lew Wasserman, had passed on *Sweet Dreams;* Wasserman, then Hollywood's most powerful movie mogul, knew that there was no Hollywood happy ending here.

Schwartz partnered with the HBO cable TV network, then owned by Columbia Pictures. Jessica Lange was as big a star as there was in Hollywood, and Patsy Cline was a known legend from Coal Miner's Daughter.[7]

JESSICA LANGE · ED HARRIS

SWEET DREAMS

WUSQ
STEREO Q-102 | **Preview**

Thursday, October 10, 1985   8 p.m.

Cinema 6 Theatres
Apple Blossom Mall
Winchester, VA.

Admit One

Proceeds to Benefit
Winchester Exchange Club

HBO PICTURES IN ASSOCIATION WITH SILVER SCREEN PARTNERS
PRESENTS
A BERNARD SCHWARTZ PRODUCTION · A KAREL REISZ FILM
JESSICA LANGE · ED HARRIS · "SWEET DREAMS"
ANN WEDGEWORTH · DAVID CLENNON · MUSIC BY CHARLES GROSS
CO-PRODUCED BY CHARLES MULVEHILL · WRITTEN BY ROBERT GETCHELL
PRODUCED BY BERNARD SCHWARTZ · DIRECTED BY KAREL REISZ
ORIGINAL MOTION PICTURE SOUNDTRACK ALBUM ON MCA RECORDS AND TAPES.
☐☐ DOLBY STEREO   AVAILABLE WHEREVER PAPERBACKS ARE SOLD FROM ST. MARTIN'S PRESS
IN SELECTED THEATRES   A TRI-STAR RELEASE
PG-13 PARENTS STRONGLY CAUTIONED   © 1985 TRI-STAR PICTURES, INC. ALL RIGHTS RESERVED
Some Material May Be Inappropriate for Children Under 13   TRI-STAR PICTURES

"Sweet Dreams Premiere Ticket"

Schwartz hired former Decca vice president Owen Bradley to make the music for *Sweet Dreams,* again remastering Cline's recordings, but this time with Lange lip-synching. Schwartz hired Ed Harris to star as her second husband, Charles Dick (his formal named, which I use throughout this book), and Ann Wedgeworth to play Hilda Hensley, Patsy Cline's mother. Rather than deal with her upbringing, the script started with Dick's initial meeting with Patsy Cline, in 1955, and ended eight years later, with her death. Absent was any examination of the first twenty-three years of Cline's life—her poverty, her learning to sing, her struggles as a woman, or her embracing of pop music.

Sweet Dreams completed principal photography on February 15, 1985, filming in Martinsburg, West Virginia, which stood in for Winchester, Virginia. Other locations included Fort Campbell, Kentucky (standing in for Fort Bragg, where Charles Dick had been stationed while in the U.S. Army), and Nashville. Lange spent three weeks in Nashville, learning to imitate Cline's vocal mannerisms from Owen Bradley. The director, Karel Reisz, was selected by Lange for his reputation based on directing the award-winning *French Lieutenant's Woman* and other serious films about women.[8]

For the movie soundtrack, MCA created an LP and an audio cassette, as something "new." As the film's soundtrack adviser, Owen Bradley, by then 70, got a second chance to redo Cline, creating new instrumentation around her voice on "San Antonio Rose," "Your Cheatin' Heart," and "Half as Much." Saying that he wanted to make it easy for 1980s audiences "to listen to," he stripped off the original instrumentation, and replaced it with a new background that included a fiddler, two trombone players, six saxophone players, two trumpet players, and new background vocals—not the Jordanaires backup group, who performed on the original recordings.[9]

Ironically, Charles Dick's ex–second wife, Jamey Ryan, provided the vocals for two new songs in the movie: "Rollin' in My Sweet Baby's Arms" and "Blue Christmas." Ryan's sound was so close to Cline's that many fans searched Cline's discography trying to find these two songs, but soon discovered that these tracks were recorded solely for the film, on October 12, 1984.

According to Schwartz, the story of Patsy Cline and Charles Dick was to be an affirmation of love and life. "The emotion I heard in Patsy's music made me think she must have been very emotional in life. And everything I read about her, everything people said about her, confirmed that," said Schwartz's Academy-Award-nominated screenplay writer, Robert Getchell (who had been nominated for *Alice Doesn't Live Here Anymore* and *Bound for Glory*). Schwartz chose not to go with a traditional "biopic," but instead to fashion a film based on Cline's rumored negative relationship with Charles Dick. This was a concession to Jessica Lange, who wanted to act in a serious drama, not another chick flick.[10]

We first see Patsy, at the age of twenty-three, singing at the Rainbow Inn, where she belts out songs by Bob Wills and Bill Monroe. Her first husband, Gerald Cline, is portrayed as a quiet, conservative, nondrinking, gentle homebody. Fictional Gerald is made to be boring, and the movie makes boredom Patsy's motivation for responding to the advances of Charles Dick.

Patsy tells Charles that her deepest personal goal as a country singer is to become a happy mother: "I want it all and I want to make it right. . . . Since I've been about eleven or twelve years old I've had my life mapped out. . . . I'm gonna be a singer. I'm gonna make some money, have some kids, then I'm gonna stop singin' and raise them kids right." Her actual struggles between being a proper full-time mother and having a full-time career are made invisible. Where did Schwartz get these words? He made them up.

When Patsy agrees to marry Charles, their union is portrayed not as all good times all the time but as a drama of martial struggle—with the predictable unhappy ending. The script is filled with errors: When she appears on the Arthur Godfrey TV show in New York City, she wears the cowgirl outfit made by her mother, not a cocktail dress the producers of the Godfrey show purchased for her. When Cline tells manager Randy Hughes that she wants to "be Hank Williams," he tells her how to go about it: "You've got a voice that was made to sing love songs. And if you work with me we're gonna take advantage of that fact."

The film drama portrays Patsy Cline as victim of random violence. In a 1961 car accident, for example, she's the only person badly injured, although in real life, her bother almost died. Here is the serious Hollywood filmmaking that Jessica Lange loved—but without any facts.

The movie's final scene of random violence—instant death in a plane crash—reinforces the image of innocence and good intentions betrayed. Rather than crashing due to pilot incompetence, as was documented in Federal Aviation Administration investigative records, the plane in the movie simply runs out of gas and then fails to clear the side of a mountain. Pilot Randy Hughes's errors were in fact far more insidious.

Sweet Dreams concludes with a dignified funeral, showing close family and a modest crowd of friends and mourners (in actuality, there were thousands in attendance), followed by Patsy's mother taking her children so that Charles can continue to work. The last scene emphasizes the tragic effects of domestic turmoil for the survivors. A grief-stricken "Movie Charlie" stands in the living room of Patsy's dream house, remembering their romantic ecstasy when he first danced with Patsy in the parking lot at the Rainbow Inn. "I'm crazy," Patsy sings on the lush soundtrack, "crazy for loving you." This last touch, integrating her most famous hit into part of the narrative, is a method that filmmakers have long used to add pathos to endings.

"Sweet Dreams Poster"

Sweet Dreams was not a hit—and critics loathed the film, only praising the "singing," which was actually Jessica Lange lip-synching Patsy's voice. In 1985, the two most famous film reviewers in the United States were Gene Siskel and Roger Ebert. Siskel wrote: "[Patsy Cline's] voice was big, throaty and hungry, the kind that sounds intense but also effortless and dignified." Ebert interprets this to mean that

Patsy Cline was a woman who called her own shots, partied hard, and had the vocabulary of a sailor. All the moviegoer would experience was that Cline had a great voice, wanted to become a star, had a boring first marriage, and a sweet-and-sour second marriage, and then died too soon. Clearly, two thumbs down.[11]

On October 2, 1985, *Variety* correctly foretold a box-office disaster, finding "no surprises in this predictable film," filled with performances not integrated into the film at all. Clearly Hollywood expected no great box-office return. And that was the case.

The *Village Voice* film critic noted the gender stereotypes: The filmmakers focused on Patsy's relationship with Charles, almost to the exclusion of her career, and in the process reduced her stature as a singer and a woman. The film never suggests that she fought back, or that she drank. If Charles is portrayed as a villainous, sexy heartbreaker, Patsy comes across as a honky-tonk angel, his female victim. What evolves on the screen is a classic battering relationship—the passion, the drinking, the adultery (his), the brutality (his), her pregnancy, and his charming speeches to win her back. Was this anything close to the truth? It seems that nothing was.[12]

The pop music critic for the *Washington Post* put it best: "Whose Life Was That, Anyway?" He found *Sweet Dreams* to be a "one-couple version of *Who's Afraid of Virginia Woolf?*" Critic Richard Harrington was right when he noted the danger that, after 1985, *Sweet Dreams* would become the "official take" on Patsy Cline as a person, performer, and key figure in music history. After a month in theaters, the studio pulled the film, as it fared poorly. But through the end of 1985 and into the spring of 1986, publicity continued, as Jessica Lange was nominated for an Academy Award as best actress. She lost but was in the news until the Awards show in March 1986. The soundtrack album did far better than the movie. The audio cassette entered the U.S. country charts on its way to peaking at number 29.[13]

In response to the movie, Charles Dick, along with brothers and Mark and Doug Hall from Canada, answered Hollywood: They created a documentary, *The Real Patsy Cline,* released in November 1986, to set the record straight. Charles Dick's co-partner, Doug Hall, told the *Toronto Globe and Mail* that "Charlie wasn't too happy with the movie *Sweet Dreams.* He felt the real story should be told." *The Real Patsy Cline* showed that Charles was a supportive husband.[14]

No documentary, however, could counteract the images offered in a feature film. *Sweet Dreams* played constantly on cable TV and was released on home video, first VHS and then DVD. The movie's repeated exposure captured new fans, who went out to purchase Patsy Cline's original recordings.

Hollywood had made Pasty Cline a poor country girl who, with sheer talent—not hard work and self-teaching—came to possess a unique pop singing style. With Hollywood's help, the world praised Patsy Cline as a skilled country singer, but one who certainly never sounded "hard country" to suburbanites. What new fans embraced was a powerful and appealing singer, one who had transformed country music to a form of popular music.

The two Hollywood movies helped Patsy Cline's *Greatest Hits* sell millions of audio cassettes during the 1980s. On January 31, 1986, *Patsy Cline's Greatest Hits,* originally released as a vinyl 33 1/3 record album in 1967, went "gold," aided by the movie publicity. On November 16, 1986, the Sunday *Chicago Tribune* headlines proclaimed, "MCA Finds New Music Talent: Patsy Cline." MCA Records' head,

Tony Brown, stated, "Those old Patsy Cline records [produced by Owen Bradley 25 years ago] still sound great, and are still selling." Thus, in August 1987, MCA redesigned and rereleased her *Greatest Hits* compilation. Boosted by the waves of publicity, it climbed into the *Billboard* listing of top country albums—and stayed there.[15]

On May 25, 1991, came the "big bang" effect of SoundScan, the tracking system that more accurately measured sales. SoundScan replaced the days of *Billboard's* calling record stores; now cash registers in stores (and later computer lines to new Web sites like Amazon), accurately estimated the sales of all forms of recorded music. There were so many specific data that SoundScan created new categories, such as "Catalog Country," defined as albums promoted as "country" that had been out for more than two years.

In SoundScan's first wave of publicity, *Patsy Cline's Greatest Hits* appeared as number 1 in SoundScan's Catalog Country. No one outside the music industry expected her retitled *12 Greatest Hits* to go to the top of that category and remain number 1 for three straight years, and then hover around the Top Ten as the twentieth century ended. In no other category did a star sustain such popularity. SoundScan thrust Patsy Cline into a Golden Age of rediscovery, and initiated her rise to iconic status.[16]

By November 9, 1996, *Country Weekly* reported to a growing number of "new" country music fans that *12 Greatest Hits* had sold more than seven million "units," with 215 weeks on the Catalog Country chart. Patsy Cline stood alone as the top-selling female country singer. And in 2004, *Guinness World Records* entered her *12 Greatest Hits* as the album by a female artist (in all genres) with the greatest number of weeks on the U.S. charts: 722 weeks total, with 251 of them at number 1. This occurred more than forty years after her death.[17]

Such sales were accomplished because a whole new generation of fans had started buying Patsy Cline. The press could not believe this phenomenon, and published thousands of articles seeking to explain it, usually starting with such phrasing as "More than [fill in a number] years after her death, Patsy Cline is still a hot property on the record charts." Yet to industry watchers, it came as no surprise. On July 24, 1989, MCA certified that *12 Greatest Hits* had sold two million units in twenty-two years, half since 1980.[18]

These sales jump-started Patsy Cline's rise from legendary to iconic status. And this rise occurred between May 25, 1991, and November 26, 1996. Her music was swept up in an era when the new popular music of the United States was either country or rap, separated by race. Patsy's biggest hits became "Walkin' After Midnight," "Sweet Dreams (of You)," "Crazy," and "I Fall to Pieces." Who was buying *12 Greatest Hits?* SoundScan's information underscored the fact that new buyers were white Baby Boomers (born from 1946 to 1964, just after World War II). The Baby Boomers had created the largest cohort in the history of the United States. These twenty-seven- to forty-six-year-olds (as of 1991) had seen *Sweet Dreams* and/or *Coal Miner's Daughter* on cable TV or home video, and so while shopping at mall stores, such as the Sam Goody chain, they bought Patsy Cline. Record companies recognized that aging white music fans had abandoned hard rock for country and new-age music. Singers like Linda Ronstadt, who helped keep Patsy Cline's reputation alive in the 1970s by singing Cline songs, gave up trying to woo teenagers in favor of wooing adults. In 1992, SoundScan and the Recording Industry Association of America certified 78 albums released before 1977 as gold (total sales of 500,000), platinum (1 million), or multiplatinum status—including Patsy Cline's *12 Greatest Hits* (with sales of 3 million).[19]

In 1995, Bruce Hinton, by then chairman of MCA Nashville, knew what the public was purchasing from his own accountants. But Hinton played off the SoundScan publicity, and called Cline a singing phenomenon. Her widower, Charles Dick, put these new sales, of which he received a percentage, metaphorically: "In 1991 Patsy got hot as a pistol."[20]

In October 1991, taking advantage of SoundScan's impact on the music business, MCA issued *The Patsy Cline Collection,* a four-CD (or four–audio cassette) box set, attesting to her soaring status. Box sets were reserved for what record companies knew were evergreens—musicians who sold continuously. *The Patsy Cline Collection* contained some 102 songs comprising her entire catalog of Decca recordings, as well as many—but not all—of her early 4 Star Records releases and some additional live recordings. (From 1955 to 1960, Patsy Cline recorded for 4 Star Music Company, and the recordings were distributed by Decca Records; in 1960, Patsy Cline signed directly with Decca.) This box set also included a forty-two-page booklet about Patsy Cline by Paul Kingsbury, of the Country Music Association. Kingsbury conducted original research, having had full access to the files of the Grand Ole Opry, including Patsy Cline's initial public relations dictation to Opry PR staff and many rare photos. *The Patsy Cline Collec*tion went to the Top Country Albums at number 29.

The press welcomed the new box set. On October 18, 1991, *USA Today* featured the headline "Patsy Cline collection glows with a legend's lasting shine." The national newspaper underscored the established image that Kingsbury had reproduced: "Patsy Cline lived hard, died young and left a lovely memory that lingers in her music. Three decades later, she is a pop/country legend." Unlike box sets assembled to focus on an artist's hits or career stages, *The Patsy Cline Collection* ($49.98 on CD, $39.98 on audio cassettes) served up a chronological ordering (from 1954 to 1963) of almost all 102 recordings made during her short career before she was killed in an air crash at age 30.[21]

On November 29, 1991, the Associated Press also spread across the United States Joe Edwards' review, which simply restated the PR released by MCA, although in a different style: "She was brassy yet tender—a woman who stood up for her beliefs and cleared a path in country music for other women to follow." Edwards recycled the public relations issued by MCA records to thousands of newspapers across the USA during the pre–Internet Age. Paul Kingsbury, with his status at the Country Music Association, assisted in the creation of an icon with a quote: "She sounded fresh then and still sounds fresh." Kingsbury never explained what technology had been used to make these records fresh, while others from the same era sound like mono monstrosities.

The MCA box set was a creation of Andy McKaie, who as vice president of catalog development and special markets oversaw all MCA reissues and anthologies. McKaie noted that, to keep the price of *The Patsy Cline Collection* under $50 for the CD package, he had MCA rent some—but not all—of the recordings she had made with Owen Bradley and were property of the 4-Star label, which by then, Sony Music had absorbed. McKaie helped MCA participate in an unprecedented boom in CD reissues in the early 1990s as he and his staff searched for extras for each box set. For *The Patsy Cline Collection,* they found rare radio recordings of limited sound quality and commissioned the Kingsbury booklet. MCA management was pleased; *The Patsy Cline Collection* box set was certified gold on March 27, 1993.[22]

McKaie also added colorized images from 1960s photographs to fashion a new image of a woman who had died nearly thirty years before. Each CD presented a different colorized photo to segment four (chronological) periods for potential buyers. On the first CD, McKaie chose a photo of Patsy Cline dressed in a tailored shirt and jacket, looking like a 1950s career girl—not in her oft-seen cowgirl outfit. On the second CD, he used a picture of her dressed in a dark lace evening gown, looking like a pop diva. On the third CD, he had her wearing a patterned shirtwaist, looking like a well-groomed early-1960s housewife. And for the fourth and final CD, called "Sweet Dreams," McKaie had Patsy Cline draped over a pillow, in a pink and black dress. McKaie chose no images of a cowgirl; he wanted her to look like an idealized suburban woman of the 1960s. He chose to sell her in 1991 as a modern pop singer; MCA research indicated that buyers of *The Patsy Cline Collection* were principally Baby Boom women.

However, MCA only owned half the copyrighted session cuts; Sony owned the rights to the 4-Star material. So, on September 22, 1992, Sony's Epic Record label issued *Forever and Always,* a compilation of 4-Star tracks. Then, on August 15, 1993, Sony issued *Loved and Again,* from additional 4-Star tracks. Moreover, from 1991 to 1996, other labels approached Sony to rent 4-Star tracks. In 1993, Rhino Records released compilations, *In Care of the Blues* and *Walkin' After Midnight.* The Baby Boom CD buyer, who looked for cheap Patsy Cline CDs, found that most stores carried at least a dozen choices, mainly from small labels that had compiled the 4-Star material leased from Sony.

On January 16, 1996, as the iconization of Patsy Cline was reaching a peak, MCA issued a CD called *The Nashville Sound: Owen Bradley.* McKaie asked the man who produced twenty-seven of Patsy Cline's twenty-nine recording sessions to select ten songs of his favorite productions across all artists he had worked with. Bradley chose one each from Loretta Lynn, Conway Twitty, Kitty Wells, Red Foley, Webb Pierce, Brenda Lee, and Ernest Tubb—but two Patsy Cline cuts: "Sweet Dreams" and "Crazy." Owen Bradley admitted that his toughest challenge was whittling down his life's work: "It was like picking your favorite children," reflected the producer who first joined Decca as an assistant producer in 1947, then piloted the company as vice president and head of operations from 1958 until his retirement in 1976. But as his selections revealed, his favorite of all the singers was Patsy Cline, since she alone rated two selections.[23]

In the notes for this important CD, Bradley thanked his Decca bosses Milton Rackmil and Paul Cohen; his assistant, Harry Silverstein; drummers Buddy Harman and Farris Coursey; guitarists Grady Martin, Hark Garland, Harold Bradley (his own brother), and Ray Edenton; acoustic bass player Bob Moore; pianist Floyd Cramer; and the backup vocal group the Jordanaires. Left unexplained, however, was Bradley's reliance on drummers and piano players—hardly the core of country instrumentation. But how did Bradley craft Patsy Cline's crossover hits? These are crucial questions that I will answer later in this book.[24]

On June 23, 1996, a small independent label, Razor & Tie, released *Patsy Cline: The Birth of a Star,* culled by CBS engineers from Patsy Cline's 1957 to 1958 appearances on Arthur Godfrey's programs. By the 1990s, Patsy Cline fans embraced any newly discovered work. *Birth of a Star* featured two live versions of "Walkin' After Midnight," with Patsy Cline backed by Godfrey's big house band—not the musicians Owen Bradley employed—and thus displaying an even stronger pop image amid brass and woodwinds. Because this was aimed at hard-core Patsy Cline fans, Razor & Tie left on the some of the recorded dialogue from the show. Fans could for the first time hear Patsy Cline speak at length. *Birth of a Star* proved to be a modest seller, for fans who celebrated all examples of her work as if they were rare artifacts unearthed at an archeological dig.

Thus, by the fall of 1996, with *The Patsy Cline Collection, The Birth of a Star,* and *12 Greatest Hits,* it seemed inevitable that some major publication would declare her an icon. The cover of the *New York Times Magazine* declared her an icon in November 1996. Rosanne Cash's profile of Patsy Cline backed up the claim. The elite culture had finally declared Patsy Cline worthy of praise, along with the likes of First Lady Eleanor Roosevelt, dancer Martha Graham, and writer Virginia Woolf. In addition, the Amusement & Music Operators Association (representing jukebox operators) announced that the most played jukebox record of all time was Patsy Cline's "Crazy." By these two measures—a profile in the *New York Times Magazine* and the number-one-played jukebox song—it seems fair to state that Patsy Cline had become an icon. The well-off elite could read about Patsy Cline in the *New York Times,* while middle-class and working-class fans who frequented restaurants and bars with jukeboxes paid to hear her in their favorite public places.

As Patsy Cline rose to iconic status, other mass media in the United States featured her—movies, TV shows, popular magazines, and even a postage stamp. She became associated with modern courtship. For example, summer 1991 yielded a hit Hollywood film called *Doc Hollywood,* starring Michael J. Fox and Julie Warner. No small, modest movie, this film was released amidst summer blockbusters. Benjamin Stone (Fox), an ambitious young doctor driving to Los Angeles, gets off the interstate to avoid a traffic jam and ends up in the small South Carolina town of Grady. He is sentenced to 32 hours of community service at the local hospital—after running down the judge's new fence. All he wants is to serve the sentence and get moving, but he gradually falls for the pretty ambulance driver, Viloula (Julie Warner). Will they fall in love? Of course. In a plot twist, she woos him while they are dancing to Patsy Cline singing "Crazy," in a sequence of just dance and music. The movie sequence lasts two hours and twenty-nine minutes, the exact length of the recording.

On June 21, 1991, the public TV show *Adam Smith's Money World* (Transcript No. 728) reported that Patsy Cline had become an economic icon in the music business. Business reporter "Adam Smith" noted the extraordinary sales of Patsy Cline's *12 Greatest Hits.* To Smith, Patsy Cline represented the ultimate example of a great "business model." And this was no fan reporting; this was an economist on a TV show aimed at the investor (read, "rich") elite of the United States. He ended this show with "[Songwriters] look for phrases that move feelings and that generate crossover hits, songs which appeal to a mass audience." Then, as an example, the producers showed a black and white video clip of Patsy Cline singing "Crazy." Patsy Cline had become the ultimate singer who appealed to everyone.

On the September 19, 1991, season premiere of *The Simpsons,* on the FOX television network, then at the peak of its cult status with young people, the father, Homer, has gotten himself into a "mental institution," and his wife, Marge, tries to call the hospital and is put on hold. What plays while she waits? Patsy Cline's "Crazy." Here her song took on a new meaning of irony simply based on its title. A year later, H. Ross Perot used "Crazy" as the theme song for his ill-fated run as a third-party candidate for president of the United States.

By December 1991, Patsy Cline was so hot that *Mademoiselle* magazine published an article about modern urban female bonding. "We drove through eight states. People thought we were crazy to want to spend a week in a car, but for my girlfriends and me, a beat-up station wagon, open windows, a tape deck and all the two-lanes between New York City and Tennessee seemed like the ideal vacation." Here was an article about young women discovering themselves in the 1990s. For them, each change of terrain demanded its own music.

On the last day of driving, during the last hour, they took an exit off the New Jersey Turnpike. "Suddenly," the author recalled, "the rigid grey skyline of Manhattan shot up before our eyes and we knew our road had almost run out. I don't remember which of us reached for the Patsy Cline tape, but it was what we were all thinking. As that skyline inched closer and closer, Patsy's sweet voice sang songs of longing and regret."

The author admitted that she needed to hear Patsy Cline then because "Patsy Cline is the music of endings. It's not just that she sings about endings, although doomed, failed and unrequited love seems the overwhelming preoccupation of her brief recording career. Just when you think Patsy has braved all the heartbreak humanly possible, she lays on another tale of woe."

On September 27, 1993, the U.S. Postal Service issued a stamp set depicting country music legends, including Patsy Cline, to complete news coverage. The "Legends of American Music Series" set also included Hank Williams, the Carter Family, and Bob Wills stamps. The postal service of the United States was going deeper into debt, and so counted on the new Patsy Cline fans to become stamp collectors and make their twenty-nine-cent contributions to the postal service.

"The Patsy Cline Stamp"

On January 17, 1994, the island nation of St. Vincent, located near South America, where the Caribbean Sea meets the Atlantic Ocean, issued its own "Legends of Country Music" stamps, which included Patsy Cline. Before the age of e-mail, images on stamps had most often been the most famous individuals in the history of the United States. These postal services were seeking to use Patsy Cline's growing fame and fan base to make money—and the fans purchased the stamps by the millions.[25]

By 1993 Patsy Cline was honored on television on a regular basis. For example, on May 8, 1993, CBS broadcast "The Women of Country Music," a special on Thursday night in a so-called ratings sweeps period, during which the network sought to maximize its ratings. With multiple clips of Patsy Cline, this special finished among the top ten TV shows of the week. On June 25, 1994, CBS aired "Roots of Country Music," a special celebrating the reopening of the Ryman Auditorium, in Nashville. Again clips of Patsy Cline graced the telecast. This became a semiannual series of TV shows, satisfying the public's desire for anything Patsy Cline. These shows were special in that CBS searched out existing rare footage of Patsy Cline singing, most often a clip of her singing "Crazy" in a dress looking like a 1960s suburban house wife. Thus fans seemed to redefine Patsy Cline not as a cowgirl but as a modern suburbanite.[26]

March 1993 marked the thirtieth anniversary of the 1963 plane crash; the Grand Ole Opry devoted one of its Saturday night televised segments to a tribute to Patsy Cline and her fellow passengers. With Cline's widower, Charles Dick, and their daughter, Julie (born in 1958), on hand, family friend Jan Howard paid tribute to Cline, singing "I Fall to Pieces" (which Howard's ex-husband, Harlan Howard, cowrote), followed by Loretta Lynn, who sang "She's Got You."

In October 1993, Dolly Parton, Loretta Lynn, and Tammy Wynette got together to create a CD called *Honky Tonk Angels*. In her rewritten rendition of "Hillbilly Heaven," Dolly Parton sang, "Patsy Cline is the best singing angel there." This project received abundant publicity and acclaim at the time of its release, and soared to number 6 on *Billboard*'s current country album charts and number 42 on *Billboard*'s top 200 pop chart.[27]

On the February 14, 1994, episode of the hit NBC series *Mad About You*, a hip New York City couple (played by Paul Reiser and Helen Hunt) related in a flashback how they came to be married. Looking younger, they are ice skating at the fabled rink in New York City's Rockefeller Center, and Patsy Cline is singing "Crazy." In the flashback, the character Paul (Reiser), anxious about proposing, remarks that he has just dreamed that Jamie (Hunt) was "Patsy Cline's crazy cousin." His actual cousin in the series storyline asks him, "Since when do you [a New Yorker] dream in country?" Still in flashback, the newly married couple move into their first apartment together. Again we hear "Crazy." Then in flashback, back at Rockefeller Center, Paul finally proposes, with "Crazy" again playing in the background. This comedy offered no Nashville connection, but by February 1994 "Crazy" was simply considered an iconic pop song. "Crazy" had become so widely associated with the difficulties of courtship that no one needed to explain. The audience for Patsy Cline was the whole United States.

Finally, even the conservative Grammys got around to honoring Patsy Cline, whom they had passed over during her lifetime. In late February 1995, Patsy Cline's mother, Hilda Hensley, flew to Los Angeles, a month before her eightieth birthday, to pick up the Grammy Lifetime Achievement Award. The ceremony took place on March 1, 1995, and the Grammys did what the Country Music Association Hall of Fame had done 22 years earlier: gave Patsy Cline its highest honor. At the time she was judged worthy of a Lifetime Achievement Award, fewer than 100 had been so honored before her. In 1995 she received a Grammy Lifetime Award with singers Peggy Lee and Barbra Streisand. That Patsy Cline was a crossover singer, who started with country music and made it popular, was acknowledged by the National Academy of Recording Arts and Sciences.[28]

On March 7, 1995, *Country Weekly,* the leading magazine for country music fans, featured a colorized image of a smiling Patsy Cline. Inside, the fanzine led with "Patsy Cline: The Legend Continues; She's Still on the Charts and Wins 1995 Grammy," and profiled Hilda Hensley and the Grammy ceremony, noting that *12 Greatest Hits* was still among the top ten on the *Billboard* Catalog Country charts. *Country Weekly* quoted Owen Bradley: "Crazy was the successful [song I produced] in walking that fine line between country and pop—which is what our [Decca] company people in New York wanted. People like her even better now."

On October 24, 1995, another Hollywood feature film, the chick flick *How to Make an American Quilt,* used Patsy Cline singing

"You Belong to Me." This film was produced by Steven Spielberg's Amblin Productions and starred Winona Ryder, Anne Bancroft, Ellen Burstyn, and Alfre Woodard. Based on a novel by Whitney Otto, the narrative centers on several women bonded in a quilting bee as they construct a wedding quilt as a gift for a member's granddaughter, Finn Dodd (Ryder). The women share their life stories, which lead the granddaughter to reflect on her own life and where she is headed. "You Belong to Me" comes in to close the narrative as the couple decides to marry.

The producers did not care (or most likely know) that Cline had covered a hit she loved. "You Belong To Me" was written in 1952 and made a hit that year by Jo Stafford. It opens with the lyric "See the pyramids along the Nile/Watch the sun rise on a tropic isle" but says to the lover, "Just remember darling all the while/You belong to me." The Stafford version first entered the charts on August 1, 1952, and remained a hit for the rest that year; the song was sung at the various venues where Patsy Cline sang in 1952 and 1953. Patsy Cline, as she had with the Willie Nelson–penned "Crazy," made "You Belong to Me" her own. With her widespread renewed popularity and sales, the producers selected it to close their film.[29]

In January 1996 poet John Reinhard published "On the Road to Patsy Cline" as a set of poems in the Minnesota Voices Project. Here Reinhard was trying to make modern an art form that was practiced mainly in universities. But Reinhard knew that his fellow poets would get the Patsy Cline reference. By 1996 she had become a universal cultural icon—so respected that she even provided inspiration to serious poets. This proved her crossover appeal: University poets were looking for ways to contend with her powerful and popular singing.

On June 12, 1996, the *New York Times Magazine* foreshadowed its praise of Patsy Cline, which would come six months later, with a profile of teenage singer LeAnn Rimes as her hit "Blue" was toping the charts. Woven into all the publicity about the song was the tale that composer Bill Mack had written "Blue" in 1963 for Patsy Cline but that Cline had died before Mack could pitch it to her. This story helped this 13-year-old sell 3 million copies. Account after account labeled LeAnn Rimes the second coming of Patsy Cline.[30]

Fans started to actively initiate and appropriate honors for the rediscovered Cline. For example, Mario Munoz, a Walmart store planner from Fresno, California, did not even like country music when he accidentally caught the movie *Sweet Dreams* while channel surfing one afternoon in late in 1991. There was something intriguing and unique about Patsy Cline's singing, so the young Californian went out and bought *The Patsy Cline Collection* box set. When Munoz did not find Cline listed in a book on the Hollywood Walk of Fame, he set out to take care of that omission. His efforts led him to the Hollywood Chamber of Commerce, which oversees the walk, where he learned how to apply. But first, Munoz needed the approval of the Patsy Cline estate; so he drove the 2,100 miles to Nashville to meet Patsy Cline's widower, Charles Dick, executor of the estate. The two men set up a breakfast on Father's Day 1995, and Dick gave his approval.

Munoz remembers how stressful it had been for him. "I looked up [Charles Dick's] number in the phone book and I was a big chicken. For three days I'd start to dial the number and stop," Munoz later said. But this young man proved nothing if not determined. It took four more years of effort, one rejection, and lots of paperwork, but on August 3, 1999, Charles Dick and his daughter, Julie, were standing on Hollywood Boulevard to unveil the new star on the walk, between the stars of actors Yul Brynner and Barry Sullivan. "It's a pretty great honor," Charles Dick said. "They put in Loretta Lynn about 10 years ago. Reba (McEntire) is in. Considering the others that are there, [Patsy] deserves to be there."[31]

The world embraced Patsy Cline. One subculture led the way: By the early 1990s, the gay and lesbian community had openly adopted her. For example, on St. Patrick's Day (March 17), the Cowgirl Hall of Fame restaurant, near New York University, held St. Patsy's Day. The Cowgirl Hall of Fame became an "in" spot and was listed in gay and lesbian travel guides, one of which stated, "It's got decor to die for and Patsy Cline is Queen here." "St. Patsy's Day" annually staged a Patsy Cline look-alike contest. Charles Dick took a bemused stance: "Patsy popular among Gays? Is that right?" he said with a smile. "Well, you don't say."[32]

Evidence from all around the world attested to Patsy Cline's international appeal. The music industry has been an international one since the coming of 78 rpm records, in the 1920s. Then, with the introduction of the CD in the late 1980s, fans restocked their music libraries and the international music industry grew steadily. Patsy Cline sales were helped as MCA, one of a handful of multinational music companies, publicized her CDs around the world. In March 1992, when teaching in the Netherlands, I entered the largest record store in central Amsterdam, and what was playing over the store's speaker system? Patsy Cline singing "I Fall to Pieces." Cline was appreciated across Europe not as a "country" singer but as a great singer—transcending musical genres.[33]

Not surprisingly, on June 27, 1996, the first Patsy Cline Web site appeared. It was begun by a Swedish fan, Per Jonsson, a high school computer teacher, who spent thousands upon thousands of hours gathering anything on her that he could find. When asked how, living in Sweden, he had become a Patsy fan, Jonsson answered, "When I heard Patsy's voice in the movie *Sweet Dreams.* Now, there's a moment to remember . . . and when I first saw her "live" in the video *The Real Patsy Cline,* I had tears in my eyes." This Swede was a pure, unabashed fan, and he had the necessary skills and motivation to construct a Web site and maintain it, making a notable contribution.[34]

In 1996, fans from around world found the site. Below are just a few of the early entries, leaving aside those from the United States, which then were in the minority:

From Russia: "I'm Russian, but I'm fond of Patsy. She's the best, she's my favourite. She's my teacher in singing. I want to find friends. I'm 25, journalist."

From Denmark: "Today I have made an interview with one of Denmark's greatest female singers Lis Sorensen. She told me, that her next project will be a record containing a selection of Patsy Cline's songs. . . . Well . . . you can't know everything, and my knowledge of Patsy Cline was rather small. So I went on the net. Found these pages, and wauwh! Now I know, what I— for this moment -- want to know about Patsy Cline. It's a splendid page. Thank you. Uffe Christensen."

From Brazil: "The first time I heard Patsy Cline singing was in 1989, and had to wait till 1992 to buy the first CD. By this time I already knew many things about her, and although impressed by her voice, by her songs, I couldn't have her records. It's very hard to find a Patsy Cline record in the city I live [in] and I had to wait 3 years. . . . She still lives in the minds and hearts of those who love her. pedro carlos de souza neto"

A special posting came in as 1996 was ending: "Hello to Per and everyone. I was just looking around and saw so many questions I just had to drop in. My name is Julie Fudge. I am Patsy's daughter. I have enjoyed reading the entries in the guestbook, and hope I can answer some of your questions. My dad is living and lives here around Nashville. When Mama died she left my dad, and myself, and my brother Randy."

The date best suited to establishing Patsy Cline's iconic status is November 24, 1996, as the date when the *New York Times Magazine* profiled Patsy Cline. The prestige of this publication among opinion leaders in the United States meant that she had officially become an icon. The magazine's subject: "Heroine Worship." The writer, Rosanne Cash, Johnny Cash's daughter, had the musical credentials and caught the moment. "My mother said her name with slightly pursed lips: "Patsy . . ."—no last name needed. Patsy Cline was wicked and fabulous when both qualities really meant something." Although Rosanne Cash is often classified as a country artist, her music draws on many genres, including pop, rock, and blues. In the 1980s, she had a string of chart-topping singles, which crossed musical genres and landed on *Billboard*'s country and pop charts, the most commercially successful being her 1981 breakthrough hit "Seven Year Ache," which topped the U.S. country singles charts and reached the Top 30 on the U.S. pop singles charts.

In 1996, Cash wrote in the *New York Times Magazine* that "[Patsy Cline] was a source of fascination, distrust and raw, if hidden, admiration." This praise came from a member of the legendary Cash family. The iconic Cline's "wild and willful personality" could not be tamed, and Rosanne Cash (and her father) knew this style. Patsy Cline had inspired both.

Rosanne Cash did her research: "To check that out, I called my Mom—not someone who would have a professional take (for that I would have called my dad) but a woman who was deeply affected by her." Rosanne Cash learned that her mom had not known Cline well, but "'your daddy and I did have her over to the house not long before she died. She had a mouth like a sailor, and she didn't put on airs. She was just Patsy, comfortable in her skin.'" Rosanne Cash admired that.

Rosanne Cash went on to note that a startling sexuality infused Patsy Cline's singing, making her "a profound source of inspiration to those of us without immediate memories of her." Cash then expressed eloquently a new generation's love of Patsy Cline: "Her confidence and lack of self-consciousness alone would have fostered myth, but because of her remarkable talent, she has become part of the fabric of our musical destiny." For Rosanne Cash, Patsy Cline had "lived a life utterly her own, messy and self-defined, and it all fed and merged with that voice."

To end this profoundly personal essay, Rosanne Cash wrote: "I couldn't help asking, 'Mom, was I at that party (with Patsy)?' 'Sure, honey! That was in, let's see, 1963? All you kids were born [by] then.' I sighed wistfully. Somewhere in the blackout of early childhood I had had an encounter with Patsy Cline. I may spend the rest of my life trying to remember it."

NOTES

Chapter 1

1   From "VH1's 100 Greatest Women of Rock and Roll" cable TV special (July 29, 1999).

2   Kimberly Potts, <u>Everything I Needed to Know, I Found from a Chick Flick</u> (New York: Citadel, 2007).

3   <u>The Christian Science Monitor</u>, March 20, 1980, 17.

4   <u>Variety</u>, February 20, 1980, 44.

5   <u>Variety</u>, October 17, 2003, 45.

6   Mark Emerson and Eugene E. Pfaff, Jr., <u>Country Girl: The Life of Sissy Spacek</u> (New York: St. Martin's Press, 1988), 73–88; <u>www.rogerebert.com</u> (accessed August 15, 2005).

7   <u>Los Angeles Times</u>, September 20, 1985: E1 (hereafter <u>LA Times</u>); <u>LA Times</u>, E1, September 2, 1984.

8   <u>Winchester Star</u>, B1, October 23, 1984 (hereafter WS); WS, October 26, 1984: B1.

9   WS, November 14, 1984: B1.

10   Sweet Dreams Press Kit, owned by Douglas Gomery.

11   The <u>Chicago Tribune</u>, September 29, 1985: A7.

12   <u>Village Voice</u>, October 8, 1985, 63.

13   The <u>Washington Post</u>, October 13, 1985: C1 (hereafter Wpost); www.the-numbers.com/movies/ (accessed October 4, 2006).

14   <u>The Toronto Globe and Mail</u>, November 27, 1986: C12; <u>The [Nashville] Tennessean</u>, November 19, 1986: 2E

15   The <u>Chicago Tribune</u>, November 16, 1986: C24.

16   Claire Folkard, <u>Guinness World Records 2005</u> (London: Guinness World Records Ltd, 2004), 194.

17   <u>Country Weekly</u>, November 9, 1996, 32 (hereafter CW).

18   The <u>New York Times</u>, August 11, 1997: C3 (hereafter NYT).

19   NYT, March 1, 1992: D3; NYT, January 25, 1996: C2.

20   LA Times, November 13, 1995: E1; WS, May 5, 2001: B1.

21   USA Today, October 18, 1991: Life 1.

22   Goldmine Annual (1994): 4–20.

23   CW, April 23, 1996: 12–14.

24   The [Nashville] Tennessean, August 7, 2008: C1

25   NYT, October 9, 1992: C4; NYT,December 27, 1992: D22; Richard Lewis Thomas, Who's Who on U.S. Stamps (Sidney, OH: Linn's Stamp News, 1991); web site www.usps.com/postalhistory/_ pdf/WomenStampSubjects.pdf#search='women'sstamps'(accessed July 23, 2009).

26   TV Guide, May 3, 1993; TV Guide, June 25,1994.

27   For events shown on mass media, the observations, unless otherwise noted, were from notes taken by Douglas Gomery.

28   www.Grammys.com -- accessed December 5, 2006.

29   Joel Whitburn, Top Pop Records 1940–1955 (Menominee, Falls, WI: Record Research, 1992).

30   Laurence Leamer, Three Chords and the Truth (New York: Harper, 1997): 304–36; www.billmackcountry.com -- accessed April 2, 2002.

31   WS, July 31, 1999: A1, A10.

32   Independent (UK), April 16, 1993: E3.

33   Robert Burnett, The Global Jukebox (London: Routledge, 1996); Michael Christianen, "Cycles in Symbol Production? A New Model to Explain Concentration, Diversity and Innovation in the Music Industry," Popular Music 14, no. 1 (1995): 55–93.

34   Web site www.patsified.com -- accessed March 2, 2002.

Chapter 2

Positioning a Poor Girl to Make Pop Music

Patsy Cline would gain millions of headlines during her lifetime (1932–63)—and even more thereafter. Few stars get front page coverage during the days before their birth, but the front page headline of the *Winchester Evening Star* on the Wednesday, August 31, 1932, edition read, "Girl Weds Man 27 Years Her Senior." The newspaper explained that Samuel Hensley, a forty-three-year-old widower from Elkton, Virginia, and Hilda Patterson, a sixteen-year-old girl from nearby Gore, had been married the previous day in the parsonage of the United Brethren Church by the pastor, Rev. George W. Stover. What the paper did not say, but all readers assumed, was that Hilda was pregnant—indeed, about to give birth any day.

The newspaper confirmed what was in the court records: The 16-year old bride was the daughter of the former Mrs. James Patterson and the stepdaughter of her mother's second husband, Frank Allanson, of Gore. Gore was just five miles from the West Virginia border, and was an town filled with so-called what city-folk called hillbillies. And only a hillbilly family would permit a girl to marry a man old enough to be her father. No one in Winchester really cared that Samuel Hensley was from Elkton, but Rev. George Stover did. Stover had long been friends with the groom's father, who was also an elder in the United

Brethren Church. Rev. Stover married the couple, a five-foot-six-inch veteran of the World War I and a very pregnant teenager, as a favor to his friend Sol Hensley.

Nine days after the marriage, on September 8, 1932, Hilda gave birth to a baby girl, whom she named Virginia Patterson Hensley. Hilda's stepfather paid the one dollar cost of having the birth in the Winchester Memorial Hospital, as the 16-year-old Hilda had had a problem pregnancy. This was no birth by the then standard practice for the poor, delivery by a midwife, but a delivery by a physician and nurses in a modern hospital. The Winchester Memorial Hospital was the fifth largest in Virginia, and Hilda got the best of care from fifty-seven-year-old Lewis M. Allen, MD.[1]

"Winchester Memorial Hospital in 1930"

When Samuel Hensley found employment at the Navy Yard in Washington, DC, and in December 1932, moved to Capitol Hill to work as a blacksmith, his disapproving parents agreed to house Hilda and her baby, Ginny, in a shack on the Hensley farm, west of Elkton and next to the Shenandoah River. But to punish Hilda and Ginny, they withheld the few dollars Sam sent from Washington. The teenage mother had to live as a subsistence farmer for the first year of marriage while supporting her baby. [2]

Throughout her career, Patsy Cline praised her mother for teaching her the same lessons that she had learned during this period. Hilda Virginia Patterson was born on March 9, 1916, the third child of James A. Patterson (b. 1885) and Goldie Newlin Patterson (b. 1890). With her older sister, Madge, and brother, Robert, Hilda lived on a small farm in Frederick Country, Virginia, about four miles southwest of Winchester. During the summer of 1918, Hilda's father had fallen off a roof and had to have his leg amputated. With her family in desperate straits, Goldie went to work at National Fruit Company's processing plant in Winchester, where the workforce consisted mostly of women and children.[3]

Then came the "Spanish flu" pandemic. On October 10, 1918, two-year-old Hilda's father died at age 33 of influenza. This was a front-page news story in the October 10 *Winchester Evening Star* *that* James Arlington Patterson well-known resident of Opequon died at 2am, after a week's illness. His case made the front page because he was unlucky enough to be the first in the area to have died from the flu, joining millions of people around the world during the worst pandemic of the twentieth century. Between October 1918 and March 1919, the Spanish influenza spread worldwide and claimed 25 million lives—more people than perished in the fighting of World War I. James Patterson had been unlucky; the *Winchester Evening Star* reported that a soldier on leave had been helping Patterson with his apple crop -- meaning that the soldier had infected him. According to the newspaper article, "A sad feature of Mr. Patterson's death is that his three little children are now ill with the influenza." Madge, Robert, and

Hilda all survived to live long lives, as this strain of influenza proved most deadly for young adults, not young children. But Hilda's mother faced a bleak future, and four days later, on October 14, 1918, she sold the family home and moved in with her parents.[4]

Two years later, in late 1920, the thirty-one-year-old widow Goldie Newlin Patterson met 28 year old Frank Allanson. As a single mother with three young children, gender expectations of the day dictated that she seek remarriage. Goldie Patterson married Frank Allanson on April 5, 1921, in Goldie's Baptist church in Gore, Virginia. After serving in World War I, Frank Allanson had come to Gore to work for the Commonwealth of Virginia, supervising the paving of U.S. 50, which ran through downtown Winchester, through Gore, and into West Virginia. Frank Allanson supervised a all–African American convict road crew that rebuilt U.S. 50 into a major east–west highway. Five-year-old Hilda Patterson now had a stepfather.[5]

Frank Allanson was none too excited to have three step-children, but he raised them as his own, while he and Goldie had their own children, as well. As each turned twelve, Frank Allanson pulled his stepchildren from school and sent them to work with just a fifth-grade education. Hilda's older sister, Madge, left home to work in 1924; three years later Hilda's brother, Robert, became a farm worker. In 1992 Hilda Hensley remembered that, starting in June 1928, "For $2.50 a week, plus room and board, I washed clothes and did household chores." She was expected to labor as a "servant-girl" until she married. No wonder she was anxious to meet someone who would marry her, even if he was forty-three years old.[6]

On October 22, 1929, Madge married Russell J. Whitacre, eight months after she turned sixteen and was legally eligible. Madge's husband was a respectable twenty-one-year-old local man. Her marriage set the precedent for leaving her stepfather's household as soon as possible. Hilda would follow three years later, when she too was sixteen years old.[7]

Samuel Lawrence Hensley was born on August 16, 1889, at the family farm, located two miles west of Elkton and 85 miles south of Gore by way of U.S. 50 South, down the Valley Pike (U.S. 11), and then east fifteen miles to the farm. Like many farmers' sons, he dropped out of school at age twelve, then apprenticed in Elkton as a blacksmith. In April 1911, at age twenty-one, he started his own blacksmith shop so that he wouldn't have to work for his father. In 1914, Sam, age twenty-five, married Wynona Jones. They had a son in 1916 and a daughter in 1919. Sam then enlisted in World War I, joining the Allied Expeditionary Force at age twenty-eight, serving as a blacksmith for the U.S. Army in France. At age twenty-nine, he returned to his first wife and children in Elkton to work in the Norfolk and Western railroad yards.[8]

His first wife was scheduled to give birth in the spring of 1927. But on February 19, 1927, Wynona, along with her unborn child, died in an automobile accident. Devastated at age thirty-seven, Samuel Hensley quit his job with Norfolk and Western, placed his two children with a local "spinster lady," (the term of that day), and took to the woods.[9]

Patsy Cline's first cousin was blunt: "Sam was running moonshine; up in the hills above Gore." The mountains behind Gore, part of the Appalachian range, offered perfect protection from law enforcement, as law officers played a cat-and-mouse game with moonshiners. In short, because those in Winchester and other nearby towns wanted liquor, local authorities turned a blind eye to illegal moonshining. Sam Hensley adapted his blacksmithing skills to making and repairing stills, and to making any necessary auto repairs to guarantee his escape from the authorities. He was an accepted figure in and around Gore by the time he met fifteen-year-old Hilda Hensley at the local general store.[10]

How did forty-two-year-old Sam woo fifteen-year-old Hilda? By automobile. Sam had one, and it was the fastest on the road. Sam was a constant presence on U.S. 50 as he sped around with his reconfigured Ford. Why get married? As 1932 began, Hilda Hensley, three months shy of her sixteenth birthday, told Sam Hensley she was "with child." Gender convention required the men of the area who had impregnated their girlfriends to marry them. Patricia Brannon, Hilda's niece, who remained close to her Aunt Hilda, stated, "Pop [her name for Frank Allanson] would not have cared, but 'Tunney'—that's what we called Grandma [Goldie]—she would have made sure she got married in a church."[1]

No one but Hilda was happy with the situation. Sam Hensley hardly wanted to start a new family. Neither sets of parents approved. But Hilda escaped her oppressive stepfather, and if she could marry in a church, her mother would be pleased, since Madge had eloped. So Sam Hensley went along, and began to look for a wage-paying job. [11]

Hilda's stepfather was not willing to house or feed his sixteen-year-old stepdaughter and her new baby. For a time, Hilda's mother insisted that her daughter from childbirth at the Allanson home. In December 1932, Sam found the Navy Yard job, and Sam's father grudgingly offered Hilda and her infant daughter a small shack on his property, away from the main house. Hilda Hensley and her e month old baby moved in December 1932, with the intention that Sam would send his father money to support Hilda and Ginny. From his rented room, ten blocks from the U.S. Capital building, Sam Hensley sent a dollar or two each week to his father for Hilda and the baby.[12]

So from December 1932 to November 1933, Sam lived in Washington, DC, and his wife and daughter remained just outside

Elkton. This was the arrangement. Hilda and her baby survived in a world of subsistence farming, accepting handouts from in-laws who loathed her and receiving meager support by her husband. Ginny Hensley started life in a difficult situation, to say the least. She and her mother struggled each day just to eat and stay warm.[13]

The Sol Hensley and his family were leading members of the small town Elkton community. Sol Hensley's father had helped create the area known as Hensley Hollow, just west of what is today Skyline Drive. Sol Hensley had been the most successful of all his brothers and sisters, owning by the end of 1932 hundreds of acres of grazing land. He was so land rich that a small crossroads town near the farm, Solsburg, was named after him. Hilda and Ginny were just an embarrassment.[14]

When interviewed in 1982, Hilda Hensley remembered, "When Ginny was born in 1932, that was a bad time. We're all poor people. We think we're good people, but we're poor people. And we had a lot of relatives in the same circumstances." In 1982, Hilda explained their relationship: "I was 16 years old when Patsy was born. All my life I'd had hand-me-downs. When she was born she was mine. We grew up together. We were hungry together." What Hilda did not mention was that, day after day, she had to work from sunrise to sundown to feed and clothe her baby. The baby who became Patsy Cline learned what the daily struggle of real poverty felt like.[15]

Hilda Hensley constantly adapted. Living next to the Shenandoah River, she taught herself to fish for food. On the Hensley farm she and her equally poor tenant neighbors traded what they gathered. Then Hilda would carry baby Virginia into Elkton and trade fish and eggs for necessary supplies. Hilda and her infant daughter had only a small stove for heat, no electricity, no running water, no telephone, no radio—no modern conveniences. By example, Hilda taught her baby survival skills on a daily basis, using used all the training that her own mother, as a subsistence farmwoman, had provided given her. At least the shack was near to the South Fork of the Shenandoah River, home to more than three hundred species of fish: bass, trout, carp, and catfish. The river also provided necessary water for drinking, washing, and cooking.[16]

Hilda's niece remembered what her aunt told her about those days. The hardest time was when baby Ginny got diphtheria as a small child. Hilda went to a local doctor, with the help of the Hensley family, who told her that her sixteen-month-old daughter was not going to live. So Hilda gathered all the help she could, including that of her mother, and journeyed by train, praying for the whole journey, back to the Winchester Memorial Hospital. The hospital supplied the necessary medication, and baby Virginia lived. Later, Patsy admitted to her family that while she smoked, she never inhaled because she was so terrified by her mother's story of that near-death experience. The brush with death probably helped Patsy Cline become a stronger singer, as she never damaged her lungs with cigarette smoke.[17]

At about this time, the construction of the Shenandoah National Park was causing problems for patriarch Sol Hensley. The U.S. government and the Commonwealth of Virginia forced Sol to sell some of his grazing land to create the park. With no legal recourse, Sol Hensley sold 313 acres for $3,190. While that was a large amount of money in the Great Depression, he did not want to sell his prime grazing land. He became a bitter old man who had pioneered the land that was being turned into a National Park for city folk up north.[18]

Like most poor rural folks during the Great Depression, Hilda, with her daughter's help, planted a vegetable garden to grow her own food. Hilda was skilled at this. Indeed, she kept up gardening her whole life, and an inventory of her household after her death, in December 1998, listed a plow. She manually plowed the backyard for her garden throughout her 50 years living in Winchester. But as her niece later remembered, "Hilda hated Elkton. She could not wait to get away from the place."[19]

But wait Hilda did. The Great Depression brought the U.S. economy to a standstill and produced untold misery for Virginians, with thousands of families living under deplorable conditions for want of clothing, medicine, and other absolute necessities. Between 1932 and 1934, the Virginia economy hit rock bottom. Dresses were made from chicken feed bags; undergarments carried the trademark of 4X flour rather than that of any department store. In March 1933, at the moment of President Franklin D. Roosevelt's inauguration, the Virginia banking system was on the verge of collapse. Hilda did not notice, as she did not have a bank account.[20]

Hilda produced almost everything she and her baby needed by living off the land. She raised chickens for food, grew vegetables, picked fruit trees, and gathered from the nearby woodlands additional food, such as chestnuts and walnuts. She offered her daughter a sense of female independence. The Patsy Cline swagger—as a self-sufficient woman—started when she was a baby, learning from her role-model mother.[21]

But at least Hilda Hensley and her daughter never had to go to a county poor farm. These tax-supported institutions were places where individuals who could not support themselves went as a last resort. Usually this occurred in temporary dire circumstances, such as illness, injury, or death of parents. Sol Hensley made sure that his family was never embarrassed by news that their daughter-in-law and grandchild failed under his care and needed to sign up at a nearby poor farm.[22]

None of the celebrated New Deal measures proved to be of any help to Hilda and her baby; they were simply not eligible for any of

FDR's programs. In August 1933, when local food stores joined the National Recovery Act, Hilda did not care, as she grew and raised almost all the food for herself and her baby. In an interview in 1995, Hilda talked a bit about those cruel days: "We weren't very happy, because there wasn't any money," she stated matter-of-factly. And there certainly was no singing, for Hilda often admitted she could not carry a tune.[23]

Samuel, working as a blacksmith at the Washington Navy Yard, held first legally paid job since quitting the Norfolk and Western Railroad five years earlier. But like many of his jobs, this one didn't last very long. By 1933, he moved back to nearby Waynesboro, 30 miles from Elkton, where he lived and worked, helping to construct an addition to the DuPont factory. Only in April 1934 did the family unite in Elkton, as Sam was hired to help build The Skyline Drive. Samuel, Hilda, and Ginny moved into an apartment in Elkton. Hilda insisted that this apartment have access to a vast backyard so that she could continue her "subsistence farming." While she and Ginny finally had electricity, Hilda still had to use a well for water and had no telephone.

In April 1936, the job on Skyline Drive ended, and the family of three moved away from the nearby wrath of Samuel Hensley's disapproving parents, to nearby Grottoes, Virginia. Sam, by then 46, worked temporally in a job overseeing the boilers at a local plant. With his skills as a blacksmith, he could deal with fire and create a necessary repair part on the spot.

Only then did the New Deal assist Sam Hensley and his family. On June 16, 1936, the U.S. federal treasury sent $500 checks to all living veterans of World War I, including Sam. Through announcements in newspapers and on radio, veterans of the Great War were told to be at home on June 16, 1936, so that they would be able to sign for the registered mail. Each veteran got an application to fill out and take to the local post office, where "certification officers" approved their applications and handed over a $500 bond. The next step was to go to the local bank for the money.[24]

"Young Ginny in Elkton"

During this three-year period, this was all the help that Samuel, Hilda, and Virginia Hensley received. So nothing really changed for Hilda and her growing daughter until August 1937, when all three arrived in Lexington, Virginia. Virginia Patterson Hensley turned five on September 8, 1937, as Washington and Lee College (hereafter W&L) started its fall session and her father began a new job supervising the new boiler system for the college. Her father had gained a steady job—and with it, free housing—with running water, indoor toilets, and electricity. Only then did a five-year struggle end, and as a side benefit, Ginny Hensley began her musical education, listening to Big Bands that played each weekend at W&L. The move to W&L at age five was the beginning of the musical interests of Patsy Cline.[25]

Lexington was 80 miles from Elkton and the rest of Sam's family. Sam Hensley had used his experience as a boilerman in Grottoes to find a permanent position as the boilerman for W&L's newly installed boiler system. The school needed a man who could deal with fire, repair iron parts on the spot, and keep the students warm through the winter.[26]

Hilda's niece remembered, "Hilda told me the Lexington home had a bathroom because it was her first." It was as if Hilda and Virginia suddenly entered the modern world. Yet Hilda never gave up her gardening. The family lived behind the campus, and thus could raise a cow for milk and chickens for food. They lived 100 feet up the hill from Woods Creek, where Hilda continued to fish.[27]

"The Hensley home in Lexington"

W&L was an elite private all-male college, an oasis of wealth in the Great Depression, which trained the sons of wealthy families to become "gentlemen." All students wore coats and ties to class, as was expected of upper-class families. Next door was the Virginia Military Institute (VMI), the "West Point of the South," where wealthy Virginians also sent their sons. Being boilerman proved a good working-class job, and the family settled in for five years and was so happy that Sam, by then fifty, and Hilda, twenty-four, added a baby brother to their family, born at home in November 1939. Virginia Hensley, age 7, helped raise her baby brother, Sam, Jr. (often called John by the family so as not to confuse him with his father). [28]

With steady work came the trappings of the modern urban United States. Hilda's niece remembers her aunt's telling her about the impact that the 1938 purchase of a radio had: "Aunt Hilda preferred country music. 'Ginny' liked all kinds of pop music." Young Ginny embraced the music she heard playing at weekend dances on campus. She became such as fan of the Big Band sound that she pestered her parents to buy her a used upright piano for her eighth birthday, September 8, 1940. She picked up chords to accompany her singing, but never took formal lessons.

Ginny responded to W&L as a musical (Big Band) paradise. Ginny could lie in bed and hear live music that played every weekend. The Big Bands played swing music in a gym less than one hundred yards from her bedroom.[29]

According to Sam's supervisor, J. Alexander Veech, superintendent of buildings and grounds, Sam's pay was free housing plus a salary of $80 a month. The used piano probably cost $5 at most. A used radio could have been purchased for less than that. Veech liked Sam, and noted that "he did good to outstanding work."[30]

Their home was officially described as a one story and part basement frame dwelling [of] wood-jointed construction covered with a metal roof. The building was supported by brick piers and the space beneath was enclosed with boards. The interior consisted of a double-joist floor, and the sidewalls, partition walls, and ceilings were insulated. (No more newspapers.) It had wiring for electricity supplied by the nearby campus, piping for running water, a toilet, and a septic field, and heat from the same system that Sam maintained for the college as a whole. It must have seemed like a mansion, with five rooms plus a separate bathroom. Young Virginia had her own bedroom with a window facing campus, and thus could easily hear the Big Bands that regularly came to campus to entertain at student dances.[31]

Sam was on call twenty-four hours a day so that, if something went wrong, Sam could immediately attend to the problem. The university had a special buzzer system to alert Sam to go down to the main boiler. The Baltimore and Ohio Railroad coal train stopped just a few yards behind the house and filled the adjacent bins with coal.[32]

With her mother's 1939 pregnancy, Ginny grew up quickly; she helped her mother during her pregnancy and then with the new baby. An only child for more than seven years, she confidently welcomed her baby brother; Sam Jr. and Ginny were close from the beginning. When you found the one, you found the other one. This close relationship started in the comfort and security of Lexington.[33]

When the Hensleys moved to W&L, the campus customs stressed fraternity-sponsored dances and all-college formal balls, with young women invited from nearby women's colleges. Weekend dances provided the center of a continuous social season, as nine hundred white male students looked for proper women to marry, ideally, soon after graduation. The essence of the W&L ethos might have been summed up in the school song "The Washington and Lee Swing."[34]

In fact, W&L was what later would be called a party school. Dance music was at its core. In December 1939, the candid report of the W&L president lamented, "The behavior of our boys has been creditable: the academic performance, though, [leaves] something to be desired." There were nineteen fraternities, where young men apprenticed to learn proper social skills, the ways to connect with young women attending nearby colleges with frequent use of their own cars, and how to schedule crammed social weekends. The total student body, 955 young men, viewed classes and course work as necessary evils.[35]

Fraternity parties came on Fridays and Saturdays, with tea dances on Sundays. The campus was openly wet. W&L was considered a gentleman's (read, well-off white elite's) club. Seniors were expected to set examples of proper behavior and good taste.[36]

W&L's main campus sat on the western edge of Lexington, then an independent city of 3,800—and rigidly segregated. The boilerman's house was actually situated in adjacent Rockbridge County, alongside the W&L athletic fields. Everywhere in Lexington were monuments to the "Lost Cause" of the Confederacy. The *Lee* in *Washington and Lee* was General Robert E. Lee himself, and in fact, the Confederate general was buried in the University chapel. Also in Lexington was the house where General "Stonewall" Jackson had lived when he left his professorship at VMI to lead the Confederate Army in its noted (Shenandoah) Valley campaign. The colleges may have made the town economy run, but Lexington also had a thriving tourist industry.[37]

White or blue button-down Oxford-cloth shirts and stripped ties were more than a custom; every student and professor walked around campus in them. Sportswear included tweed jackets and Shetland sweaters in solid brown, gray, or neutral shades. Gray flannel or neutral gabardine slacks completed the gentleman's wardrobe. For formal evening wear, all students owned a double-breasted midnight blue tuxedo and a white dinner jacket, but only seniors were permitted, according to custom, to wear white tie and tails. Students embraced the formal attire as the dress of a proper gentleman. Robert E. Lee had established the dominant code: "We have one rule here, and it is that every student must be a gentleman."

Lexington was white elite paradise. Neither VMI nor W&L had an African American, a Jew, or a woman enrolled. White downtown Lexington included everything from grocery stores to car dealerships to department stores. The few African Americans, who lived near downtown, worked as servants or domestics and lived in a small ghetto just east of the white central business district..

Former U.S. Supreme Court Justice Lewis Powell, Jr., earned two degrees at W&L less than a decade before the Hensleys arrived. Powell provides an ideal example of the W&L gentleman, a young man from Richmond who sought a college community drenched in the hagiography of the Old South. He remembered being impressed by the W&L buildings, known as the Colonnade, all lined up on the crest of the ridge, featuring a succession of neoclassical porches and white columns. For the well-mannered and cosmopolitan Powell, the principle activities at W&L were drinking, carousing, and sneaking young ladies past the fraternity housemothers. In his senior year, Powell became president of the student body, in which office his main responsibility proved to be hiring top Big Bands for W&L's fabled Fancy Dress Ball, an annual January extravaganza, for which students wore expensive costumes. Women came in from Randolph-Macon Women's College, in Lynchburg (45 miles away); Sweet Briar College, just north of Lynchburg (40 miles away); Hollins College (70 miles away); and Mary Baldwin College (35 miles north). From September 1937 to June 1941, almost every notable Big Band of the era showed up at least once to perform at W&L. (It took a world war to temporarily call a halt to this tradition.) Young Ginny listened, and learned to love the Big Band sound.[38]

Ginny Hensley could not have chosen a better spot for her musical education. Less than a month after moving in, the five-year old girl heard the local Don Bestor Orchestra and Dean Hudson and his Floridians, the first bands booked for that academic year (September 1937–June 1938). The music came from the W&L gym, and since the Hensleys' house was just across a steep valley, that music would have seemed to be amplified by modern stereo speakers.[39]

Each week, bands came, played, and created a crescendo toward the top event each year, January's Fancy Dress Ball. In January 1938 W&L student leaders booked Jan Garber (1894–1977), a jazz bandleader known in his heyday as The Idol of the Airwaves. He was only slightly less famous than Paul Whiteman and Guy Lombardo, and like those renowned bandleaders and their orchestras, Garber's and his orchestra played "sweet" dance music—meaning, he hired violins, as well as brass and woodwinds. (Later Big Bands dropped strings to go "hot.") But for W&L bookers, it was enough that Garber appeared as a big star on NBC radio. Ginny had listened to Garber on WNBC, from New York City, which she picked up on the family radio.[40]

In May 1938, to end the school year properly, W&L brought in the Hal Kemp band and singer Dolly Dawn. Kemp (1904–40) had just made a hit with "Got a Date with an Angel," and was another Paul Whiteman knockoff, but Kemp included noted jazz trumpeter Bunny Berigan. The Kemp band later would be seen as transitional, since it played both sweet and hot music. Every important band featured a female singer, and none at the time was more famous than Dolly Dawn. The diminutive and ebullient Dawn was, in fact, the focal point of the Kemp band. Her version of "Dawn Patrol" ranks high among the best loved recordings of the era. She proved to have an equally deft touch with both hot, jazzy tunes and tender ballads. By 1936, Dawn had already starred in a Warner Bros. Vitaphone short subject. She was known for her infectious sense of swing and the strategically employed trill in her voice. The twenty-two-year old delivered ballads with sweet passion, and jazz-inspired songs with spontaneous bounce and teasing wit. No less an authority on popular singing than Ella Fitzgerald expressed admiration for Dolly Dawn's work, once recalling that she used to skip school to hear Dawn sing. Ginny simply had to lie in bed and listen. If anyone inspired the six-year-old to become a singer, it was Dolly Dawn.[41]

"A typical Washington & Lee Dance"

On September 27, 1938, Paul Whiteman kicked off the next W&L social year. While he was not so "hip" in the late 1930s, compared with the innovative Benny Goodman, Artie Shaw, Tommy and Jimmy Dorsey, and Glenn Miller, Whiteman nonetheless remained very popular. His radio show proved to be a big hit for Chesterfield cigarettes. Thus, the then president of the student body and his advisors played it safe by bringing Whiteman to campus.[42]

Although called the King of Jazz, Paul Whiteman was not the "King of Swing." Anything but. During his long career as an orchestra leader he rarely ventured into swing territory. He played sweet music. (No wonder that, when producer Owen Bradley introduced strings to Patsy Cline records, his star had heard how well they could work.) At W&L, Paul Whiteman came with his twenty-six-member orchestra and six vocalists. His star was Mildred Bailey, who offered young Ginny another role model for her later career. .[43]

In January 1939, Hal Kemp and his orchestra returned for the Fancy Dress Ball, and Dolly Dawn returned to inspire Ginny. Kemp was a safe choice, but on February 28, 1939, the W&L student newspaper reported that a crisis had hit W&L's "big men on campus," since next- door rival, VMI, was getting more famous bands through its contract with its talent agency, the Music Corporation of America (hereafter MCA). So W&L student leaders also signed with MCA, which represented such stars as Jimmy Dorsey and his vocalist, Helen O'Connell. The big men on the W&L campus wanted the hottest bands that MCA could book for them—and the most popular of the Big Bands and their female vocalists.

This move to MCA expanded the selection of bands and female vocalists that Ginny would hear. That very next weekend, W&L booked Bunny Berigan and his hot band. The W&L student newspaper praised the new policy in bold type on its front page. Bunny Berigan

(1908–42) was one of the greatest trumpeters in the world of jazz. His range, virtuosity, and tone set the standard by which all other white trumpeters were judged. In 1937, MCA helped him create his own band. Ginny Hensley pressed her parents to tune into and listen to CBS Radio's "Saturday Night Swing Club" broadcasts, a forum from which Berigan helped popularize jazz as the hot new swing music. Berigan appeared at W&L with his own eleven-piece outfit, with four female singers—Kitty Lane, Ruth Gaylor, Gail Reese, and Jayne Dover.[44]

With the backing of the mighty MCA, Harry James and his band appeared at W&L on the weekend of March 21 and 22, 1939. In spring of that year there was no hotter band than Harry James's—unless it was Benny Goodman's. But James was almost as famous. MCA had formed the Harry James Band in January 1939. As a (white) trumpet player, James ranked at the top his profession. In 1937 James had joined Benny Goodman's band as featured player. James developed a simple, sweet style, his cool trumpet with a mass of strings. His performances ranged from blues to boogie-woogie to Viennese waltzes—all with the technical wizardry of his own trumpet. His solo singer was a young man—Frank Sinatra.

In May 1939, the hot drummer Gene Krupa and his band came to W&L, with Anita O'Day as the "girl" singer. Krupa was probably the most famous Big Band drummer in the United States, known for his high energy and flamboyant style. MCA found him in Chicago, and made him a member of Benny Goodman's band, where his featured drum work, especially on the hit "Sing, Sing, Sing," made Krupa a radio star. In 1938, MCA formed the Krupa band, with singer Anita O'Day. Jazz critic Will Friedwald has written, "When you think of the great jazz singers, I would think that Anita O'Day is the only white woman that belongs in the same breath as Ella Fitzgerald, Billie Holiday and Sarah Vaughan."[45]

In September 1939, as the W&L students reappeared from summer vacation, Ginny returned to her music education; there had been no dances or parties during the summer months. On September 12, 1939, Virginia Hensley started first grade at West Lexington School, a short walk from her house. She attended West Lexington through June of 1942 (the end of third grade—her longest stay at any one school before she dropped out in the tenth grade. The West Lexington School had three rooms and a central space with a piano. In at least one term, spring of 1940, she made the honor roll. This seems to have been a happy period of her life; indeed, she came back to Lexington for a visit in September 1953 with her first husband, Gerald Cline.[46]

In September 1939, the W&L campus leaders tried to rebook Hal Kemp, with the Jack Teagarden band as a second choice. Instead, these new big men on campus had to settle for another MCA client, the band headed by Ozzie Nelson, with his wife and female vocalist, Harriet Hilliard (yes, they were the Ozzie and Harriet of 1950s TV show fame, parents of David and Ricky Nelson). In 1939, Nelson was a full-time bandleader and Hilliard was the band's vocalist; so in September of that year, Virginia Hensley listened to yet another popular female Big Band singer.[47]

MCA then came through for the January 1940 Fancy Dress Ball with radio star Kay Kyser. MCA's Lew Wasserman had arranged for Kyser to be broadcast nationally over the CBS radio network, directly from W&L, as then there was no more popular radio star at the time. Kyser (1905–85) was purely an MCA radio creation. W&L leaders hired him not for his fabulous sound but for his radio celebrity. MCA and Kyser came up with an act that was part musical quiz and part singing, and it ran on NBC radio from 1939 to 1949 as Kay

Kyser's *Kollege of Musical Knowledge*. He played cover versions of hits by other, more creative Big Bands, but was booked all over the United States because he was a radio star. That W&L was even considered for a remote broadcast meant that the Hensleys could listen live or tune in on the CBS radio network and hear the same music. Kyser showcased his "girl singer," Ginny Simms.[48]

The battle of the bands between W&L and VMI came out into the open again for the 1940 Easter weekend dances, when the W&L big men on campus could consider MCA clients Tommy Dorsey, Harry James, Gene Krupa, and Woody Herman. W&L took Krupa again, and also Woody Herman. VMI countered with Glenn Miller—on the same Saturday night (April 20, 1940). Ginny Hensley may actually have heard Miller if her parents allowed her to walk a hundred yards from her house to sit across from the VMI gym and listen.

At W&L, she heard Woody Herman, who headed "The Band That Plays the Blues." In 1936, Woody Herman acquired the remains of Isham Jones's orchestra, after Jones decided to retire. On April 12, 1939, Herman had recorded his top hit record, "Woodchoppers' Ball," and then appeared at W&L with one of the most famous Big Bands in the United States—and with his vocalist, Francis Wayne.[49]

For the final dances of 1940, held on June 5, 6, and 7, Ginny Hensley heard the Eddy Duchin Orchestra play on three consecutive nights. The sweet-sounding Duchin was a popular pianist and bandleader of the 1930s and 1940s, famous for his engaging on-stage personality and his elegant piano-based style. One of the first pianists to lead a commercially successful large band, he became widely popular, thanks to regular radio broadcasts. Playing sweet music rather than hot jazz, Duchin's 1938 cover of Louis Armstrong's "Ol' Man Mose," with vocalist Patricia Norman, zoomed to number 2 on the *Billboard* charts. Duchin was at his peak when he arrived at W&L with his singer, Durelle Alexander.

Also in early June 1940, Jimmy Dorsey and his singer Helen O'Connell entertained at W&L. The Dorsey brothers, Jimmy and Tommy, helped promote swing music. And Ohioan Helen O'Connell was one of the most popular a singers at the time. After working for several regional bands, her big break came during a stay in New York in 1939, when Jimmy Dorsey heard her sing. She was a female crooner, popular with radio audiences for her hit "All of Me." In fact, she was voted best female vocalist in a 1940 Metronome poll.[50]

By then Ginny Hensley was hooked. She loved the music she was hearing and wanted to be the next Helen O'Connell or Dolly Dawn. She regularly listened to them on the radio and copied down their lyrics. And she wanted her own piano. Her parents could now afford this luxury, and they treated Ginny to one for her eighth birthday, just as the W&L 1940 social season was starting. Ginny wanted to play the tunes she heard played on the radio and also live on campus. If there was a genesis of "Patsy Cline," it was on September 8, 1940.

She remembered the date fondly, as she revealed in a letter to fan club President Treva Miller dated October 29, 1955. A parade of "girl singers" had inspired her, and Eddy Duchin made her want to learn the piano. Her father approved because he could play a little. Her cousin remembered, "She'd hear something once and then play it. She taught herself by listening." This self-teaching would become the hallmark of Patsy Cline. She had no formal training, and could not read music, but she trained her brain to focus on the melodies and words, and practiced and practiced.[51]

The new 1940 academic year at W&L was supposed to start with Benny Goodman, but this MCA client's saw band had broken up over the summer, and MCA pulled him. Instead came Larry Clinton, a trumpeter who became a prominent bandleader between 1937 and 1941. His hook was to rearrange the works of famous classical composers like Debussy and Tchaikovsky, and add lyrics to "swing the classics." His version of Debussy's "Reverie" featured female vocalist Bea Wain, and became a hit on the *Billboard* charts.[52]

For the January 25, 1941, Fancy Dress Ball, Goodman finally appeared. He was so popular, even with his new African American band members, that W&L authorities let the integrated band appear on the stage in the gym. In the 1941 W&L yearbook, there appears a photo of African Americans Lionel Hampton and Teddy Wilson on stage, playing at the Fancy Dress Ball. Conservative W&L campus leaders finally embraced hot swing music, which was redefining pop music in the United States. Three decades later , aspiring lyricist Alan Bergman, then fifteen, described the Goodman sound of that year as "the most amazing thing I had ever heard in my life. I had never heard music like that before—no one had." Bergman described the Goodman Orchestra of the early 1940s—when nine-year-old Virginia Patterson Hensley heard it live—as "Benny's all-time greatest band." As W&L had no Jewish students, Benny Goodman, a Jew from Chicago, also broke a religious barrier with his appearance. Gender, however, had never been an issue, as long as women "kept their place," either as dates or Big Band singers. W&L gentlemen had no problem with Goodman singer at that time, Louise Tobin; the following year, Louise Tobin and the Goodman band would create a major hit, "There'll Be Some

Changes Made." She stood off to the side, and when Goodman called she took her place before the microphone and sang.[53]

News of the European war in June 1941 began to restrict Big Band bookings at W&L. More important for the Hensley family, as Ginny finished third grade, in June 1941, her father learned that the U.S. government was accelerating ship repair activities at the Norfolk Navy Yard, located in Portsmouth, Virginia. The government was looking for blacksmiths, and offered twice what her fifty-one-year-old father was making at W&L.

On July 15, 1941, Sam Hensley applied. Soon after the attack by Japan on Pearl Harbor, the Navy Yard his application and so Ginny Hensley finished out the school year, then moved with her mother and brother to Winchester to be close to Hilda's ailing mother. On July 17, 1942, her father left by train for Portsmouth, 230 miles away. As he had in Washington, DC, Sam, Sr., found a room a few blocks from the Navy Yard. Hilda (age twenty-five), Ginny (age nine), and Sam, Jr. (age two) rented a small bungalow on Winchester's east side and awaited Sam, Sr.'s, call that he had found family housing. Hilda was pregnant when Sam, Sr., left to earn $9.60 per day for a 6 day week, more than $3,000 a year— the most he had earned in his life. [54]

The move to Winchester proved disappointing for Ginny. Her education in live Big Band music ended, and she lost her beloved piano. And her mother was pregnant. But Ginny was so hooked on Big Bands that she insisted on keeping the radio. While the family waited to join Sam, Sr., in Portsmouth, Ginny, turning ten in September of 1942, attended fourth grade at the John Handley School. While many standard authorities have her dropping out of John Handley High school, she actually never attended the high school, only (September 1942 through February 1943) the temporary grade school set up during the World War II,

The John Handley School had pianos, but only for high school students in another part of the building complex. She entered a city school that taught "good" (meaning classical) music, and earned average grades (Cs), as she struggled with being the "new girl." That a Handley fourth-grade teacher gave Ginny a grade of C in music seems both ironic and telling. She loved Big Band music, but the teacher graded her on her ability to appreciate classical music.

Virginia Hensley's response was to focus on listening to the radio as her interest in formal education decreased. She continued to teach herself popular tunes by taking notes on lyrics and then teaching herself to sing the tune with daily practice. Radio turned out to be her musical instructor , teaching her Big Band singers' newest hits.[55]

Making family life worse, in October 1942, Hilda's beloved mother died and Hilda grieved with her brother and sister. In 1934, her stepfather had paid $850 for a farm one mile from Gore, where Goldie and her six Allanson children lived. On October 9, 1942, the *Winchester Evening Star* noted on its obituary page that Goldie was but fifty-two years old and that she had died at about 1:30 a.m. at her home in Gore, from the lack of a medicine (unnamed), on which she was dependent for a chronic condition. Frank Allanson, who was by then employed at the Virginia Glass Sand Corporation open pit mine, in Gore, survived her. So did Hilda's older sister, Mrs. Russell (Madge) Whitacre, and older brother, Robert. Goldie Allanson had been a long-time member of the Baptist church in Gore, where she was buried. Thereafter, Hilda would turn to her sister and brother for family support. Hilda's niece noted how hard Hilda took her mother's death at such a relatively young age. Hilda's own husband was a year older.[56]

During this short stay in Winchester, Ginny listened to network radio broadcasts from Washington, DC. In January 1943, the most popular network radio program was

The Pepsodent [toothpaste] *Show,* on NBC, starring Bob Hope with frequent female guest singers, including Jo Stafford, who was just launching her solo singing career. If there was any solace in the eight-month Winchester stay, it was that Ginny discovered a new role model for her singing. As Jo Stafford (1917–2008) became more and more popular, Ginny began to imitate her sound. At the same time, Hilda grew ever larger with her pregnancy, turning to Ginny for help, and hence Ginny missed many days of school. Hilda and Ginny worked together running the growing family.[57]

Sam, Sr., worked at the Norfolk Navy Yard, located on the Elizabeth River, in Portsmouth. This area had long been a key base of the United States Navy, as it possessed a good, deep port. By the time of World War II, there were almost four hundred military bases, offices, depots, annexes, air stations, and shipyards in what was called the Hampton Roads area. In 1942, with the buildup in ship repair for the naval battles of World War II, the Norfolk Navy Yard was hiring a thousand new workers a month. To make room for the construction and repair of ships, the Norfolk Navy Yard expanded from 352 to 746 acres. City buses, restaurants, and hospitals filled to capacity. To the rest of the United States, the area became the prime example of wartime overcrowding.[58]

While boarding alone, Sam, Sr., spent a great of his free time (a few hours a day) seeking a spot in new federally funded housing for war workers with large families. That the Hensleys would soon be a family of five qualified them for a place in the new Alexander Homes project, three miles west by bus from the Navy Yard. He achieved a reserved spot sometime early in 1943, as Hilda approached her expected April delivery date. All three thousand of the Alexander Homes were identical, with insulated wallboard and redwood siding, built quickly from prefabricated parts and with mass-production methods. All had two bedrooms, in addition to a living room, a kitchen, a bath, storage space, and an average of six closets. After the war ended, the builders of Alexander homes, The Levitt Company, used the same mass-production techniques to create whole prefabricated towns, such as Levittown, New York, and Levittown, Pennsylvania.[59]

Hilda hated Portsmouth, and grew nostalgic for rural living. She had no garden, and her niece remembered Hilda stating that Portsmouth was "too crowded; and noisy all the time." In the evening, Hilda missed sitting on the porch, listening to the birds and crickets. Hilda learned to hate cities and would never live in a big city again. But she was able to find a midwife to help with Sylvia's April 1943 home birth.[60]

Sam, Sr., did dangerous work. On January 6, 1943, a couple of months before his family arrived, he lacerated a finger while trimming a piece of steel to make a repair part. In the rush to war, blacksmiths worked as all-in-one mechanics who could fabricate a part, as well as fix or repair rivets on older ships. The Navy preferred welders, but there simply was no time to train enough welders for the tasks at hand. So the Navy went with the second-best solution -- employing aging blacksmiths.[61]

Again Ginny entered a new school, but one where chaos defined the so-called school day. She was in class with sons and daughters of shipyard workers from all over the South. If everyone knew everyone at the school in Lexington, no one knew anyone in Portsmouth. The only constant was that everything, including school was crowded with unknown faces. By November 1, 1943, the civilian population of Hampton Roads was 505,119 persons. The Hensleys did far better than most with housing, but had to deal with inadequate, overtaxed utilities, bus transportation, and even access to running water as well as shortages of food. Rationing meant Ginny looked after her baby sister and small brother while her mother waited in line to use her ration coupons to buy food to feed the family.[62]

With all this chaos, Ginny again retreated to her radio. Later her second husband remembered, "Patsy told me that when she was young, she used to hum or sing with just about every song she'd hear on the radio." When at home, taking care of her sister and brother, she had total control of the radio, and as she was turning eleven in September 1943 and twelve in September 1944, Jo Stafford was her favorite—and the nation's favorite—female pop singer. Stafford was all over the radio on regularly scheduled shows and as a guest star in the highest demand. Her popularity has never been properly understood or explained. It might have been that she had a way of letting a song happen, rather than shoving it at the listeners, soaked in her personal style. Jo Stafford had gone solo in November 1942, and by 1944 she began a string of hits. She won the *Downbeat* magazine award for top singer of 1945.[63]

Young Virginia Hensley was hardly the lone singer inspired by Stafford. Judy Collins grew up in Colorado and listened to KOA radio from Denver and heard Jo Stafford. Later labeled a "folk" singer, in interviews Collins revealed that it wasn't the sound of the Weavers or Woody Guthrie, but that of Jo Stafford, that inspired her. As an eleven-year old, Collins heard Stafford sing "Barbara Allen" —a ballad of unrequited love, death, and grief, and she modeled her singing ever after on Stafford's. Ginny Hensley used her radio listening to also become inspired by Stafford..[64]

On January 12, 1945, the U.S. Congress saw that the European war was about to end and began to investigate inactive workers at the Norfolk Navy Yard. The Senate issued a report that found "excess manpower," and out-of-power Republicans demanded a response. The Norfolk Navy Yard top brass knew that good PR was key, and in February 1945 started terminating last-hired workers. That put Sam, Sr.'s, job in jeopardy. He was by then fifty-five years old, and his trade had gone down in value as welders had been trained to replace him. Blacksmiths, particularly those aged fifty-five, were simply not needed. Thus, he lost his job in March 1945. He had an unknown contact back in the Shenandoah Valley, in Edinburg (population 500), so the family of five returned to the Shenandoah Valley.[65]

By then, his twelve-year old daughter knew what she wanted to do—become a singer like Jo Stafford. Ginny loved the latest pop music and the family prospects seemed good after the war, as her father, like many war workers, had saved a great deal of money, since the U.S. Navy forced him to purchase war bonds. In March 1945 he cashed them in. From September 1937 to March 1945, Ginny's working-class life would prove to be the peak of family prosperity, which she would not attain again until 1957. Steadily, the Hensleys slipped back into economic hardship. Young Ginny was optimistic about her prospects as a budding pop singing star, but had never appeared before an audience. Her lack of formal training did not bother her, as she figured that Jo Stafford, Helen O'Connell, and company had not needed advanced education—only a break.

NOTES

Chapter 2

1   William O. Stevens, <u>The Shenandoah and Its ByWays</u> (New York: Dodd, Mead, 1941).

2   The Military Record of Samuel L. Hensley, on deposit at the Regional National Archives, St. Louis, Missouri (hereafter, Military Record).

3   Charles R. Alton and Samuel L Hensley v. Sylvia M. Wilt , in Circuit Court for the City of Winchester, Chancery Number CH99000084, March 1, 2002 (hereafter TRIAL); Stuart Brown, Patsy Cline Archive, held in Handley Archives, Winchester, Virginia (hereafter Brown Archives).

4   Frederick County [VA] Deed Book 138/ 292; Deed Book, 142/413; Deed Book, 121/459, on file at Judicial Center, Winchester, VA; Alfred W. Crosby, <u>America's Forgotten Pandemic: The Influenza of 1918</u> (New York: Cambridge University Press, 1989).

5   William L. Selke, <u>Prisons in Crisis</u> (Bloomington, IN: Indiana University Press. 1993), 55.

6   Richmond Times-Dispatch, July 5, 1992, .

7   ORAL HISTORY, Patricia Brannon and Rebecca Williams; ORAL HISTORY -- April 2007) (hereafter Oral History); WS, August 30, 1923, 1; WS, January 23, 1988: A2.

8   S. Collins and J. Lehman, "Excess Deaths from Influenza and Pneumonia and from Important Chronic Disease during Epidemic Periods 1918–1951," <u>Public Health Monographs,</u> No. 10 (1953).

9   Military Record; Kathy Hensley Caswell, <u>Hensley Descendants</u> (Fenton, MO: No Waste Publishing, 2008), 201.

10   ORAL HISTORY, May 1, 2009, Patricia Brannon and Rebecca Williams, (hereafter ORAL HISTOY [May 1, 2007]).

11 Military Record; <u>Valley</u> [Elkton, VA] <u>Banner</u>, October 8, 2008, 5; Sam Lehman, ed., "Gore," Chap. 8, Pt. 2, in <u>The Story of Frederick County</u> (Winchester, VA: Frederick County Board of Supervisors, 1989.

12 Marial S. Kaplan, <u>Frederick County, Virginia</u> (Winchester, VA: The Winchester–Frederick County Historical Society, 1999).

13 Rudy Abramson and Jean Haskell, eds., <u>The Encyclopedia of Appalachia</u> (Knoxville, TN: University of Tennessee Press, 2006).

14 Kathy Hensley Caswell, <u>Hensley Descendants</u> (Fenton, MO: No Waste Publishing, 2008).

15 <u>WS</u>, B1, September 8, 1982; Radio show, March 1975, on deposit at Celebrating Patsy Cline (hereafter CPC).

16 ORAL HISTORY (May 1, 2007); Patricia Brannon and Rebecca Williams, Oral History (July 31, 2007) (hereafter Oral History [July 31, 2007]; Trial.

17 Trial.

18 ORAL HISTORY – Herman Longley, Jr. (October 20, 1995. (Longley was the son of Sam Hensley's sister and a local historian of Elkton, VA.)

19 <u>The [Elkton, Virginia] Valley Banner</u>, April 2, 2009:1; Virginius Dabney, <u>The Last Reunion</u> (Chapel Hill: Algonquin Books, 1984); Charles Reagan Wilson, <u>Baptized in Blood: The Religion of the Lost Cause</u>, 1865-1920 (Athens: University of Georgia Press, 1980); ORAL HISTORY – April 10, 2007.

20 Ronald L. Heinemann, <u>The Great Depression and New Deal in Virginia</u> (Charlottesville: University Press of Virginia, 1983); Nancy J. Martin-Perdue and Charles L. Perdue Jr., <u>Talk about Trouble: A New Deal Portrait of Virginians in the Great Depression</u> (Chapel Hill: University of North Carolina Press, 1996).

21 Tony Waters. <u>The Persistence of Subsistence Agriculture: Life Beneath the Level of the Marketplace</u> (Lanham, MD: Lexington Books. 2007).

22 James D. Watkinson, "The Treatment of the Poor in Antebellum Virginia," <u>Virginia Cavalcade</u> (Winter 2000): 21–29; David Wagner, <u>The Poorhouse: America's Forgotten Institution</u> (Lanham, MD: Rowman & Littlefield, 2005).

23 <u>The Harrisonburg [Virginia] News-Record</u>, March 28, 1995: 9.

24 Paul Dickson, and Thomas B. Allen, <u>The Bonus Army: An American Epic</u> (New York: Walker and Company, 2004).

25 Military Record.

26 Military Record; Lester G. Telser, "The Veteran's Bonus of 1936 and the Abortive Recovery from the Great Depression," MA Thesis, University of Chicago, 1949.

27 Military Record; ORAL HISTORY – April 10, 2007.

28 TRIAL; ORAL HISTORY – April 10, 2007.

29 ORAL HISTORY, April 10, 2007.

30 Military Record.

31 In a Report on file at the W&L Lee Special Collections entitled "Inspection and Survey report: property of Washington & Lee University Engineering Department, issued February 1941, "DWELLING .. BUILDING NO 50 – The Bolilerman's House"

32 ORAL HISTORY – Raymond E. Bryant – January 2, 2001; The W&L student newspaper named "The Ring-tum Phi" in its 20 May 1937 issue had a news story about the new boiler system on its front page. Lisa S. McCown, of Special Collections, guided me through the W&L collections.

33 ORAL HISTORY – April 10, 2007.

34 Papers at the W&L Leybourne Archive and time line as prepared by the university in 2001.

35 A copy of the December 1939 President's report rests in the W&L Special Collections.

36 The following is based upon the only history of the University -- self published in 1998: <u>Come Cheer for Washington and Lee: The University at 250 Years</u> – found at W&L Library special collections.

37 Winifred Hadsel, <u>The Streets of Lexington</u> (Lexington, Virginia: The Rockbridge Historical Society, 1985); Rockbridge Retired Teachers Association (ed.), <u>A Brief History of Public Education in Rockbridge County</u> (Lexington: privately published, 1980).

38 John C. Jeffries, Jr., <u>Lewis Powell</u> (New York: Charles Scribner's Sons, 2001):26-39.

39 This is from a weekly campus newspaper called The Ring-Tum Phi which the author read from the time the Hensleys arrived a three person family in September 1937 to June 1942 when Sam Sr. left for Portsmouth and Hilda, Virginia (aged 9) and Sam Jr. (aged 2) went to Winchester. See also images from the 1938-1942 W&L Yearbooks.

40 web sites: www.swingmusic.net & www.downbeat.com – accessed March 23, 2007.

41 George T. Simon, <u>The Big Bands</u>, (New York: Schirmer Books, 1981).

42 William E. Studwell and Mark Baldin, <u>The Big Band Reader</u> (New York: Haworth Press, 2000):201-204.

43 Joshua Berrett, <u>Louis Armstrong and Paul Whiteman: Two Kings Of Jazz</u> (New Haven: Yale University Press, 2004).

44 Robert Dupuis, <u>Elusive Legend of Jazz: Bunny Berigan</u> (Baton Rouge: LSU Press, 1993).

45 http://www.drummerworld.com/drummers/Gene_Krupa.html – accessed March 16, 2005.

46 TRIAL; The Rockbridge County News, 2 February 1940: 5.

47 Ozzie Nelson, Ozzie, (Englewood Cliffs, NJ: Prentice Hall, 1983).

48 Philip K. Eberley. Music on the Air (New York: Hastings House, 1982).

49 Gene Lees, Leader of the Band: The Life of Woody Herman (New York: Oxford University Press, New York, 1995); Woody Herman, The Woodchopper's Ball: The Autobiography of Woody Herman (New York: Dutton, 1990).

50 Leo Walker, The Wonderful World of the Great Dance Bands (Garden City, New York: Doubleday, 1964).

51 ORAL HISTORY, May 1, 2007.

52 web site http://fancydress.wlu.edu – accessed March 22, 2002.

53 Brown Archives.

54 ORAL HISTORY – May 1, 2007; Military Record; Jonathan J. Wolfe, "Virginia in World War II," Unpublished Ph.D. dissertation, University of Virginia, 1971.

55 The John Handley High School Archives – accessed by CPC on July 13, 2006.

56 ORAL HISTORY - January 18, 2008.

57 Harrison B. Summers, editor, A Thirty-Year History of Programs Carried on National Radio Networks in the United States (Columbus: The Ohio State University, Department of Speech, January 1958).

58 National Archives, Records of the Committee for Congested Production Areas 1943-1945 (NARA - Record Group 212), College Park, MD; Patrick Evans-Hylton, Hampton Roads: The World War II Years (Charleston, SC: Arcadia Publishing, 2005).

[59] NYT, February 11, 1942: 12; <u>Hill's Norfolk and Portsmouth City Directory</u>, Volume XCIII: 1386 – found at the Local History Room of the Portsmouth Public Library.

[60] ORAL HISTORY – April 10, 2007.

[61] Communication from Dave Allen, Appalachian Blacksmiths Association [web site: http://www.appaltree.net – accessed 9 December 2003; Military Record.

[62] Marvin W. Schlegal, <u>Conscripted City</u> (Norfolk: Norfolk War Commission, 1951); Patrick Evans-Hylton, <u>Hampton Roads: The World War II Years</u> (Charleston, SC: Arcadia Publishing, 2005).

[63] The University of Arizona School of Music, "The Paul Weston and Jo Stafford Collection, Collection" Number: MMS 6; Gene Lees, <u>Singers and The Songs</u> (New York: Oxford University Press, 1999); Jim Cox, <u>Music Radio</u> (Jefferson, NC: McFarland, 2005).

[64] NYT, April 23, 2009: C5.

[65] Military Record.

Chapter 3

A Career as a Singer Begins

On Wednesday, April 4, 1945, Sam Hensley, Sr., turned in his tools at the Portsmouth Navy Yard and the family of five moved back to the Shenandoah Valley of Virginia. As World War II had not yet ended, men with Sam, Sr.'s, skills were in demand on the home front. The Hensleys journeyed 250 miles to the town of Edinburg (population 500), some thirty-seven miles north of where Sam, Sr.'s, brothers and sisters lived, in Elkton, and some forty-eight miles south of where Hilda's brother and sister lived, near Winchester. The final entry in Sam, Sr.'s Military Record notes, "This employee states as he is getting older he wishes to establish himself in business where he wouldn't have to work so steady."[1]

The war work provided the Hensley family with some savings, but hardly enough to look forward to retirement. As Sam, Sr., realized that his dream of retirement would never come true, he grew bitter. Patsy's cousin reflected, "They moved so often because he'd run his mouth. That's why he could not hold a job." But in addition, few wanted to hire a man nearing sixty years of age who had been trained as a blacksmith.[2]

At first he was able to gain a job to his liking, maintaining a cooperative electric system. With this job came a house with electricity, running water, indoor plumbing, a radio, and even a telephone. The Edinburg, Virginia, electric cooperative had come into being because of the Rural Electrification Administration, part of FDR's New Deal. The U.S. Department of Agriculture subsidized its construction of a dam, and then the REA installed poles and wires. Edinburg proved to be a rare small town where everyone had electricity.[3]

Edinburg also had a two-story school building that accommodated all rural grades, first to eleventh. (Only in 1950 did the Commonwealth of Virginia require rural school systems to add kindergarten and twelfth grade.) Ginny's fifth-grade elementary school room had a glass cabinet that held the 50 textbooks. The school was a New Deal Works Progress Administration (WPA)–built project. But the Hensleys' stay in Edinburg proved short lived. The town's electrical grid maintenance man came back from the war and reclaimed his job. Thus, by the beginning of 1946, the family of five had moved twenty-four miles up U.S. 11 (the Valley Pike), relocating on a tenant farm in Middletown, Virginia (population 500), closer to Hilda's extended family and forever disconnecting them from the Hensley side of the family.[4]

———————————

Moving to Middletown in time for the spring planting of 1946 represented a significant step down the economic ladder. Herbert Larrick rented the Hensley family one of his farm's houses, for a split of the crop. Larrick offered the house gratis, but guaranteed Sam, Sr., and Hilda—and the three children—no wages. Thus, the Hensleys moved into the cycle of nature: agriculture boom and bust. They lived at "the Larrick place" for just one planting season, spring through fall 1946. Hilda retooled her subsistence-farming skills. Middletown was the same size as Edinburg but had no electric cooperative, so the family returned to the preelectrical age. The home had no plumbing, and so they returned to an outhouse and hauled water from a well. Middletown had one special trait—Frederick County's biggest rural school. Opened in 1909 as part of the agriculture training movement, the Middletown school taught boys agriculture skills and girls "domestic science." By the time Virginia Hensley attended the school, it had built two separate additional buildings, one used by the girls to learn proper "housekeeping," and one for the boys to learn agricultural skills.[5]

H. Dennis Hoover was principal from 1939 through 1950. He was strict. When Mildred Brumback attended Middletown in the 1940s, she and her classmates could tell when Principal Hoover was coming. "Most of the high school was upstairs," she said. "When he taught class, you would hear the steps screeching. We knew when to get quiet." In 1997, Hoover remembered that "back then" the students started in the first grade and attended until they either dropped out to work on the farm or graduated. Virginia Hensley entered the sixth grade in the spring of 1946, and then attended the seventh grade that fall. Always the outsider, she was the only one of her class of twenty who had not lived in Middletown her whole life. Moreover, the Larrick Place bestowed a special lower-class status, as attorney Larrick drove away tenant families yearly. But Larrick did supply a piano, as did the Middletown school. Ginny took up her piano playing (and singing) in earnest.[6]

Middletown, like Edinburg, consisted of but one main street (the Valley Pike), with a dozen buildings housing stores to sell staples to local farmers. In Ginny's spring and fall school sessions, according to her classmate Virginia Dicks (Gruver), the teachers stressed letter writing. This would give rise to invaluable data, as Patsy Cline became an obsessive letter writer and correspondents saved her letters. Gruver also remembered, "Ginny would play piano and sing at both home and school."[7]

Ginny attended classes in domestic science, social studies, English, history, and mathematics. But perhaps the most valuable benefits of her Middletown School experience were the regular medical and dental examinations that Frederick County schools provided. These would prove vital to Ginny, as she never had the long-term dental problems so common among the poor.

When Ginny attended the Middletown school, the Domestic Science Building contained three rooms, a kitchen, a work room with sewing machines, and a bedroom. Girls learned everything from first aid to sewing pillow cases. Their first project was fashioning an apron from a feed sack, something Ginny Hensley had already learned from her mother. The girls also prepared a meal from scratch and invited parents as guests. There were few extracurricular activities, as the students went home early in the afternoon to help with chores.[8]

After just one growing season, Herbert Larrick and Sam Hensley, Sr., severed their agreement, and the Hensleys moved yet another step down the economic ladder. In November of 1946, Sam looked for a new position, one that would pay wages; so over the Christmas season, he took a position as a salary worker for the High Hill Orchard, located just outside Round Hill, Virginia, thirty miles to the northeast. Round Hill barely offered a crossroads for a downtown, but three miles to the east, on Virginia Route 7, lay Purcellville (population 700). Virginia Hensley again started at a new school, but records state that she usually stayed home to help her mother and father—and to listen to the radio.

The family was hired to help Elizabeth Sleeter maintain the sixty-acre orchard. In 1941, she and her husband, Colonel Frank Sleeter, had moved to rural Loudoun County for the country lifestyle and because housing in Washington, DC, proved so scarce. Col. Sleeter carpooled for the sixty-mile journey to the nation's capital and left management of the orchard to his spouse. The Sleeters had purchased a vast stone home for their family, and the tenant house came with it in the deal. Elizabeth Sleeter revived the small orchard with the help of hired men whom she offered free housing and wages paid biweekly.

Ginny first went to the Round Hill Elementary school, and then, after the summer of 1947, attended the Lincoln school for the eighth grade. As at Middletown school, she took traditional classes in English, history, and mathematics. The Hensley's two-story home on the Streeter property contained a full kitchen, dining room, and living room on the first floor, and bedrooms and a sewing room on the second floor. In the fall, Ginny again most often stayed home to help her family pick apples. Sam, Sr., was a low-paid employee, and so the family depended on Hilda's subsistence-farming skills in order to eat. But the family had electricity (for a radio), a well, and even a "leach field" (a gravel filled cesspool) for indoor plumbing[9]

Lincoln School was the largest school Ginny had ever attended, and it even had a stage and a small basketball arena at its core, surrounded by individual classrooms, each holding about twenty-five students. Both Round Hill Elementary and Lincoln Schools had pianos, but with family work requiring her to be at home, Ginny had only her radio, which played the popular songs of the day, allowing her to write down the lyrics and learn the songs, thus continuing her musical self-education.[10]

"Lincoln School"

But one cold December day, Virginia Hensley was gone. Fellow student Carroll Jones remembered this, since they usually rode the bus together: "Just before Christmas break, she was no longer on the bus." As was always the case in the Hensley family postwar moves, the nomadic family owned little and could pick up and leave for what Sam, Sr., and Hilda thought might be a better job.[11]

The Hensleys always felt isolated in Loudoun County, forty miles on a two-lane road from Hilda's relatives in Gore. At age fifty-eight, Sam Hensley, Sr., finally gave up any aspirations to making it on his own. He turned to his thirty-one- year-old wife, who contacted her brother; Robert "Buck" Patterson was working at the open-pit sand mine near Gore, and he got Sam a job requiring blacksmith skills. Sam worked the midnight to eight a.m. shift, running a sand dryer. In December 1947, the Hensley family rented a house three miles west of Gore on U.S. 50. The "Bock place" had electricity, a well, and was twice the size of the tenant house in Round Hill.[12]

Ginny reentered the eighth grade in late December 1947 at the smaller Gore School. The Frederick Country school system reported that Virginia Hensley withdrew from Gore High School in November 1948, ending her formal education.

It was a turbulent time, as Ginny's family was coming apart at the seams. Sam never adjusted to the graveyard shift. He started running behind on his bills. Sometime in the spring of 1948, the Hensleys were tossed out of the Bock house for nonpayment of rent, and they moved to the "Turner Dunlap place," more than five miles down Back Creek Road from the Gore school, a house with no electricity, toilets, or well. Patsy lost her access to radio.[13]

"The Turner Dunlap House"

But at least the school had a piano. So did the only church in town, the Mt. Hebron Baptist church. Charles Hoak was her classmate at Gore School. He got to know her because she "attended the youth functions of the Baptist church— particularly the Royal Ambassadors." On Sunday evenings they met and sang, as prescribed by the rules of the Royal Ambassadors for Christ. Hoak remembered singing hymn duets with her: "I sang with her—two nobodies when the youth director would say for 'Charlie and Virginia' to sing together." Hoak also remembered waiting for school in the morning at his mother's general store, and seeing Sam struggling home from work at eight a.m.: "He was always dirty after night shift. We kids assumed he was mean as he often yelled at us."[14]

"Mt. Hebron Baptist Church"

At the isolated Turner Dunlap house, Hilda and her children were overwhelmed. During the day Hilda had to take care that five-year-old Sylvia would not disturb Sam, Sr.'s, sleep. Ginny took Sam, Jr., to Gore School on the bus, and returned in the late afternoon. Then came the hardest part of the day, from four p.m. until eleven p.m., when the whole family was stuffed into the small house, catering to their weary father's moods as he prepared for his graveyard shift. Like all nearby families, Hilda and Ginny tended a vast garden, fetched all the water, cleaned the outhouses, and raised chickens. Charles Hoak saw the strain on the Hensleys and later recalled, "Mr. Hensley was famous for his hot temper, and often came out of the town's general store cussing. I know because my mother co-owned the store and Sam Hensley left her with a $300 bill."

The graveyard shift at the Sand Mine proved to be grueling work. To make the sand, first workers had to dynamite the rock, blowing sandstone off the hill, and then hauling it to a crusher, which ground the rock into wet sand. Next workers converted the wet sand into sellable sand by heating it with fire—and Sam Hensley operated what was called the dryer. This was dangerous work, for the buildings were all wooden and the fire was constant. And to make working conditions even worse, Sam labored on the same shift as Hilda's stepfather, a watchman. It must have been uncomfortable, to say the least.

"The Sand Mine where Sam Hensley worked"

In short, Hilda Hensley had fallen back into the conditions that had driven her out of the Gore area in the first place. Here again was daily grinding poverty, reminding Hilda of the 1930s. Hoak recalled, "Families were poorer the further down the road you went." And at the end of the macadam road—just before it turned to a dirt by-way—lived the Hensleys. It was just another rental place, with bare wooden floors, a kitchen where Hilda cooked in the fireplace. With no electricity, there was no refrigerator. Back Creek was literally across the road and so for refrigeration Hilda kept her milk, and preserved vegetables, in the creek." Hilda returned to fishing, and Ginny learned to catch squirrels for meat. In 2004, Loretta Lynn published *My Favorite Recipes and Memories* (Nashville: Thomas Nelson), and she confirmed that Patsy Cline loved squirrel meat.[15]

In September 1948, Frank Whitacre arrived as the new principal; he remembered Virginia Hensley as an outgoing but average student. He remembered her because she constantly pestered him to use the school's piano. Whitacre recalled, "I'd say, 'Virginia sing us a song,' and she'd step up and do it." She was now focused on her sole ambition, to become a professional singer.[16]

Whitacre remembered her love for Al Jolson. At the time, the vaudevillian was making a comeback based on two movies about his life. While Larry Parks portrayed Jolson on screen as a young man, Jolson rerecorded his past hits: "Rock-a-bye Your Baby," "California, Here I Come," "You Made Me Love You," "Sonny Boy," and "Avalon." Hollywood's Columbia Pictures released *The Jolson Story* in late 1946, and the film made its way to theaters in the Shenandoah Valley in 1947 and 1948. Ginny's principal and Gore school classmates were fans.[17]

But singing even uptempo Jolson songs at school could not mask the troubles at home. One of Ginny's classmates put it bluntly:

"Hilda got fed up, and took the kids and left Sam and went to Kent Street [in Winchester]." At age fifty-nine, Sam, Sr., wanted a day job; Hilda wanted a return to electricity, running water, and indoor plumbing. And Ginny wanted a radio. So in late November 1948, just before Thanksgiving Day, the thirty-two-year old Hilda sent Sam, Sr., packing, and moved the family—Ginny, age sixteen; Sam, Jr., age nine, and Sylvia, age five—into Winchester.[18]

Rumors circulated about abuse by Ginny's father, but the facts seem to justify an interpretation of a simple breakdown of the family dynamics. In Winchester, South Kent Street was where poor whites lived, and Hilda reasoned she could at least pay her bills and jettison the constant complaining of her increasingly dysfunctional spouse. Hilda finally settled in Winchester, after three years of seemingly constant moving, and never left. She raised her children by making all their clothes, raising much of what they ate, and using the monies from work as a seamstress to enable her family to live just above the poverty line.[19]

Hilda Hensley took a bold gamble by moving, but she really had no choice. While forcing her husband of sixteen years to leave did not constitute the behavior of a "proper woman," she wanted the best for her children and knew she could not raise them with Sam, Sr., around. She dared to run headlong into the most rigid of gender stereotypes—that of a faithless, unsuccessful wife. Thus she often stated that Sam, Sr., "deserted" the family.[20]

That Hilda Hensley chose to become a single mother is incontestable, as two handwritten letters from Sam, Sr., to Hilda's brother document. In both these letters Sam begged "Buck" and his wife to influence Hilda to take him back. But Hilda never considered reconciling. Ginny, at age sixteen, agreed to go to work to supplement the family income and help support her brother (attending the second grade) and sister (only ready for school in September 1949). Sam, Sr., lived out the rest of his life first in Staunton, Virginia (ninety-five miles south of Winchester), and then Harrisonburg, Virginia (seventy miles south of Winchester).[21]

Quoting a letter of July 16, 1949, from Sam, Sr.'s, job at the Western State Hospital, in Staunton, to the Pattersons: "Well it's a job and there is few jobs now for an old man. It is a place to eat and sleep. I have no home, no friends, and no place to go. You *know* my family has thrown me out, cast me aside. I do wrong." Hilda and her son and daughters would not again encounter Sam, Sr., until his death, in December 1956. On [original language] December 12 of that year, the *Winchester Evening Star* ran Sam Hensley, Sr.'s, obituary, noting that he had died at age sixty-seven in the Newton D. Baker Veterans Hospital, in Martinsburg, West Virginia. Sam, Sr., did not live to see his daughter become a successful singer. He was buried at the expense of the United States government in Winchester's National Cemetery because he was a veteran of World War I. Hilda, when asked if she wanted to reserve a plot for herself—as was her right as the surviving widow—she signed up for one. It would be forty-two years before she would need it.

Ginny at this point still very much wanted to be a pop singer. Her next-door neighbor at the time, then sixteen-year-old Donald Elliott, remembered "[Ginny] singing in the backyard." But Ginny needed a day job to pay the rent for 608 South Kent Street, which had running water, an indoor toilet, electricity, and a radio.[22]

The first floor had three rooms, a parlor, a dining room (which doubled as Hilda's work room), and a small kitchen. The lone bathroom -- was in a converted closet -- had been installed well after the home had been built in the late nineteenth century. Upstairs there was but one sleeping room, where all four of the Hensleys slept in partitioned spaces. This sleeping area contained one double bed for Hilda and her five-year-old daughter, a cot for Ginny, and another for Sam, Jr.

Once settled, Ginny, as a sixteen-year-old high school dropout, immediately looked for work. Winchester was a compact walking city, a mile wide and a mile long, holding about 12,000 citizens. And the central city provided the shopping hub, which was just a mile walk from their home. Winchester had strict neighborhood divisions: South Kent Street for poor whites; North Kent for African Americans; Washington Street for the families of doctors, lawyers, and bankers. By early 1949, Virginia Hensley was working downtown as a waitress, her uniform labeling her an "uneducated poor white woman." Her sister Sylvia would repeatedly stated Handley High School students never let Ginny forget her place. The elite teenagers all entered a college track, and hung out at People's Drug store downtown. They became lawyers, physicians, businessmen and their wives. Sylvia trained to become a secretary. The one occupation that was not segregated by class (or race) was radio broadcasting, and Ginny listened, copied down lyrics, and practiced as much as she could.

Proper young women were supposed to graduate from high school, learn social skills from their mothers, and then marry. Virginia Hensley never attended a day of high school in Winchester. With Hilda as her single-mother role model, Ginny did not aspire to immediate marriage, and so most people in Winchester labeled her a "loose" girl. The polite talk condemned Ginny as "brash" and "having a foul mouth." The elite whispered that the Hensley women "did not know their proper place."[23]

Hilda's sewing skills soon became well known and in demand. She never left a record of what she did, save in the costumes she made for her daughter. Hilda's sewing, like her daughter's music, was self-taught and well practiced. She used her creativity to meet the desire of the Winchester elite for custom made garments. If a Winchester family was wealthy enough, the mother had clothes home sewn. Winchester matrons shared the belief that the custom sewn was precisely what made their clothes special—better than those the average person could purchase at Sears or J. C. Penney's.[24]

Hilda reconfigured her dining room into a sewing work space. A pedal-driven Singer sewing machine, with which Hilda had long made clothing for her growing family, made her home dressmaking possible, and replacement parts were available at the Singer store downtown. And Hilda did not have to pay taxes on the money she earned, as her customers paid with cash.[25]

Hilda's sixteen-year-old daughter entered the labor force as soon as Hilda moved them to South Kent Street. The family of four needed two steady incomes, but Ginny's choices were limited, as we can see from the classified ads in the *Winchester Evening Star* on December 12, 1948. There were but ten "Classified Ads Female:"

1. Maids at George Washington Hotel (African Americans)
2. Clerks at Bakers Drug store
3. Settled woman for light housework to help two adults
4. Soda jerk at People's Drug store
5. Soda jerk at Brook's Pharmacy
6. Waitress at Golden Glow restaurant
7. Laundress for couple
8. Cook for family
9. Maid
10. Waitress at Greyhound bus terminal.

It was no wonder that Virginia Hensley would take up waitressing and soda-jerking.[26]

First, however, she did try factory work. She walked to the other end of Kent Street to the Rockingham Poultry slaughterhouse, where she got a job standing all day in rubber boots and butchering chickens. The slaughterhouse workers killed and processed 10,000 animals a day. It was literally a bloodbath. In 1992, Hilda Hensley remembered, "They gave her the worst job in the plant, killing the turkeys. She would come home with blood on her clothes and her hands cut from having to stab turkeys in the neck all day." Ginny lasted a week.[27]

Then she returned to the want ads, and took the advertised job as a waitress at the Greyhound bus station. One hundred buses entered and exited Winchester every twenty-four hours. This was chaotic at best, and as the constant advertising in the newspaper want ads indicated, few waitresses stayed very long. If she was going to work for minimum wage—seventy-five cents an hour— she could at least seek a quieter, nicer place to work. Many rumors abound about her trying other waitress jobs, at the Capitol and Red Wing restaurants downtown and the Triangle Diner near her home, but none of these can be verified.[28]

"Patsy Cline in her waitress outfit."

One can. From April 1949 until summer 1950, Ginny worked at the downtown Snack Bar, as coworker Ruth Grim attests. It was just up the street from the Palace movie theater, and eight doors from the defined center of town. The Snack Bar served pies, Cokes, hamburgers, and foot long hot dogs; it had a grill in the front, so people could see Ginny perform as the short order cook as they passed on the sidewalk. Owned by Carl Lewis, who according to Grim, never fired anyone, this employment offered a less hectic atmosphere that waiting tables and a kind boss, who let her adjust her schedule to try singing.[29]

Ruth Grim was the same age as Ginny but was still in high school. So Ginny worked days, and Ruth worked evenings. As both cook and server in a narrow counter "joint" about two doors wide, Ginny, was in full control—and not working on an assembly line. Grim remembered that Ginny quit in June 1950 (when Grim graduated from high school) to soda-jerk at Gaunt's drugstore.[30]

In time, owner Hunter Gaunt became her patron, giving her day hours to accommodate her singing. Gaunt and his wife owned this independent Mom and Pop drug store. As the soda fountain attendant, Ginny served vanilla Cokes, and root beer frosties; she wore a white uniform, bobby socks, and loafers. Virginia Snapp, who worked at Gaunt's in the evenings, remembered: "Mostly Ginny stayed behind the soda fountain – serving a dozen patrons." Gaunt's was no vast emporium, just a small neighborhood store.[31]

Betty Jean Grove (later married as Robinson) lived on the working-class south side of Winchester, and as a teen, was a frequent patron of Gaunt's. She recalled, "Ginny was friendly and always started a conversation. She then made my favorite—crushed ice, chocolate syrup, and whipped cream, a 'Chocolate Unique.'" The soda fountain was located in the rear of the store, and was a hangout for white, working-class teens. During the spring of 1952, Grove visited 608 South Kent Street and remembered a piano in the parlor, with another guest, William R. "Jumbo" Rinker, playing and entertaining.[32]

In the *Washington Post* of March 6, 1963, for a report on Patsy Cline's death, a reporter called druggist Hunter Gaunt, who claimed that she had worked there for two years, from June 1950 to June 1952. When she worked in the food and beverage industry, Ginny learned always to be friendly in order to retain loyal customers. She needed a good memory to avoid confusing customers' orders, and to recall names and preferences of frequent patrons. This memory training proved vital to Virginia Hensley as she became Patsy Cline.

She also learned the reality that, due to the relatively small size of most food-serving establishments, opportunities for promotion were limited. After gaining experience, the position of waitress (or soda-jerk) was as far as she could go. That she exhibited no desire to work at a higher class restaurant, where she could have made more money, demonstrated her continuing goal to become a professional singer. Once she quit Gaunt's to join Clarence William "Bill" Peer's band, she never returned to the food service industry. In this sense, she was typical: As 1950 census discovered, women working as food and beverage servers in the United States at the time were primarily sixteen to nineteen years old.[33]

————————————

Jim Riley, who grew up in Winchester as the son of elite parents, wrote 50 years later, "It was always a great adventure to go downtown. Often, we were headed to one of the two movie theaters in town. The Palace was located on South Loudoun and a big neon sign hung over the street from the theater to a building directly across with big letters that read: P-A-L-A-C-E. The Capitol [restaurant] was located at the corner a couple of blocks away." Because it did not fit proper nostalgia, Riley failed to mention that both theaters had "colored-only" balconies. He also left unstated that he never dared to venture to North Kent Street, the African American ghetto, or South Kent Street, where "poor white trash" lived. These were spots in town that his well-to-do parents warned him to avoid—or face stiff punishment.[34]

Ginny loved movies and live entertainment when finances permitted. So on July 31, 1949, sixteen-year-old Virginia and her mother went to hear gospel star Wally Fowler at the Palace Theater. An ad ran in the *Winchester Evening Star*: "ON STAGE—IN PERSON—WALLY FOWLER & HIS OAK RIDGE QUARTET FOLK SONGS!" Palace Theater owner, Herman H. Hable, presented stage shows at 3:15, 5:20, 7:25, and 9:30 p.m. to boost his revenue. On July 31, 1949, Ginny boldly approached Fowler after the show, and Fowler later recalled, "I thought at the time 'This little girl is really something—she might have potential to be groomed for bigger and better things.'" Later that evening, in the living room at 608 South Kent Street, Fowler asked Hilda to bring her daughter to Nashville for an audition.

So for a tryout during early August of 1949, Ginny, Hilda, and her two siblings (age nine and six) traveled six hundred miles to Nashville for the promised audition. Fowler took her to meet Roy Acuff, and Ginny Hensley appeared on his *Dinner Bell* radio show singing songs she had learned from the radio. But the Hensleys did not have enough money to stay a second night. They made the long trip back to Winchester, never to hear from Fowler again. Previous writers interpret at the Fowler incident as the first clue of the ambition of Patsy Cline as a country singer. Yet she was simply taking advantage of this one-time offer. Ginny still loved singing pop music.[35]

In September 1949, Herman Hable initiated a Saturday afternoon amateur show. Jack Fretwell was the master of ceremonies; Ken Windle played the piano; and Hable gave out the prizes—sometimes five dollars and more often food or merchandise from a local store. In the *Winchester Evening Star* of September 21, 1949, Hable first advertised: "WANTED! AMATEUR ENTERTAINERS TO APPEAR ON THE STAGE AT HABLE'S PALACE—EACH SATURDAY AFTERNOON—CASH PRIZES TO THE WINNER—COME HELP CHEER AND ENCOURAGE YOUR LOCAL FUTURE STARS."

Ginny thus started entering amateur shows at the Palace, from September 1949 to November 1950. Richard Reid, then assistant manager, grew familiar with seeing her as a constant contestant. Ginny would get Ruth Grim to sub for her at the Snack Bar on Saturday afternoons, and when Ginny's performance time came, she'd hustle down to the Palace, don a costume made by her mother, and sing her favorite pop songs, which she'd learned from radio listening. (Much as the myth of "natural talent" would lead us to expect that she was a constant winner, she rarely earned the top prize. An African American tap dancer Ben Brown, then age nine, did.) Reid recalled Ginny's singing the songs of Al Jolson, such as "Rock-a-by Your Baby with a Dixie Melody" and "I'm Sittin' on Top of the World." Her audience was half black and half white, as dozens of the African Americans turned out to see young "Benny" Brown and filled the balcony of the Palace to cheer on his victories.[36]

"Amateur contestants (Ginny Hensley with tall hat)"

Amateur show master of ceremonies Jack Fretwell was a well-known bandleader in 1949. Recalling his Saturday afternoon work at the Palace amateur shows, Fretwell said, "Little Benny Brown was the real star and he went on to almost win Ted Mack's amateur contest; Virginia needed the money." Brown's father, who knew Ginny from her work at the bus station, was a beloved figure in Winchester, working at the bus station, servicing only African American passengers in the cramped building. He wanted his son to go to college and so stashed any winnings into his college fund. With Brown's steady job, his family epitomized the middle-class African American family.[37]

Ginny learned important skills both from Fretwell and pianist Ken Windle. Both had pop bands that appeared at such spots as the Candlelight Club, in Martinsburg, West Virginia; the John Marshall Inn and Skyline Terrace, in Front Royal, Virginia; and private parties of the Winchester well-to-do, often held at the Winchester Country Club. Both Fretwell and Windle covered Big Band hits and encouraged Ginny to sing like Jo Stafford, not Al Jolson.[38]

The Palace amateur contest started Ginny Hensley's radio career. Herman Hable, lifelong resident of Winchester, crafted a deal with the only local radio station, WINC-AM, to have these amateur shows broadcast as radio remotes.[39]

John Lewis' family owned the WINC radio station, and he later remembered that WINC also would rent out slots on Saturday mornings back then, and the renter—a band—would sell the ads and then plug its upcoming gigs. Lewis stated, "In reality, 'Patsy Cline' really had nothing to do with the station." She appeared on these remote broadcasts paid for by Herman Hable.[40]

Ginny was ambitious, and she looked for larger venues. She found them at monthly amateur shows held at the 1,300-seat theater at John Handley High School. These shows were where Ginny got her start as a pop singer, as covered by the local press. Starting on October 19 and 20, 1949, Jack Fretwell ran a Kiwanis Club amateur show, in which Virginia Hensley did a pop star imitation of Margaret Whiting. During the summer of 1948, Whiting's "A Tree in The Meadow" had gone to number 1 pop.[41]

On January 28, 1950, the *Winchester Evening Star* printed on its front page that Virginia Hensley had passed an audition to perform in the finals of an amateur show, to be held on February 2, 1950. Twenty-five female and male pop singers, pop vocal groups, and tap dancer Ben Brown competed in the finals. (There were no country and Western [C&W] singers.) A twenty-four-year-old African American singer, Ellen Marie Gant, of Middletown, won singing "Summertime" from *Porgy and Bess*. (Later Gant received an invitation to Ted Mack's *Original Amateur Hour*, but she could not afford to leave her two children or to pay the price of a ticket to New York City). Virginia Hensley sang a current Jo Stafford hit, but failed to finish among the top six prize winners.[42]

This show did not launch Ginny's career, but it did launch Ben Brown's. He would go on to appear on WNBW-TV (Washington, DC), where he defeated all area winners. This led to Brown's appearing on national television and earning second place on the Ted Mack *Amateur Hour*. Brown also toured with Mack, and with the money he earned and saved, he was able to gain a college education and serve in a distinguished military career. Ginny remained in Winchester, still competing to become a winner of a local amateur contest and still seeking to launch a career singing pop music.[43]

On October 3, 1950, at the Third Annual Amateur Minstrel Show, sponsored by a local Softball League, Ginny sang "After You're Gone," a 1918 Tin Pan Alley composition, made famous in 1942 by Judy Garland in the movie *For Me and My Gal*. The show was not a contest, and it ended with a grand finale featuring all the performers. Again, there was no C&W singer.[44]

On October 11, 1950, Ginny appeared in another amateur show, the Kiwanis Club's musical revue "Ridin' High," to raise funds for "underprivileged children." This was yet another organized show, not a contest. Ginny Hensley, along with others who volunteered, rehearsed a variety show around the theme of a transcontinental airplane flight, set at LaGuardia Field, New York City. There were vocal groups, dancers, and singers, with Virginia Hensley singing the "St. Louis Blues." (In 1996, Jack Fretwell recalled: "We had rehearsed songs like "Stardust" and "That Old Black Magic," but chose "St. Louis Blues.") The *Winchester Evening Star* of October 12, 1950, in reviewing the night's events, reported, "Virginia Hensley got a rave review from the audience."[45]

Her break came as 1950 ended and Jack Fretwell hired her to sing pop songs at the John Marshall Inn, in Front Royal, Virginia. She threw herself into her songs, but she was hamstrung by the stationary microphones of the era and so just stood there and used her voice. Here Jo Stafford inspired her. Frank Sinatra praised Stafford: "She's one of the great women singers for technique. She can hold notes for sixteen bars if she wants to. Jo Stafford was a crystal-clear-toned singer." And Stafford was the first female singer to go platinum with a disc selling more than two million copies. In Jo Stafford's recordings, with smooth, vibrato-free purity of tone and a sensuous sound, we can recognize the inspiration for Patsy Cline's pop vocal stylings.[46]

On February 21, 1951, *Warren* (County) *Sentinel* published a vast ad for the John Marshall's new singer: "Virginia Hensley our vocalist will appear every Saturday night and she has got the umph....." There was a cover charge for Jack Fretwell and his orchestra, which played from 5:30 p.m. to 9:30 p.m.; then Virginia Hensley did her sets. Fretwell remembered, "We were playing at the John Marshall in Front Royal. Roland Payne, the owner, felt we should have a female vocalist.

So I talked to [Ginny] and she was tickled to death." So Fretwell went to 608 South Kent Street, and went over some pop songs she could sing with his band. He had a band built on the Glenn Miller model, just with fewer members. Ginny sang "Embraceable You," "Melancholy Baby," "Blue Moon," "Moonglow," and other pop standards.[47]

The *Winchester Evening Star* reported that Fretwell—and his new girl singer—also played at assorted fraternal organizations, like the Winchester Eagle's Club. For these pop gigs, Virginia wore a white satin dress that Hilda had made her. She remained with Fretwell for about six months, until mid-1951, when Fretwell ran into a fallow period and had to let Ginny go. The Korean War was playing havoc with the economy.[48]

"Virginia Hensley playing the piano"

Even with Fretwell, Ginny never quit her day job at Gaunt's. Fretwell did not quit his day job, either. But once Fretwell let her go, Ginny looked for a steady singing job. This would lead, after a year's search, to Bill Peer, who led a C&W band. As Richard Reid, assistant manager of the Palace Theater, who knew Ginny from her dozens of appearances at the amateur shows, reflected, "She did it for the money. One had to sing country to make it around here."[49]

By 1952, there was money to be made in covering C&W. Tony Bennett and Jo Stafford were covering Hank Williams songs, and selling millions of records. Ginny tried for two years to become Winchester's Jo Stafford. But she never made enough to quit Gaunt's. It took Ginny a year to find such steady work—covering C&W hits.

Virginia Hensley struggled. Winchester-based C&W booker Jim Kniceley later observed that she took irregular bookings at clubs in West Virginia that featured C&W. The Commonwealth of Virginia did not have "liquor by the drink," and so as a consequence, no public restaurant could sell anything but beer. The middle class and upper class had their private parties and brought their own liquor (referred to as "brown bagging it"). But in West Virginia, a short ten-mile drive to north, there were road houses that sold all types of liquor to almost anyone who looked old enough. Ginny turned nineteen on Saturday, September 8, 1951, probably singing in a "hot spot" up the Valley Pike (U.S. 11) in Ridgeway, West Virginia.[50]

One name that popped up in the ads for Ridgeway, West Virginia, clubs was Winchesterite Sonny Frye, who headed a C&W band. During the summer of 1951, Ginny Hensley became a regular entertainer at George and Katherine Frye's Rainbow Inn, with a country band made up of the sons of the owners called "Sonny Frye and Playboys." This gig offered up the first image of the future "Patsy Cline" in a western outfit. The Fryes ran a Texas-style outdoor dance hall, with beer and country music. Frye also took Virginia Hensley to Ridgeway's, Chuck and Ray's Western Club to sing. But no regular bookings came with the Fryes.[51]

During this transitional period—late 1951 and early 1952—Virginia Hensley sang wherever she could. In August of 1951, she sang from the back of a truck at the annual meeting of the ham radio clubs of Virginia, held near Front Royal. Some two hundred people showed up, and she received only five dollars. She did numerous gigs like this to supplement her job at Gaunt's, but she affiliated with no single band. Ginny wanted to acquire a regular relationship with a working band, as she had with the Jack Fretwell Orchestra in early 1951.[52]

In her work to sell herself as a country music cover artist (so called because she did not write her own music but sang hit tunes by the likes of Eddy Arnold and Hank Williams, Sr.), Virginia Hensley allied herself with Winchester piano player William R. "Jumbo" Rinker. He booked himself and Hensley in West Virginia. But Rinker, like many a local musician, kept his day job and just used these bookings for added income. He helped Ginny gain experience, but like Fretwell, Rinker could not enable her to earn enough to quit Gaunt's.[53]

As she worked with different bands, she learned a repertory of memorized songs but had no idea what key they were in. So she sought help from a local piano teacher and performer, Nettie A. Carbaugh (1914–1990). Jack Fretwell often asked Carbaugh to substitute for Ken Windle at the Palace amateur shows. Ginny frequently called on Miss Nettie for help. Carbaugh, who worked as a secretary during the day, played piano up and down the Shenandoah Valley at night and on weekends. Carbaugh told Ginny that professional musicians hated it when someone came to sing and did not know the major key of the song. Thereafter, Virginia Hensley carried a little black notebook with her, with her keys written in it.[54]

Gradually Ginny Hensley, inspired by Jo Stafford's hit covers of country music, dropped her aspirations to become a pop star, and settled in as a C&W singer to make a living. She learned that there was a fraternal club circuit and Bill Peer was the king of this so-called Moose Hall circuit. These fraternal clubs regularly held dances and Peer also played sporadic dates during the rest of the week. That would mean more money than she was making at Gaunt's. Jumbo Rinker made the necessary introduction to Bill Peer.[55]

Hilda Hensley recalled that Ginny auditioned for Peer sometime during the summer of 1952, and then began working Moose Halls in Brunswick and Hagerstown, Maryland. These towns were filled with unionized workers who had steady working-class incomes and C&W tastes. Brunswick functioned as a rail center; Hagerstown workers had steady employment at the Fairchild airplane factory. Bill Peer gave her a steady job, and she quit Gaunt's as a soda jerk. As she celebrated her twentieth birthday, on 8 September 1952, she had finally achieved her goal of becoming a professional singer.[56]

Peer, a member of the Brunswick Moose Hall, played there every Saturday night. This was a small step toward Ginny's professional ambitions. The Brunswick Moose Hall is not a large building; rather, it seats one hundred people, and its stage is a simple, tiny triangular riser, holding but six musicians. The weekly *Brunswick Blade-Times* from 1952 to 1954 makes it clear that the Brunswick Volunteer Fire Hall, not the Moose Hall, was the center of entertainment at that time. The fire hall had a full stage, able to hold Guy Lombardo's thirty-six piece orchestra. And when Tex Ritter came to Brunswick, in April 1952, just months before he became famous for his theme music for the 1952 movie *High Noon,* he played the Brunswick Volunteer Fire Hall.

"Patsy and Bill Peer singing together"

Finding no advertisements for the small Brunswick Moose Hall in the local newspaper, I turned to the *Hagerstown* [Maryland] *Daily Mail* of November 3, 1952, for the first ad for "Patsy Hensley" performing with Bill Peer's Melody Boys and Girls at the local Moose Hall. Thereafter, the Hagerstown Daily Mail contained regular advertisements for Peer's band, with Patsy as featured singer. Peer and his band later played at the CIO Union Club, in Hagerstown. Peer named her Patsy after his infant daughter; she added the *Cline* with her March 1953 marriage to Gerald Cline, whom she met at the Brunswick Moose Hall. Throughout 1953, Peer and his band—featuring Patsy Cline—regularly played the Brunswick Moose Hall on Saturday nights and the CIO Union Club on Friday nights.

There were 10,000 CIO members in Hagerstown, and the CIO Club proved a high-paying gig. The club was located in the center of Hagerstown, and was five times the size of the Brunswick Moose Hall. The front page of the March 14, 1953, *Hagerstown Herald* described the CIO Club as part of a three-story building in the heart of downtown Hagerstown, with union offices on the top two floors and the social club filling the first floor. This regional CIO headquarters dealt with all CIO locals from Winchester, Virginia, to Shippensburg, Pennsylvania. A regular gig there meant no more day jobs for Patsy Cline, as Peer paid her seventeen dollars per appearance at the CIO Club.[57]

In 1952, Bill Peer lived in Charles Town, West Virginia, with his wife and two children—son, Larry (born 1945), and daughter, Patsy (born 1951). He did a live Saturday morning radio show, *Bill's Melody Time*, from Martinsburg, West Virginia (twenty miles from home). When not working Hagerstown (forty miles from home), and Brunswick (fifteen miles from Charles Town) Peer looked for bookings elsewhere. For example, he appeared at the Marine Corps NCO Club, in Quantico, Virginia (some hundred miles from Charles Town).

Peer employed Patsy to cover the top C&W and pop hits of the day, so that folks could dance. She learned her cover versions by taking notes from radio broadcasts. Peer played the rhythm guitar, and he hired a lead guitar, a bass player, and at various times, a fiddler, an accordion player, and steel guitar player. Patsy sang, often duets with Peer. Venues within a hundred-mile radius hired Peer and his band and female singer to give people a chance to dance to live music.[58]

Ray Fields, of Loudoun County, Virginia (located across the Potomac River from Brunswick), remembered that people danced at that local Moose Hall, from nine p.m. to one a.m. Peer regularly covered the tunes of Hank Williams, Sr., the hottest singer-songwriter the C&W field had ever fashioned , with a dozen number 1 hits such as

"Why Don't You Love Me?" "Moanin' the Blues," "Cold, Cold Heart," "Hey Good Lookin'," "Jambalaya (On the Bayou)," "Kaw-Liga," "Your Cheatin' Heart," and "Take These Chains from My Heart." Such fare attracted young men like Ray Fields, who with his friends, regularly journeyed to Brunswick. The audiences were all white and young, looking for fun. All had to join the Moose—which they could easily do when they first attended, as the Moose club made its money selling liquor.

Bill Peer's son, Larry, later a bandleader like his dad, has stated that his father's band projected a cowboy image and so Patsy became a "cowgirl," wearing colorful western outfits her mother made, to offer a non-threatening female image. Peer taught her how to sell her songs to local audiences.[59]

Patsy remained inspired by Jo Stafford, who had her fifth number 1 hit in 1952, her cover of "You Belong to Me," a tune written by Pee Wee King and Redd Stewart (who were responsible for Patti Page's country-pop hit, "The Tennessee Waltz"). "You Belong to Me" would become Jo Stafford's greatest hit, topping the charts in the United States. Stafford's version first entered the U.S. charts on August 1, 1952, and remained there until late January of 1953. Patsy Hensley sang this country-pop cover at all her gigs that winter, and a decade later, Patsy Cline recorded "You Belong to Me" for Decca.[60]

Patsy's cousin remembered her performing style, saying, "While later imitators jump around, she was very dignified when she sang. Ginny always stood still in front of the microphone." Later films recorded this singing style. She did not entertain with her dancing; she inspired others to dance. Indeed, she was no master of the dance. Her cousin continued, "She stepped on my foot in Paul Jones." Patsy, tied then to bulky microphones, imagined herself as a dignified Big Band singer.[61]

Soon Peer devoted himself to promoting Patsy; for example, he spent six thousand dollars he received from his mother's estate to boost her career. Peer managed to have Patsy try out (unsuccessfully) for *Arthur Godfrey's Talent Scouts,* a national TV show, paying for the band and Patsy to journey to New York City for the audition. Peer's son even admitted to the press that his father had fallen in love with Patsy, despite the fact that he too was married and had two children. All this caused Peer's wife to divorce him in 1954. Even though he had "discovered" Patsy Cline, Bill Peer never amounted to more than a regional talent. He taught Patsy all he could, and then she moved on. But learning on the job was what Patsy needed at the time. Peer would school her for three years, and out of this experience she emerged as Patsy Cline, a professional and popular regional singer.[62]

Peer also helped her dig herself out of poverty, particularly during busy summers with nearly daily appearances at local fairs and carnivals. For example, on Thursday, June 22, 1954, Peer and Patsy performed at the Middletown, Maryland, Fireman's Carnival; then later that summer they played the Woodsboro, Maryland, Volunteer Fire Department Carnival and the Clear Spring, Maryland, American Legion Carnival. All featured amusement-park rides, plus live entertainment for dancing under the stars. Then Peer and Patsy went to the regular gigs: Friday nights at the Hagerstown CIO Club and Saturday nights for the Brunswick Moose Club.[63]

Bill Peer was an average guitar player—he would hire better players—but he was a skilled promoter. He was able to get Patsy Cline into Winchester's 1954 Apple Blossom Parade. The April 27, 1954, *Winchester Evening Star* printed "Music-Makers for Festival Square

Dances," with a photo of Bill Peer (guitar), Pete Miller (drums), Patsy Kline (sic) (vocalist), Charles Anderson (guitar), Joan Anderson (guitar), and Ken Windle (piano), whom Patsy knew from her days at the Palace Theater. This ad-hoc group then appeared in the festival's Grand Feature Parade. The Grand Parade drew one hundred thousand attendees, with Ed Sullivan, of Sunday night television fame, at its head.

This is how Patsy Cline learned to sing—with "practice, practice, practice." She rode the wave of the rise of postwar fraternals (the Moose, the Eagles, the Elks, and the Veterans of Foreign Wars [VFW]), and the rise of union social centers after the Second World War. Every town had a VFW Hall, for example. And where large factories existed, there was a union hall. When live entertainment was presented, the beer would flow without the constraints of public law, as these were private clubs, able to set their own hours and enforce their own age limits. They stood at the core of working-class culture. The fraternal hall was the place to meet, to drink, dance, and have fun.

In a 1995 book called *Bowling Alone,* Robert D. Putnam, a Harvard University political science professor, argued that fraternals helped create the social trust that pulled the United States together during the 1950s. Along with union clubs, these institutions helped create a unified working-class culture. Friends met every Friday and Saturday night. Patsy Cline was fortunate that she started her career when fraternal halls existed in every town with a stable working-class population.

Why would working-class Marylanders want to hear country music? Maryland in the 1950s is best understood as the northern edge of a "fertile crescent" of interest in country music. Using geographical and sociological analyses, two scholars have argued that country music prospered from Texas to Maryland, a fertile crescent where most

C&W stars had been born. Brunswick may have been a railroad town and Hagerstown a factory city, but both sat on the northern edge of this crescent. Many of the workers had grown up in the South and developed a love of C&W music. Patsy Cline worked to entertain those who lived right on the border of the cultural South and North of the United States. Fans of Bill Peer did not demand that Patsy sing with a twang; nor did they mind a pop hit as long as they could dance. Singing, drinking, and dancing—that was the whole purpose of the fraternals and union halls.[64]

Patsy sang every Saturday morning on Bill Peer's radio show to publicize upcoming appearances. Gene Edwards, of Eldersburg, Maryland, confirmed this: "In 1953, I was a senior at Martinsburg (West Virginia) High School and worked weekends for radio station WEPM. Bill Peer and his Melody Boys and Patsy Cline sang on the station regularly." To high school student Edwards, Peer and Cline were local celebrities.[65]

During this period, Patsy Cline developed her crossover style, and with Peer's constant bookings, she spent the rest of her time listening to the radio, writing down lyrics, finding out the keys from her band members and Miss Nettie, practicing, and then learning on the job to please audiences. Bill Peer gave her regular work, and she took her cues from her audiences. One Brunswick old-timer told me, "We'd shout out a request and she'd say 'I never heard that one yet, but I'll learn it!'" Peer provided a platform for Patsy's interest in pop music to jump to country audiences—and for her to ascend from amateur to professional level. Peer offered a necessary condition for her move to iconic status—but not a sufficient one. She would have to move up to a more demanding professional level.

Work with Peer paid better than any job she had held in Winchester, but a traditional, socially approved means—marriage—helped considerably more. Some time during the fall of 1952, Patsy Hensley (age 20) met Gerald Edward Cline (1925–94), a five-foot-eight-inch, 220-pound, twenty-eight-year-old divorced son of a millionaire building contractor from Frederick, Maryland. Thereafter, Cline wooed her (and Hilda), and he and Patsy married on March 7, 1953. Cline was smitten, and he lavished the Hensleys with gifts. He arranged to drive to Winchester to pick Patsy up and drive her to work. Patsy was glad to finally have a steady ride, as she did not own an automobile. Gerald Cline won Hilda over with gifts of kerosene to heat her family's home and a household full of furniture. Hilda and her extended family full well knew that he—and his money—could make a difference. Cline was the son of Earl H. and Lettie Cline, and the scion of his father's construction company. The family lived in a twelve-room mansion on the edge of Frederick.

"Patsy and Gerald Cline"

On February 27, 1953, Gerald Cline and Virginia Hensley applied for a marriage license at the Frederick, Maryland, courthouse. The license was granted on March 2. The ceremony took place on Saturday afternoon, March 7, at the Reformed Church, one of the oldest churches in Frederick.[66]

Patsy Cline's cousin remembered that "her brother [Sam, Jr.] gave her away and few were invited to the wedding." Cline's family did not attend. Yet the Clines never denied their elder son any means of support. Indeed, Earl H. Cline, if anything, always indulged Gerald.

For Patsy and Hilda, Gerald offered up more money than they had seen since their days in Portsmouth. And to the world of entertainment, thereafter, Ginny would forever be known as Patsy Cline.[67]

The Cline-Hensley marriage was hardly stable. The couple lived together, then separated, and then reunited: first to the Linden Hills area of Frederick County, Maryland, where Earl H. Cline owned property and offered Patsy her first new home. Then they to a flat in a duplex at 824 East Patrick Street, several blocks from the Cline family home but to save money Patsy and Gerald's moved into his parents' home. Patsy and Gerald would end their cohabitation in a trailer park west of Frederick. When they temporarily split up, Patsy would move back to 608 South Kent with her mother, sister and brother.

At first Gerald lavished Patsy with a new Buick Roadmaster in her favorite colors, red and white. All the Hensleys agreed that Gerald was a nice man who dearly loved Ginny, but she was less smitten because of his continual demands that she give up singing. As her career grew more successful, she chose career over marriage and security.[68]

In a November 9, 1955, letter to her fan club president, Patsy Cline claimed to have lived in Frederick, Maryland, for "two years." However, the separations were noted in the 1957 divorce proceedings. The Cline marriage was an on-again, off-again union. Gerald Cline claimed that she left him four times between their marriage in March 1953 and March 1956— the last time, for good. He stated in a March 11, 1957, deposition, "The first time she was gone a week or two, the second time about the same. The third time we separated for six months." The last time, in March 1956, proved to be the permanent separation. In all, they lived together as husband and wife for only twenty-nine months. In a May 28, 1956, letter, Patsy Cline complained that her husband had stopped supporting her. Unstated in that letter was that in April of 1956, Patsy Cline had met Charles Dick.[69]

Patsy's cousin put it this way: "Gerald had no career but had family money; he loved her dearly, but his love got to be controlling. Gerald wanted her to travel with him, and not sing. Patsy wanted to sing."[70]

In the divorce proceedings, Gerald Cline blamed Hilda Hensley. For the record, answering the question his lawyer posed—"What broke up the marriage?"—Gerald Cline answered, "Her mother seemed to agitate her whenever she talked to her." Gerald Cline also blamed Bill Peer:

Q: Did these activities take out of your normal home life and divert her? A: Yes, they did. Q: Did the acquaintances she made in this work have any influence on her? A: Yes. For instance, Bill Peer wanted to act as her agent for making records. He came to our apartment and in some months ran up a $90 or more on the telephone bill.

Lois Troxell, who lived next door to the Cline family home, blamed Gerald Cline's mother. Lettie Cline was a stern woman who hated Patsy because of her reputation as a "loose" woman. "Nobody on the street liked [Lettie Cline]. She was as nasty as she could be."[71]

Gerald Cline was never really part of the family business, save as a minority owner, but he was pampered by his father. In contrast, Gerald's younger brother, Nevin, was the "good" son and eventually took over and ran the family business. Nevin Cline served in the U.S. Army in World War II, unlike his brother, who married to avoid military service. Once Patsy and Gerald Cline divorced, Gerald moved to Martinsburg, West Virginia, remarried, and lived off his family money.[72]

Before the marriage officially ended, however, Gerald Cline supported his wife in the next vital step on the road toward becoming an icon: He helped her get a record contract, which she signed on the last day of September in 1954. Gerald Cline had set this event in motion on August 7 of that year, when he took Patsy to compete at the Fourth Annual National Championship Country Music Contest, held in Warrenton, Virginia, and sponsored by impresario Connie B. Gay. Patsy Cline won $100 as best female vocalist, covering a C&W classic, "Faded Love," a western swing song written by the brothers Bob and Billy Jack Wills.[73]

This earned Patsy Cline a weekday job for Gay's WMAL-AM radio show in Arlington, Virginia, a suburb directly across the Potomac River from Washington, DC. At first she sang advertising jingles. What Connie B. Gay's connection did offer was a record contract with William McCall, owner of the 4-Star label, of Pasadena, California.[74]

McCall, as he did with all first contractees, exploited Patsy Cline. But she understood that the first step in a career in music was to record—anywhere. She knew the label from Jimmy Dean's hit "Bummin' Around." And like Dean, Patsy Cline signed with the only label to offer her a contract; at least it was a recording contract. No new and unknown singer ever gets a favorable initial contract.[75]

Bill McCall's gift to Patsy Cline was that he subcontracted the actual recording sessions to others. McCall approached Paul Cohen, Decca's man in charge of Nashville, to record Cline and distribute her on Decca. McCall would make his money on his contract with Patsy by dictating that she use his copyrighted songs. Cohen assigned her to the best producer in Nashville, Owen Bradley. Patsy Cline's success would never have been possible without Bradley. In retrospect, Patsy Cline could not have gotten a better deal, as Owen Bradley was only beginning to prove himself Nashville's best producer, and he accepted all work. For his day job, Bradley was still leading a Big Band in Nashville, so he had sympathy for Patsy's love of Big Band music. No one knew it at the time, but this signing was the next big step in Patsy Cline's march on her ascent to stardom. She could have not gotten a better, more sympathetic producer-teacher.[76]

NOTES

Chapter 3

[1] Military Record.

[2] Military Record; ORAL HISTORY – 10 APRIL 2007.

[3] Edinburg history files, Shenandoah County Library, VA; ORAL HISTORY- 10 April 2007; D. C. Brown, Electricity for Rural America (Westport, CT: Greenwood Press, 1980).

[4] ORAL HISTORY – 1 May 2007.

[5] Cathy McNeely Sutphin, "History of Virginia Congressional District Agricultural High Schools" unpublished Ph.D. dissertation, Virginia Tech, 1999.

[6] Virginia Division of Landmarks, Survey Form, Middletown School, on deposit at the Handley Library Archives; WS, 16 April 1997, Page E1; WS,13 August 1997, Page E1.

[7] Isabel Hammack Davis, Long Glaces Back : A History of Middletown Agriculture High School (Stephens City: Commercial Press, 1981); WS, 1 January 2000: F1; WS 12 June 2000: B2; WS, 17 May 2000: E1.

[8] WS, 30 August 1995: E4.

[9] ORAL HISTORY – John Sleeter, 9 January 2010.

[10] Ann Thomas Research Papers, 1836-2005, Thomas Balch Library, Leesburg, VA folder 9; The Loudoun Times-Mirror, 6 June 1962: 1

[11] 110. Ann Whitehead Thomas, A Story of Round Hill, Loudoun County Virginia (Leesburg, VA: Friends of the Thomas Balch Library 2004); ORAL HISTORY – 10 APRIL 2007.

[12] The Loudoun Times-Mirror, 31 July 1980: B1.

[13] ORAL HISTORY – 31 July 2007.

[14] ORAL HISTORY - Charles Hoak – 10 June 2004

15 ORAL HISTORY – Charles Hoak – 21 November 2003; WS, 30 August 1995: E4.

16 Letter to author from Frank Whitacre, postmarked 4 June 2000; WS, 16 May 1947: 1; WS, 2 April, 1948: 1; WS, 4 April 1948:1; WS, 16 May 2000: C6; WS, 4 June 1948: 1.

17 Joseph Murrells, The Book of Golden Discs (London: Barrie & Jenkins, 1978): 32-45.

18 ORAL HISTORY – Charles Hoak – 21 November 2003.

19 TRIAL.

20 ORAL HISTORY – 1 May 2007.

21 ORAL HISTORY– 10 APRIL 2007.

22 ORAL HISTORY – 10 APRIL 2007.

23 Margaret Ripley Wolfe, "The Southern Lady," The Journal of Popular Culture, 11 (1977): 18-27.

24 Barbara Burman (editor), The Culture of Sewing (London: Oxford University Press, 1999).

25 Katherine Cranor, "Homemade Versus Ready-Made Clothing," Journal of Home Economics 12 (May 1920): 230-233; Helen Hall, Simplified Home Sewing (New York: Prentice-Hall, 1943).

26 Cindy Hazen and Mike Freeman, Love Always, Patsy Cline: Patsy Cline's Letters of a Friend (New York: Berkley Books, 1999), 29 October 1955 letter [hereafter H&F].

27 ORAL HISTORY – 10 April 2007; The Richmond Times-Dispatch, 5 July 1992: C2; WS, 18 September 1946: 12.

28 Brown Archives.

29 ORAL HISTORY – Ruth Grim Wingfield – 6 July 2006.

30 WS, 12 November 2003: B1.

31 ORAL HISTORY – 1 May 2007; Brown Archives; CPC video interview – 1996 – Virginia Snapp.

32 ORAL HISTORY - Betty Robinson – 22 June 2004.

[33] Debra Ginsberg, <u>Waiting: The True Confessions of a Waitress</u> (New York: HarperCollins, 2000)

[34] WS, 22 June 2005: B1.

[35] Walter Carter, "Wally Fowler's Big Idea," <u>The Journal of Country Music</u>, XII/ 1 (1987): 34-42; H&F, 29 October 1955; H&F, 9 November 1955.

[36] WS, 22 November 1997: B1; ORAL HISTORY – Richard Reid – 20 August 1999; WS, 28 AUG 1993: B2; Herbert G. Goldman, <u>Jolson: The Legend Comes to Life</u> (New York: Oxford University Press, 1988).

[37] ORAL HISTORY – 1 May 2007; WS, 7 May 1948.

[38] Brown Archives; WS, 12 APRIL 1948: 1; ORAL HISTORY – Ben Ritter by Douglas Gomery - 8 December 1999; WS, 25 October 1997: A2; WS, 28 August 1993: B1.

[39] WS, 14 July 1932: 6; <u>Motion Picture Herald</u>, 13 January 1945: 54; WS, 6 August 1994: F2; WS, 22 November 1997: B3; WS, 20 August 1949: 10; WS, 4 May 1949: 10; WS, 13 July 1949: 10; WS, 4 January 1950: 10.

[40] ORAL HISTORY – John Lewis - 15 July 2004.

[41] Brown, Archives; Whitney Balliett, <u>American Singers</u> (New York: Oxford University Press, 1988).

[42] WS, 4 February 1950: 12.

[43] WS, 2 October 1950: 1; ORAL HISTORY – Ben Brown – 3 February 2009.

[44] Brown Archives.

[45] WS. 7 October 1950: 12; WS, 11 October 1950: 12; WS 12 October 1950: 12 ; WS, 8 November 2000: F2.

[46] ORAL HISTORY – Jack Fretwell by Fern Adams – 9 September 1993 – at Handley Archives; Roy Hemming, <u>Discovering the Great Singers of Classic Pop</u> (New York: Newmarket Press, 1991).

47 ORAL: HISTORY – Jack Fretwell on deposit at archives of The John Handley Memorial Library, Winchester, Virginia.

48 WS, 7 April 1951: 3; WS, 30 August 1995: F1; WS, 21 February 2006: B1.

49 WS, 15 DEC 1999: F3.

50 ORAL HISTORY – Michael Foreman, 15 December 2007; WS, 10 July 1999: B1.

51 WS, 26 April 1951: 12; WS, 4 July 1951: 14; WS, 13 July 1951: 12; WS, 26 July 1951: 12, WS, 7 November 1951: 12; WS, 19 September 1998: F1; WS, 21 April 1992: F2; Brown Archives

52 ORAL HISTORY – William Poole - 30 June 1992.

53 WS, 8 January 1998: A2.

54 ORAL HISTORY – Bernetta Jenkins – 30 November 2006; WS, 8 October 1985, B2; WS, 11 December 1990: F2.

55 The Keyser (WVA) Times-News, 5 March 1990: B1.

56 WS, 8 September 1982: 1.

57 Issues of the newspaper from 1952-1955 from newspaperarchive. com; Robert H. Zieger, The CIO 1935-1955 (Chapel Hill: University of North Carolina Press, 1995).

58 The Spirit of Jefferson-Advocate [newspaper published in Charles Town, West Virginia] 26 September 1968: 1: web site of son Larry Peer: www.ho-kisspo-kiss.com – accessed 4 July 2007.

59 Wpost, 1 September 2003: T3.

60 Joseph Murrells, The Book of Golden Discs (London: Barrie & Jenkins, 1978), page 62.

61 ORAL HISTORY - Patricia Brannon and Becky Williams – 18 January 2008.

62 In Circuit Court of Jefferson County, West Virginia, Virginia M. Peer v. William Peer, 22 September 1955; The Spirit of

Jefferson-Advocate, 26 September 1968: 1; The Martinsburg (West Virginia) Journal, 22 October 1984: B1.

63 Issues of the newspapers from 1952-1955 from www. newspaperarchive.com; Robert H. Zieger, The CIO 1935-1955 (Chapel Hill: University of North Carolina Press, 1995).

64 Richard A. Peterson and Russell Davis, Jr., "Country Music's Fertile Crescent," Journal of Country Music, volume 6 (spring, 1975): 19-27; Alvin J. Schmidt, Fraternal Organizations (Westport, CT: Greenwood Press, 1980): 220-223.

65 The Baltimore Sun, 23 January 1994: M3.

66 Marriage Application No. 17280, License No. 0718, Frederick County Court House, Frederick, MD; The Frederick Post, 7 June 1994: A5; Brown Archives.

67 ORAL HISTORY - 1 May 2007.

68 TRIAL.

69 H&F, 25 January 1956.

70 Gerald E. Cline v. Virginia P. Hensley Cline, Divorce, Equity No. 18,568, on deposit at Frederick County Court House, Frederick, MD.

71 ORAL HISTORY - Lois Troxell - 27 August 2007.

72 The Frederick (MD) Post, 8 June 1969: A4; ORAL HISTORY – Mrs. Ronnie West (aka Nevin Cline's daughter) – 9 December 2007.

73 The Connie B. Gay papers, Country Music Association Library, Boxes 1&2 [hereafter CMA -GAY]; The Washington [D.C.] Evening Star, 8 August 1954: A14 [herafter WashStar]; Wpost, 8 August 1954: 3.

74 ORAL HISTORY - 1 May 2007.

75 Jimmy Dean and Donna Meade Dean, Jimmy Dean's Own Story (New York: Berkely Books, 2004): 25-30; Galen Gart, The

American Record Label and Dating Guide, 1940-1959 (Milford, NH: Big Nickel Publications, 1989): 88-89.

[76] Goldmine, 4 December 1987: 22–26.

Chapter 4

Patsy Cline Sings to Fame on TV and Starts to Record

After Patsy Cline signed her record deal, on September 30, 1954, DJ and radio entrepreneur Connie B. Gay only hired her occasionally and Bill McCall worked out his deal with Paul Cohen, of Decca. She prepared to record, but would have to wait eight months for her first recording session.

MEET THE MEN BEHIND THE MIKE

780 KC **WARL** 1000 WATTS

CONNIE B. GAY

PHIL LONG

DON OWENS

RAY ARMAND

HOWIE FISHER

"Connie B. Gay of WARL"

However, during the first weekend in December of 1954, Peer, Patsy, and the band members journeyed to WFVA-AM in Fredericksburg, Virginia (75 miles from Winchester), to record a demo of four songs that 4-Star president Bill McCall had sent her. Band member Roy Denton remembered the Fredericksburg radio station as having the "only decent recording facility in the region." Patsy Cline recorded demos of "Hidin' Out," "Honky Tonk Merry Go Round," "A Church, a Courtroom and Then Goodbye," and "Turn the Cards Slowly," all of which on June 1 of the following year, she would formally record with Owen Bradley in Nashville. To earn money for the trip and to rent the studio, Bill Peer and His Melody Boys and Girls played the Popular Tavern, near Fredericksburg, and the Fredericksburg Armory.[1]

For additional funds, Patsy Cline ended up working gigs with Peer closer to Washington, DC. For example, she sang at the VFW Hall in Oxon Hill, Maryland, a small community in Prince George's County, an as-yet-undeveloped suburban area just outside Washington. In a letter to Treva Miller, president of her new fan club, Patsy wrote of Peer's expanding list of venues, including drive-in movie theaters and union halls all over Maryland and Virginia. On March 6, 1955, Peer's band, with Patsy Cline singing, began to appear every Sunday afternoon at Strick's, a roadhouse in Prince George's County. Her audiences were working-class whites who had started to move to Prince George's to escape the desegregation of the capital's schools under the *Brown v. Board of Education* Supreme Court ruling, issued in May of 1954.[2]

Working at Strick's led to interaction with Connie B. Gay's star Jimmy Dean and Dean's guitar ace, Roy Clark. On one ordinary July, 1955, night, three future country music superstars sat together in a Bladensburg, Maryland club called the Dixie Pig. Jimmy Dean and Roy Clark regularly performed there, and Patsy Cline worked at nearby Strick's. All had all come to listen to Chick Hall, a guitarist who had a local reputation equal to their own at the time. He was "one of the most creative and innovative guitar players around," recalled Clark, whom Hall had tutored. However, Hall—unlike Clark, Dean, and Cline—never made any records; so generations later, his music only exists as legend. Hall chose job security, but Patsy Cline, with her recording contract in hand, was not going to make Hall's mistake.[3]

Patsy also began to freelance, apart from Bill Peer. She even began to appear as a solo act in clubs in Washington, DC, as she did on January 5, 1955, when according to the *Washington Daily News,* she sang at the Famous Club, in Washington. The Famous had become the most important haunt for C&W fans in the still-segregated downtown DC. In the 1950s, there were two distinct urban live music corridors in the District: an uptown African American jazz scene, which thrived in afterhours joints and where vanguard African American jazz musicians like Charlie Parker and Thelonious Monk met jazz veterans like Art Tatum and Earl Hines; and the corridor along white downtown 7th Street, where one could hear C&W in a string of servicemen's bars. The Famous was near the two interstate bus stations, where white southerners (typically GIs on leave) streamed into the city for "rest and relaxation." Roy Clark stated in 1986, "I'll never forget that night [in 1955] I was working The Famous, and in came this dark-haired girl [Patsy Cline] from Winchester. She blew the place apart."[4]

But some ties continued with the smitten Bill Peer. In early May 1955, Peer again got Patsy Cline into Winchester's Apple Blossom Parade. Peer secured a handsome 1955 black Cadillac Coupe de Ville convertible from a Martinsburg, West Virginia dealership and decorated the car with crepe paper streamers shaped like musical notes. Patsy Cline and Peer's musicians, in their finest C&W costumes, sat and waved as the parade wove past the homes of the Winchester elite.[5]

In September of that year, Patsy formally spilt with Bill Peer. She wanted no part of the divorce proceedings initiated by his wife. In addition, Connie B. Gay had told Patsy that he would soon be getting her more bookings. So with Gay's promise of TV appearances, she formally broke with Peer.

On June 1, 1955, Patsy Cline first stepped into Owen Bradley's new recording studio on Nashville's Music Row—eight months after she had signed with Bill McCall. She had only this one Nashville recording session in 1955, and then three others in 1956, recording a total of sixteen songs, all produced by Owen Bradley. Patsy's cousin confirms that, in April and May of that year, Ginny practiced at the small studio in the G&M Music Store, in downtown Winchester. Patsy would go into the booth on the second floor, record, listen to the playback, and record the song again and again until she got what she wanted. Her determination never wavered. A successful record could make her rich—not financially dependent on a husband.[6]

With the June 1 session, Patsy Cline became one of the first singers to record at the new Bradley studio. Producer Owen Bradley and his brother, Harold, purchased a decrepit Nashville mansion and later added a steel-frame and metal-covered Quonset hut to the rear of the house. This created Bradley's Film and Recording Studio. Owen Bradley's son, Jerry Bradley, recalled how his father and uncle improvised the sonic space, using old curtains, pieces of wood made into louvers, and raw insulation covered with burlap. "My dad had a way of dealing with materials to acoustically fix a room," Jerry Bradley said. "Owen and Harold, they tuned that room by trial and error, and with their ears." This was their third try at creating their own studio, and this time they created a new acoustical standard for Nashville recording. No studio in Nashville at that time could claim to be superior to the Bradleys'.[7]

The Bradley facility could record both film and audio. Indeed, in 1955, Owen Bradley saw the future in television: "I was Music Director at WSM-AM. I felt like my days were numbered since television was going to wipe us off the face of the earth. [In 1955] I hoped to be a film producer." But his plans proved misplaced, and by June 1, 1955, although the Bradley facility did house some filmmaking, audio recording bookings overwhelmed the studio. Ironically, the wooden sets built for making syndicated TV shows, which lined the walls of the Quonset hut studio, made a unique acoustical contribution, enhancing the studio's reputation. According to Owen Bradley's younger brother, guitarist Harold Bradley, "The studio sounded so good we left [the sets] in there and we never took them out. It made the acoustics as close to perfect as you could get them."[8]

Here Owen Bradley, recorded Patsy Cline singing "Hidin' Out," "Turn the Cards Slowly," "A Church, a Courtroom and Then Goodbye," and Honky Tonk Merry Go Round." Bradley remembered that, when Patsy first reported to him, she listened closely to his instructions: "She did anything I asked." Patsy and Owen Bradley cooperated -- contrary to rumors stated later.

Bill McCall chose the songs; Owen Bradley produced the sessions; and Decca's Paul Cohen, Owen Bradley's boss in New York City, approved the take and chose two songs for two 45 rpm records.. Initially Patsy recorded in the small studio created out of the center of the former mansion; later, as Bradley added more musicians, they all moved into the Quonset hut behind the mansion.[9]

"Owen Bradley (left) and Paul Cohen (right)"

On July 29, 1955, even the *Winchester Evening Star,* although well inside the newspaper, on page 12, underlined the significance of her first record: "Miss Virginia Hensley [sic], who sings under the name of Patsy Kline [sic], has had a record released by Coral Records [a division of Decca], of New York City, where she is under contract [sic]." The record Cohen approved was of "A Church, a Courtroom and Then Good Bye." and "Honky Tonk Merry Go Round." A month earlier, Decca arranged for her to sing in Nashville's Centennial Park, as a special guest of Decca star Ernest Tubb and his Texas Troubadours, featuring fiddler Tommy Jackson, who had played in Patsy Cline's first recording session, Patsy performed for a crowd estimated at fifty thousand, but *Billboard* listed her as "Patsy Kline." Then, in an October 29 letter to fan club president Treva Miller, Patsy related that she had appeared on the Grand Ole Opry, again with Tubb, singing "Just a Closer Walk with Thee."

With Paul Cohen's help, Patsy obtained her first national fan magazine exposure in the October 1955 issue of the magazine *Cowboy Songs,* in the "Women in the News" column. The column noted her experience with Bill Peer. Paul Cohen of Decca Records predicted big things for Patsy very soon. Ernest Tubb, Eddy Arnold, Roy Acuff, Owen Bradley, and many others said Patsy was destined to become one of the country's great stars

In January 1956, *Cowboy Songs* promoted Patsy's second recording session, just held on January 5. As a result, one month later, Decca's Coral brand released "I Love You Honey" and "Come On In." Still pushing Patsy Cline, Paul Cohen had Owen Bradley scheduled a third recording session, for April 22.[10]

On January 16, 1956, from 608 South Kent Street Winchester, Patsy wrote to her fan club president about her first airplane ride and her performance at Nashville's Plantation Club with Tony Bennett, Ray Price, Audrey Williams (Hank's widow), and Eddy Arnold. She performed two songs, and then the crowd demanded a third.

Patsy Cline was starting her recording career with a significant push by the Decca PR department, but no hits had emerged. Only with her fourth recording session, on November 8, 1956, did Bradley, his session players, and Cline create her first big hit, "Walkin' After Midnight." On November 18, Patsy wrote her fan club president from Winchester that she was proud of the new recordings, and had had "a ball" at the annual disc jockey convention held in Nashville. Patsy described the fourth recording session to her fan club president in a letter and predicted that "Pick Me Up on Your Way Down" might become a C&W hit. Patsy considered "A Poor Man's Roses" a lively pop tune, but Paul Cohen preferred "Walkin' After Midnight."[11]

As we listen to Patsy Cline in the twenty-first century, we realize that she never sounded hard country, even in the beginning. Decca session master Owen Bradley already had Kitty Wells to record in that style, and so Decca did not need another girl singer with a twang. From the beginning, Owen Bradley took the piano parts for himself and asked Farris Coursey (from Bradley's Big Band) to fashion the beat on the drums. Both these instruments were associated with pop music, not hard country. And they served to give Patsy Cline a new and different platform for her singing. No fan would mistake her for Kitty Wells. Pianist Bradley and Patsy Cline had bonded over their love of the piano and Big Band music, and so the germination of "the Patsy Cline sound," which led later to her iconic status, began during those four early sessions.

"Patsy Cline early publicity photo"

For the first four Patsy Cline sessions, all taking place before her January 21, 1957, appearance on Arthur Godfrey's national TV show on CBS.7 Owen Bradley used only seven instrumentalists to back Cline: an electric guitar (Grady Martin), an acoustic guitar (Harold Bradley), a steel guitar (Don Helms), an acoustic bass (Bob Moore), a fiddle (Tommy Jackson), a drum kit (Farris Coursey), and a piano (played by Owen Bradley himself). Within the world of country music at the time, the Grand Ole Opry did not permit a drummer on its stage, so Bradley was making a radical break, encouraged by Paul Cohen.

Owen Bradley employed the best musicians in Nashville from the very beginning. For example, Grady Martin (1929–2001) was as skilled an electric guitarist as any session player. He came off a Tennessee farm unable to read music, but by age twenty-one, he was developing a style of his own, hard edged without being abrasive. (Think of the opening riff of Roy Orbison's "Pretty Woman.") Paul Cohen changed Martin's life in 1949 by recording the guitarist's marked, raunchy, bluesy chords on Red Foley's mega-hit "Chattanoogie Shoe Shine Boy," one of Decca's 1950s top pop hits. During this time, Grady Martin continued to fine-tune his guitar playing, contributing impressive solos to Foley's hits, such as the biting lead on "Birmingham Bounce" (1950), the haunting, blues solo on "Midnight" (1952), and the screaming break on "Plantation Boogie" (1955).

By 1955, Martin had become the lead guitar of choice for Owen Bradley. Indeed he was so successful with Bradley that he was fully booked day and night doing sessions at the Bradley studio. "I'd sleep where I could, sometimes," Martin later told Jack Hurst. "I slept under the piano bench for a few hours a few nights. You'd start out [the session] early in the morning and might not get through until early the next morning. But I always considered myself lucky, because I was able to work and still [live] at home." Among the most important innovations in Martin's session recording was his frequent use of a nylon-string classical guitar in a medium that was built on the steel-string guitar sounds. He was part of what made Patsy Cline sound innovative as his skilled playing of a nylon-string guitar graced her "Walkin' After Midnight."[12]

On acoustic guitar was Harold Bradley, Owen Bradley's youngest brother. Owen was always in charge, but Harold helped create the Bradley–Decca sound. Harold Bradley had played alongside Grady Martin in classic Owen Bradley sessions that produced Red Foley's "Chattanoogie Shoe Shine Boy," Bobby Helms' "Jingle Bell Rock," and Brenda Lee's "I'm Sorry," as well as Patsy Cline's "Walkin' After Midnight." Engineer Mort Thomasson and Owen and Harold Bradley were not studio architects, but they felt that there would be a demand for quality audio recordings, and Paul Cohen was willing to promise them Decca sessions. In later years, Harold Bradley related that recording Patsy Cline proved to be a different experience. "We had no headphones. We had no musical scores. My brother came up with the arrangements." Harold Bradley remembered Patsy Cline as being "very very intense about her music." She learned from Owen Bradley and was at ease in the presence of a master producer.[13]

If we listen closely for the beat in the original 1956 recording of "Walkin' After Midnight," the acoustic bass playing of Bob Moore becomes readily apparent. Moore played the acoustic bass in the first Patsy Cline session and would play in all but one of her Nashville sessions. Born in Nashville in 1932, Moore could not afford an instrument as a youngster, but when he spied a used acoustic bass in the school band room, he grabbed it. By age seventeen, in 1949, high school dropout Moore was sharing a boardinghouse room with future guitar great Hank Garland, and was regularly jamming with another young guitarist— Grady Martin. Then Moore, like Martin, began busy years, juggling work with Red Foley at the Ozark Jubilee in Springfield, Missouri, eight hours from Nashville, and for Owen Bradley back in Nashville.[14]

Moore noted that while he was happy for the money, he loved working for Owen Bradley: "I can tell you, Owen had soul. He was . . . a great piano player." Moore's musical training and expertise came from having worked in Owen Bradley's Big Band for twenty years. He not only became Bradley's preferred session player, but later credited Bradley for teaching him music and recording, opening his mind up "to the inside of the chords," and to seeing music as more than melody and rhythm. "It was a real musical education," Moore later said. Patsy Cline created masterpieces for Owen Bradley as a result of the same education she received under his tutelage.[15]

While Patsy Cline has become synonymous with the Nashville Sound, defined as "no fiddles, no steel guitars," this characterization is ahistorical. Both a fiddle and a steel guitar were included in her first four sessions. Owen Bradley hired experienced steel guitarist Don Helms to give her recordings a country feel. No steel player had greater credentials; Helms had been the steel guitarist for Hank Williams' Drifting Cowboys band, and by the time of Williams' January 1, 1953, death, had recorded more than one hundred songs with Williams, including "Your Cheatin' Heart" and "Cold, Cold Heart." Thereafter, Helms played in Nashville sessions. "Walkin' After Midnight" was just another job.[16]

Helms was born in New Brockton, Alabama, in 1927, and as a child, he fell in love with the sound of the steel guitar. As an adult, he created a steel guitar sound that echoed the bluesy timbre of Hank Williams' voice. In the first four Patsy Cline sessions, Helms added a piercing, forceful steel guitar, defining the bluesy Patsy Cline sound. His two steel solos on "Honky Tonk Merry Go Round," gave the recording its distinctive, country feel. Later Helms provided the dirgelike, weeping notes for "Walkin' After Midnight."[17]

These first four sessions also included fiddler Tommy Jackson. He is subdued in "Walkin' After Midnight" but leads off in her very first recording, the underappreciated "Hidin' Out." Born in Birmingham, Alabama, in 1926, Jackson and his family moved to Nashville, where his father, a barber, had gotten him jobs on the Grand Ole Opry by the time he was seventeen. But like all Owen Bradley session players, Tommy Jackson loathed the grind of the road and lived on session work, also with Decca's Red Foley, for whom Jackson virtually invented the standard country fiddle backup style. If there was a Jimi Hendrix of country fiddlers, it was Tommy Jackson. And if square dance music had its Eric Clapton, then it was Tommy Jackson. Thus, he was Owen Bradley's logical choice for Patsy Cline's first four sessions.[18]

To this mix, Owen Bradley added his own Big Band touches. First, he used drums. With no session drummers in Nashville, Bradley hired the drummer from his own Big Band, Farris Coursey, nicknamed Sap. Coursey played in the first four Patsy Cline sessions. Sap added a hard beat to the early 4-Star sessions. Born in Mt. Pleasant, Tennessee, in 1911, Coursey had become a session star because Paul Cohen liked a beat on his records. In fact, Cohen used Coursey on "Chattanoogie Shoe Shine Boy."

Harold Bradley remembered the creation of "Chattanoogie Shoe Shine Boy," this way: "My brother had a dance band, with a drummer named Farris Coursey. Owen and him were boyhood friends. Owen came up to [Farris and me] in the hallway [at WSM] and said, 'We're going to do this song about a shoeshine boy, and see if you can come up with a sound like a rag popping sound.'" Coursey played his thigh for the Red Foley number1 hit.[19]

The final session player, on the piano, was Owen Bradley himself. If we listen closely to the original "Walkin' After Midnight," we hear a tinkling piano. That's Owen Bradley. Indeed, he produced all his sessions—from Patsy Cline's to Brenda Lee's to Loretta Lynn's—on a piano. Here Bradley differentiated his sound from the other famed Nashville producer, guitarist Chet Atkins.[20]

Owen Bradley told Paul Kingsbury that Paul Cohen never lost faith in Patsy Cline. "Owen, she's got it," Cohen said. "She's special." Paul Cohen (1908–70) was Decca's country music head until 1958, when he moved to run Coral and turned the Nashville operation over to Bradley. Cohen had first entered the record business with Columbia in the late 1920s, but in 1934, he joined Decca's newly formed U.S. operation, organized by Jack Kapp. During World War II, he took over Decca's "hillbilly" Nashville division, which he ran from New York City. In 1947, Cohen hired Owen Bradley to represent him in Nashville. Cohen was still a New York City–based Decca vice president when Decca founder Jack Kapp died, in 1949, but Cohen was passed over as the new president and stayed on as vice-president to sign Kitty Wells, Webb Pierce for hard country, and Brenda Lee and Bobby Helms for pop. According to Owen Bradley, Cohen liked country music because of its melody. Jack Kapp was notorious for his insistence on musicians' following melody – not approving any recording with improvisation. Kapp even had a sign in the Decca lobby in New York, reading, "Where's the Melody?" Cohen enforced this rule with Patsy Cline.[21]

Through 1955, Patsy had not created hit records. Back home, on October 1, 1955, Connie B. Gay started *Town and Country Jamboree,* a three-hour live local Saturday night TV show, broadcast by the ABC affiliate, WMAL-TV (Washington, DC). The ABC network offered no national programming during that time period, so WMAL-TV, owned by the most popular newspaper in DC, the *Washington Evening Star,* initiated a bold experiment: Starting at ten p.m. Saturday nights, it broadcast *Town and Country Jamboree* live—for three hours..[22]

WMAL-TV handled this as a remote broadcast from Turner's Arena. This venue was the size of a small college basketball arena, with the stage set at the east end of the building, and at the other end, Connie B. Gay erected elevated bleachers for fans. In between about 100 couples danced. In front of the stage were three TV cameras and to the left of the stage, through a side door, stood a TV remote truck in an adjacent alley. Since the arena had been built for wrestling and boxing, the dressing rooms were former locker rooms.[23]

Turner's Arena was located in an all-white working-class neighborhood two miles north of the White House. Turner's Arena (later named Capitol Arena) was the biggest neighborhood building, among grocery stores, five-and-ten-cent chain stores, Greek restaurants, and gasoline stations. Across the street from the arena, fans passed a Chevrolet dealership. African American DC was only a few blocks away, but the segregation in Washington was as rigid as that in Winchester. This was a remote TV show done by whites for whites.[24]

Turner's Arena was easy to get to by street car from Washington's bus stations, and many servicemen filled the audience on weekend evenings. Opened in 1935 by professional wrestling promoter Joe Turner, it held 1,880 people in a multipurpose space. During its thirty-year history, besides the Connie B. Gay show, the arena held seven boxing championships. And every professional wrestler from Gorgeous George to Bruno Samartino entertained there. Turner's Arena also housed union meetings and political rallies. During the two-season run of *Town and Country Jamboree,* Vince MacMahon, Sr., the father of successful professional wrestler of the late twentieth and early twenty-first centuries, took ownership of the arena, and changed its named to Capitol Arena. Mac Mahon guaranteed Connie B. Gay a Saturday night exclusive.[25]

For his October 1, 1955 TV premiere, Gay booked as guest stars Bob Wills and the Texas Playboys, a C&W Big Band led by the composer of "Faded Love" and "San Antonio Rose." Gay's local star, and the master of ceremonies of the show, was Jimmy Dean, later of sausage-selling fame. The *Jamboree,* during its fifteen-month run, filled Turner's Arena and proved an overwhelming success in the local TV ratings.[26]

"Patsy Cline with Jimmy Dean"

The director of *Town and Country Jamboree,* Thomas Winker, did his job from the remote truck parked next to the arena, instructing three camera operators working directly in front of the stage, and a fourth in a side room, where Jackson Weaver did the announcing and commercials, with slides for advertisers ranging from local beer companies to automobile dealers. Winkler coordinated these live feeds, like football telecasts, for three hectic hours. Local sponsors bought fifteen-minute segments from independent producer Gay. Like other observers of Connie B. Gay, Winkler noted, "If there was a buck to be made, Connie had a part of it." One of the ways he did this was to film the three-hour show and then show repeats, as indicated by the local *TV Guide*s of 1956 and 1957. Sadly none of these films seems to have survived.[27]

By January 21, 1956, *TV Guide* described the newest local TV phenomenon. Star Jimmy Dean would emcee and sing, but by this point the show had picked up additional talent—notably, three girl singers, Mary Klick, Dale Turner, and Patsy Cline. There was also regular dancing on stage by the Echo Inn Cloggers, from Gay's native North Carolina. But the energy came from the five hundred dancers, following the teen-dance-show model most often associated with Dick Clark, from another ABC affiliate in Philadelphia.[28]

Indirectly, it was Mary Klick (married as Robinson), the singer and acoustic bass player for Jimmy Dean's band, who gave Patsy Cline a chance. In September 1955, she gave birth to a daughter, opening a slot for a replacement singer. Gay tried a couple of others but settled on Patsy Cline, who started in December. With her cowgirl outfits (made by her mother) and pop singing style, Patsy Cline was no Mary Klick, who sounded more like Kitty Wells and was always properly dressed in a gingham frock. Patsy proved an ideal crossover star—like emcee Jimmy Dean, an ex-soldier from Texas, whom *Variety* compared to Bing Crosby for his crooning style.[29]

"(left to right) Mary Klick, Patsy Cline
and Dale Turner"

Patsy learned to entertain the dancers shown on TV and ignore the TV cameras. This practice would provide invaluable experience as she implicitly prepared for her real goal: an appearance on Arthur Godfrey's national network showcase, *Talent Scouts*. Godfrey commanded a larger percentage of the mid-twentieth-century national TV audience than *American Idol* would in the twenty-first century, and he took pride in his ability to find as-yet-undiscovered professionals. Patsy had failed to make the cut when Bill Peer was backing her, but she knew that this was her path to national prominence.

On December 26, 1955, Patsy Cline noted in a letter to her fan club president that she was now appearing every Saturday night on *Town and Country Jamboree*. To introduce his new star, Gay arranged for Patsy Cline, along with girl singers Mary Klick and Dale Turner, would appear on the cover of the January 1, 1956, *Washington Sunday Star's Televue* magazine, the newspaper's weekly guide to TV shows. Cline's appearance on the cover of *Televue* had been easy for Gay to arrange, since the newspaper owned the TV station. The color image introduced Patsy Cline to a regional audience.

Since Gay had arranged Patsy Cline's recording contract with 4-Star, he willingly had her sing her new recordings. On February 4, 1956, she sang "Turn the Cards Slowly," which she had recorded on June 1 of the previous year and Decca had released shortly thereafter. Unlike other *Town and Country Jamboree* performers, Patsy had records that fans could actually go out to buy after hearing the tunes on TV. On February 25, 1956, Patsy Cline sang "Come On In," which she had just recorded, on January 5. In the summer of 1956, she promoted her new recordings "I Love You Honey," "Come On In," "I Cried All the Way to the Alter," and "I Don't Wanna" on *Town and Country Jamboree*. But with only a handful of songs available on 45s, Patsy had to learn new songs, covers of hits by others. On March 3, 1956, she sang "High Ballin' Daddy" (Tiny Bradshaw, 1949), the following week "If You Want Some Loving," (Teresa Brewer, 1951), and so on.[30]

On February 22, 1956, Patsy Cline wrote her fan club president that Gay had arranged for her to be the only TV personality in the upcoming Winchester Apple Blossom Parade. And Patsy told of the new live appearances that Gay had booked. On Thursday, March 1, 1956, Patsy Cline headlined as a single at Quantico Marine Base, backed by Jimmy Dean's Wildcat band (composed of a fiddler, a couple of eclectic guitar players, a steel guitar, acoustic base player, and Dean on the accordion). Dean and his band were TV regulars, appearing not only on Saturday nights but on a fifteen-minute early evening show Monday through Friday. In anticipation of this appearance Patsy Cline designed a new costume, a cowgirl outfit with white horses set in rhinestones on deep purple cloth, which her had mother skillfully sewed for her.[31]

With regular TV appearances, Patsy Cline started getting a lot of fan mail, and so on March 18, Gay convinced the *Washington Evening Star* editors to do a cover piece on Patsy alone for the Sunday magazine. Gay wrote the copy and portrayed Patsy as a "Hillbilly with Ommmph." "Pardner, there's a purty li'l thrush in a cowgirl outfit (she's more at home in boots than high heels), who's making city slickers pine for country music. She's a feminine singing sensation." Gay ended the story with "Patsy has brought a brand of showmanship and rhythm to hillbilly music that's as welcome as a cool country breeze in springtime. She creates the mood by the lilt of her voice, reaching way down deep in her soul to bring forth the melody." This was pure PR-speak, but would make its way into story after story for decades. Gay even staged a Patsy Cline Night on *Town and Country Jamboree.*

On April 1, Gay's PR machine arranged for the *Country Song Roundup* fan magazine to print a note about his "new" star in a column entitled "Hillbilly Queens." Fans read another Connie B. Gay public relations creation: "She began to sing and play the piano at eight (fitting the child prodigy myth); she sang anywhere for experience (showing her work ethic); she and Bill McCall were working to make her a recording star (showing her drive). Absent were the roles of Paul Cohen, and Owen Bradley. Gay did get her first record releases right, though—"A Church, a Courtroom and Then Goodbye," coupled with "Honky Tonk Merry Go Round," and "Hidin' Out," backed with "Turn the Cards Slowly."[32]

Steady work meant new money. On April 10, Patsy Cline wrote her fan club president that she had purchased a 1951 Hudson, and so the break from Gerald Cline was now permanent. (She left unmentioned meeting Charles Allen Dick and her loss of the expensive Buick that Gerald Cline had made payments on.) Ironically, the very next day the *Winchester Evening Star* printed on page 6 that, in her Hudson, "Virginia Hensley Cline of Winchester, known to television fans as Patsy Cline, was uninjured when her car collided with a truck on US Rt. 50 west." Patsy was not hurt, but she now needed a new ride. This transportation need supplied the opening Charles Dick, whom she'd just met, needed to woo her. He promised her regular rides to Washington, DC.[33]

Patsy Cline used her TV celebrity to obtain other gigs, and so on Friday nights she appeared with the Kountry Krackers band at the Berryville, Virginia, Armory. (This is where she met Charles Dick.) Kountry Krackers' leader Bud Armel offered her a percentage of the door, and on Friday nights, she usually made about one hundred dollars for singing from 9:30 p.m. to 1:00 a.m. Fans paid a dollar admission. The Kountry Krackers covered everything fans liked to dance to. Technically, the Armory served no alcohol, but fans regularly slipped out to the Red Fox, around the corner. Armel would let her go if Gay booked something better for her. So on July 20, 1956, for example, Gay booked Patsy Cline and Jimmy Dean at the Upper Montgomery County (Maryland) Volunteer Firemen's Carnival. Finally Patsy Cline was making it on her own, as a female solo singer, backed by Jimmy Dean's band or the Kountry Krackers.[34]

Life got easier for Patsy Cline as a performer. Connie B. Gay was a businessman who scheduled the lives of his stable of stars. Roy Clark remembered working for Gay: "Connie ran everything. We knew where to show up every night and every day, we knew where we were going a week from Monday, what time, and for how much. We did a lot of free functions for Connie, who often booked us to play at political rallies and barbecues for politicians, where everyone would be dressed in blue jeans with kerchiefs around their necks for a hillbilly day." Patsy Cline was now helping her family meet its needs and rise to working-class status.[35]

Gay knew that if his stars got national TV exposure, more fans would tune into *Town and Country Jamboree*. So, on April 21, Patsy Cline appeared on the nationally televised *Ozark Jubilee* on the ABC television network. For this show, she flew to Springfield, Missouri, home of the *Jubilee*, then flew to Nashville for a Sunday recording session, and then back to Washington's National Airport on Monday afternoon. At the *Ozark Jubilee*, she got to meet Eddy Arnold and sing with him. She also met the "female Elvis," Wanda Jackson. At that show, Decca producer Paul Cohen promised to take her to New York City to record "Just a Closer Walk with Thee" and "Life's Railway to Heaven" with a twenty-one piece orchestra and fifteen-man chorus. [This session did not take place.] Cohen told Patsy that Red Foley had sold four million with "Just a Closer Walk with Thee," and she could replicate his success with a female version. While Cohen had Owen Bradley record Patsy Cine in Nashville classified as "country music," he envisioned her matching Decca's Red Foley, who at that time was host of the *Ozark Jubilee*, as a crossover star.[36]

Connie B. Gay placed Patsy Cline in Winchester's 1956 Apple Blossom Festival parade, on April 26 and 27. Gay made a deal that she would serenade the Apple Blossom Queen and her court, backed by Claude Thornhill and his Big Band. Gay knew that news crews would film this for newsreels that would appear in movie theaters across the United States. In Winchester, Patsy Cline sang at the Apple Blossom Festival's Thursday night square dance and Friday night's Young

People's Dance. For the Grand Feature Parade, the car was draped with a banner that read, "Town & Country T.V. Star PATSY CLINE."[37]

Two weeks later, on May 14, she wrote her fan club president that she was working five nights a week. And she was saving her money to buy a new Oldsmobile in the fall. This Olds Super 88 is now considered a classic among the large, sleekly designed cars of the mid-1950s. In May 1956, Patsy Cline was still hoping for a hit record, but "Walkin' After Midnight" was eight months away.

Meanwhile Connie B. Gay had Patsy regularly covering pop hits on *Town and Country Jamboree*. On the May 26, Patsy Cline sang "Nobody but You," which had premiered as a pop song in the MGM musical *Hollywood Revue of 1929*. On the same TV show, Jimmy Dean rendered "John Henry," Billy Grammar sang "Wabash Cannon Ball," and guest Grandpa Jones sang a medley of his hits including "Mountain Dew," "Rock Island Line," and "Are You From Dixie?" In other words, Patsy Cline represented the pop side of *Town and Country Jamboree* and guests from Nashville and other regulars handled the country side. Ironically, on that same show, Gay had Mary Klick, back from maternity leave, cover Don Gibson's hit "Sweet Dreams"—the song that, by the twenty-first century, had been wholly remembered as a Patsy Cline song.[38]

For the June 2 *Town and Country Jamboree* show, Jimmy Dean opened, as usual, singing "Riding Down to Sante Fe," the show's theme song. Patsy came next, the second performance of the evening, with "Honky Tonk Merry Go Round," the fourth song she had ever recorded. But Gay was cognizant of the changing tastes in pop music and had Herbie Jones, of the Jimmy Dean band, cover Elvis' "Heartbreak Hotel." Presley had released his version five months earlier, and by June 2, "Heartbreak Hotel" sat atop the rock charts. Baltimore's Gunther Beer paid top dollar to sponsor the first hour of the *Jamboree*.[39]

On June 16, Gay permitted Patsy Cline to appear as a guest star on the Grand Ole Opry, where she sang "A Church, a Courtroom and Then Goodbye" on the *Prince Albert Show*, the portion of the Opry that was broadcast over the NBC radio network. Longtime Opry star Little Jimmy Dickens introduced her, and a comic routine by Minnie Pearl followed her performance. Then Dickens called Patsy back to sing "I've Loved and Lost Again," her forthcoming Decca release.[40]

On June 17, 1956, while in Nashville, Paul Cohen arranged for the United States Navy to hire Patsy Cline to guest star on two episodes of the syndicated radio show *Country Hoedown* and sing "Come On In (and Make Yourself At Home)," "Turn the Cards Slowly," "Yes, I Know Why," "Stop, Look and Listen," "The Wayward Wind," and "For Rent." These two episodes included a thirteen-minute radio broadcast shipped to stations for free, leaving two minutes for local advertising. While this show was labeled "country," "The Wayward Wind" was a pop lure for young recruits. Faron Young hosted both shows. His career was at a peak that year, and the following spring Young would cover "Sweet Dreams" and take it to number 2 on the country charts.[41]

However, trips to Nashville and Springfield, Missouri, were still the exception for Patsy Cline. Gay booked her and Jimmy Dean, his two top stars, all over the local area where fans could see them on TV. For example, on June 29, Gay booked them, along with Dean's band, the Texas Wildcats, to ride in the Volunteer Fireman's parade in Damascus, Maryland, sponsored by Count's Western Wear, of Damascus. (Dean and Cline then received free cowboy hats from Count's.) This small town was 30 miles from Washington, DC, well within TV range of *Town and Country Jamboree*. Three days later, Patsy Cline, backed by a local band, sang at the nearby Boonsboro, Maryland, Carnival. Here were two of her typical Connie B. Gay paydays, but Gay demanded that she get there on her own, provide her own costume, and return to Winchester in her own car—all for the $120 she earned. Her life was far better economically, but she could not yet afford to move her family out of 608 South Kent Street.[42]

On July 14, 1956, Connie B. Gay expanded this musical empire to include George Hamilton IV to become his Pat Boone. Hamilton had recorded "A Rose and Baby Ruth" as a student at the University of North Carolina, and was discovered by Connie B. Gay's son, Jan Gay, who attended nearby Duke University. Connie B. Gay helped Hamilton sign with ABC Records, and to the surprise of all, "A Rose and Baby Ruth" started rising on the *Billboard* pop charts, peaking at number 6 in November of 1956. Hamilton was straight pop, complementing the crossover style of Patsy Cline.[43]

The August 1 issue of *Country Song Roundup* printed its top seven female singers of 1956: (1) Kitty Wells, (2) Jean Shepard, (3) Goldie Hill, (4) Wanda Jackson, (5) June Carter, (6) Charline Arthur, and (7) Patsy Cline. At the time the magazine conducted this survey, Patsy had only three records out, and she had not yet had a hit. She had a fan club, but was simply a regional star.

Still, Patsy aspired to break out of her regional mold. In a September 4 letter to her fan club president, Patsy reported a scheduled trip to New York for her second audition for *Arthur Godfrey's Talent Scouts* TV show. This time her new boyfriend, Charles Dick, drove her the three hundred miles to New York City and then drove her back after the audition. Dick was a linotype operator at the *Winchester Evening Star*, and together, he and Patsy funded the trip. She was comfortable working on TV and knew Godfrey liked solo singers who could be backed by his house band and thus formulated to appeal to the Godfrey audience. But Godfrey's producer, Janette Davis, did not commit one way or the other as to when Patsy Cline might appear.

Gay was pleased, however, and on the September 8 telecast of *Town and Country Jamboree,* he had Patsy sing nostalgic pop standards, notably "Some of These Days," made popular by Sophie Tucker, first as an Edison cylinder recording in 1911. During her lengthy career, Tucker sang "Some of These Days"—the tale of a person who starts at the bottom of the ladder and never gives up—as her theme song. "Some of these days you're going to be so lonely" would turn out to be a theme that Owen Bradley would tap into when freed from the 4-Star contract. Tucker, a single woman who stood her ground, served as a role model for Patsy Cline, with appearances on Ed Sullivan's *Toast of the Town,* Edward R. Murrow's *Person to Person,* and Steve Allen's *Tonight Show.* And Gay's request that Patsy Cline learn this standard and sing it on *Town and Country Jamboree* showed that, while Patsy dressed like a cowgirl, she sang like a pop star.[44]

On September 15, 1956 the start of the new TV season, the Washington, DC, edition of *TV Guide* contained an article on *Town and Country Jamboree,* which detailed preshow preparations for the live Saturday night broadcast. Patsy Cline had to be at Turner's Arena at 8:00 p.m., arriving as the crowd was already dancing to tunes played by Jimmy Dean and his Texas Wildcat band. Then at 10:30 p.m., as Turner's Arena filled, the broadcast commenced. Gay carefully plotted his three-hour extravaganza, and so each performer did a segment, took a break, and then did another set later. On average, Patsy Cline sang a half-dozen songs that she was told to learn for that week's show.[45]

On September 22, with *Town and Country Jamboree* one week short of being a year old, Gay experimented with Mary Klick as the emcee. Gay liked his female stars. Klick introduced Patsy Cline singing one of her records "I Love You Honey" (recorded on January 5, 1956), plus covers of Marty Robbins' "It's a Long Long Ride" and Hank Thompson's "We've Gone Too Far." (Patsy Cline never recorded either.) Indeed, the show was littered with covers: Dale Turner doing "China Doll" (later covered by George Hamilton IV), and George Hamilton IV singing the Doris Day hit "Que Sera Sera," from Alfred Hitchcock's movie hit *The Man Who Knew Too Much*. Doris Day's pop tune had reached *Billboard*'s charts in July 1956, and would, in the spring of 1957, receive the Academy Award for Best Original Song. A close examination of the show's script demonstrated that, as the second season of *Town and Country Jamboree* commenced, Connie B. Gay had carefully crafted his *Jamboree* as a mixture of pop and country singing and dancing.[46]

By late September, Patsy Cline was well off enough to buy a used 1956 Oldsmobile 88. Patsy got a good deal, as this was the end of the model year; Oldsmobile was announcing its new 1957 models, and dealers were clearing their lots of the 1956 models. Cline was continuing to earn money doing local events, and she even flew to Los Angeles for appearances on Friday, October 12, and Saturday, October 13, telecasts of *Town Hall Party*. This local Los Angeles TV show was the *Town and Country Jamboree* of Southern California. Paul Cohen arranged this gig to help expand Patsy's record sales.[47]

For the second season of *Town and Country Jamboree*, Connie B. Gay grew ever bolder with his pop music offerings. On October 27, Gay had Patsy sing "That Crazy Mambo Thing." Earlier in 1956, Prez Prado had ignited a mambo dance craze in the United States. And indeed, to demonstrate the crossover appeal of this dance craze, Hank Snow had also covered it and RCA had released it along with Snow's version of "Hula Rock," the latter reaching the *Billboard* country charts. No one seemed to care that "That Crazy Mambo Thing" had been written by a Jewish, Tin Pan Alley pop songwriter, Cy Cohen.[48]

And Patsy Cline's bookings became crossover, as well. On the final day of October 1956, she appeared in the Public Square of

Hagerstown, Maryland, to kick off the annual Mummer's Day Parade. Here backup included saxophone, accordion, and glockenspiel players. Patsy Cline was learning to sing any style of music.[49]

Patsy Cline's career on *Town and Country Jamboree* was hardly as a pure country singer, despite her western duds. On December 29, she sang "I Don't Wanta," which she had recorded, and "Nobody but You," a standard by George Gershwin, written in 1919. Thus, as 1956 drew to a close, Patsy had promoted her four singles of 4-Star songs and anything else Connie B. Gay thought would appeal. But only Patsy Cline could sing George Gershwin.[50]

While it seems obvious more than a half-century later that she should have striven to get to Nashville, it was not clear in 1955 that Nashville would become "Music City USA." Cities like Cincinnati (King Records) and Los Angeles (Capitol Records) had TV shows like *Town and Country Jamboree* and recording studios that Washington, DC, lacked. It only seems clear looking back from the twenty-first century that Owen Bradley's new Nashville studio would be a success and would redefine Nashville as a recording center equal to Los Angeles or New York City. With Bradley's connection as Decca's exclusive recording studio in Nashville, Patsy caught a fabulous break, as Paul Cohen and Owen Bradley made Nashville into a major recording center.

Also by good fortune, Patsy Cline caught the crest of the Connie B. Gay entertainment empire. She did not know that it was about to end. In 1957 Gay joined Alcoholics Anonymous and took the proceeds from his Washington, DC, operations to purchase a string of radio stations. Nevertheless, as indicated by his induction into the

CMA Hall of Fame, in 1980—eight years after Patsy Cline received that honor—Connie B. Gay did help turn the C&W genre into "country music," a modern entertainment subset of pop music.[51]

Indeed, Gay was making so much money that on September 23, 1955, he announced his eventual retirement as a radio DJ. In a notice to all his employees, he wrote, "On November 5, 1955, I will have served nine years as the conductor of *Town and Country Time* on Station WARL, Arlington. On that day, I plan to have my farewell broadcast and kiss that microphone goodbye forever on my broadcast between 12 Noon and 3pm." *Town and Country Jamboree* proved the apex of his TV success. Then, in 1957, Gay jumped out of his league and made an agreement with the CBS television network to do a morning show to compete with NBC's long- running hit, the *Today Show*. While his radio stations always made money, his network show on CBS lasted only three months.[52]

On November 18, 1956, Patsy wrote her fan club president that she had just recorded new songs: "Pick Me Up on Your Way Down," "A Poor Man's Roses"—a pop tune done with hillbilly music. ("I sound like Jo Stafford. But the Decca men [Paul Cohen and Owen Bradley] stated they liked . . . 'Walkin' After Midnight.'") Patsy ended the letter: "Mr. McCall, my bossman, called and stated he was talking to Kay Starr and there was only one girl singer she feared and it was Patsy Cline."

In the end, Patsy Cline used Gay's promotional skills to learn to perform in front of TV audiences, ideal training for an appearance on *Arthur Godfrey's Talent Scouts*. On October 15, 1956, George Hamilton IV appeared on Godfrey's *Talent Scouts*. Hamilton recalled: "Connie [B. Gay] helped me get on 'Talent Scouts.'" Hamilton sang "A Rose and Baby Ruth"—and won.[53]

Gay later did for Patsy what he had done for George Hamilton IV, but first Godfrey wanted to see her perform on his own show. At this point Godfrey lived in Leesburg, Virginia, on a vast estate about thirty-five miles from the WMAL-TV transmission tower. So one Saturday evening during December of 1956, most likely the 22nd or 29th, Godfrey watched *Town and Country Jamboree,* and that following Monday he ordered his producer, Janette Davis, to work Patsy into the January 1957 schedule. We do not know the exact date when Davis called Cline in Winchester to set up the details of her appearance on Monday January 21, 1957, but during the call, Jeanette Davis asked Patsy who her scout would be and what song she wanted to sing.

Thus, in turn, Patsy called Owen Bradley, who called his boss, Paul Cohen, and they selected "Walkin' After Midnight" for her to sing, so that Decca could release "Walkin' After Midnight," backed by "A Poor Man's Roses," in late January, to take full advantage of Patsy's national TV network exposure. There was some discussion about who her scout should be until Patsy Cline proposed "Hilda Hensley, of Winchester," whom of course she had known all her life. This was a ruse, as relatives were not usually scouts. But as Patsy was technically still Mrs. Gerald Cline (and would be until her March 1957 divorce), Davis and her staff assumed she and Hilda Hensley were not related.[54]

What had Patsy Cline sung on *Town and Country Jamboree* to impress Godfrey so? The December 22, 1956, show had adopted a Santa Claus theme. Patsy Cline sang "I Saw Mommy Kissing Santa Claus," yet another cover, the original recording by Jimmy Boyd having reached number 1 on the *Billboard* pop charts in 1952. This pop song was commissioned by Dallas department store Neiman Marcus to promote its Christmas sales, and was as pop as pop could be. Then, on December 29, Patsy Cline sang "Nobody but You," by George Gershwin, and "Pepper Hot Baby," a 1955 Jaye P. Morgan hit. Whatever the exact song was, it was Patsy in a cowgirl outfit singing in pop style that had impressed Arthur Godfrey. Patsy had passed the ultimate audition.[55]

Gay recognized that Patsy Cline, along with Jimmy Dean and George Hamilton IV, were skilled pop singers. On December 21, 1956, Gay booked the trio into the Casino Royal nightclub in downtown Washington. This was a coat-and-tie nightclub—indeed, (white) downtown DC's most posh nightclub. The three singers did three shows that night: 8:00 p.m., 10:30 p.m., and 12:15 a.m. After appearances on Town and Country Jamboree on the following night, the trio returned for the same booking on Sunday night, finishing early on Christmas Eve morning. Patsy Cline was a crossover star, able to sing pop before sophisticated audiences and still star on *Town and Country Jamboree*.

"Advertisement for appearance at Casino Royal"

When Patsy Cline was booked by Arthur Godfrey on January 21, 1957, she had been singing professionally for six years, and performing on local TV for one year. This practice placed her at a point where she sounded like exactly what the Godfrey *Talent Scouts* show claimed it wanted: rising young professional pop singers able to appear on national television. In her November 8, 1956, recording of "Walkin' After Midnight," Patsy sounds like a seasoned professional pop singer who had been coached by the best producer Nashville had to offer, Owen Bradley. After years of struggle and thousands of hours of practice, she was in a place to finally gain a national audience—and to win.

NOTES

Chapter 4

1   ORAL HISTORY – 1 May 2007.

2   H&F, 9 November 1955; Brown Archives; <u>The Washington Daily News</u> ads – every Friday from 1 March 1955 to 16 September 1955; <u>The Cumberland [MD] News</u>, 20 September 1968: 2.

3   Wpost, 21December 2008: C8.

4   Brown Archives; Joe Sasfy, "Connie B. Gay: The Hick from Lizard Lick," <u>The Journal of Country Music</u>, XII/1 (1987): 16-24.

5   Brown Archives.

6   ORAL HISTORY – 1 May 2007.

7   http://countrydiscography.blogspot.come/2009/06/patsy-cline. html provides a vital source of her recording sessions, her albums, compilation albums, and singles [hereafter countrydiscography].

8   David N. Black, "Television from a Third Coast," unpublished Ph.D. dissertation, University of Tennessee, 1996: 82-88.

9   countrydiscography

10 countrydiscography.

11 countrydiscography.

12 Rich Kienzle, "Grady Martin: Unsung and Unforgettable," <u>Journal of Country Music</u>, X/2 (1985): 54-60; <u>The [Nashville] Tennessean</u>, 4 December 2001; A13.

13 "History of Music City," <u>Mix</u> magazine, May 2008; Lindell Gentry, <u>A History and Encyclopedia of Country, Western, and Gospel Music</u>, 2nd edition (Nashville: Calirmont Group, 1969); Michael Kosser, <u>How Nashville Became Music City, U.S.A.</u> (Milwaukee: Hal Leonard, Inc., 2006).

14 <u>Bass Player</u>, April, 2007:13-15.

[15] Bob Moore's home page – www.nashvillesound.net - accessed 13 March 2006.

[16] The Associated Press, 12 August 2008 [hereafter AP].

[17] NYT, 17 August 2008: A18.

[18] Charles Wolfe, "Tommy Jackson: King of the 50's Fiddlers," The Journal of the American Academy for the Preservation of the Old-Time Country Music, #26, (April 1995): 17-19.

[19] Rich Kienzle, "Owen Bradley, "The Journal of the American Academy of Old-Time Country Music, #24 (December 1994): 13-15; Paul Kingsbury, The Encyclopedia of Country Music, (New York: Oxford, 1998): 114.

[20] TRIAL.

[21] Ronnie Pugh, Ernest Tubb (Durham: Duke University Press, 1998): 209-211.

[22] TV Guide, 24 September-1 October 1955 [all cites from DC-Baltimore edition]; Wpost, 1 October 1955: 39.

[23] ORAL HISTORY – George Hamilton IV – 13 September 1997.

[24] Bill Donaldson post on www.innercity.org – accessed 23 Febuary 2004.

[25] WashStar, 30 September 1955: B12.

[26] Wpost, 27 June 1965: C1; Cowboy Songs No. 45; March 1956.

[27] ORAL HISTORY – Thomas Winkler - 9 June 1993.

[28] TV Guide, 21 January 1957: A14-15; TV Guide, 4 February 1957: A14.

[29] Wpost, 21 April 1957: F3.

[30] GAY-CMA, Box 2.

[31] TV Guide, 21 January 1957: A14-15; Arbitron TV Ratings Collection, Hargrett Library, University of Georgia, Athens, Georgia.

[32] Country Song RoundUp, April 1956, #43: 21.

[33] ORAL HISTORY - Charles Dick - 9 May 2009.

[34] Brown Archive; The Frederick [MD] Post, 20 July 1956: 15; TV Guide, 3 December 1955: A-1; CPC collection, card from Winchester Memorial Hospital X-Ray Dept. X-Ray no. 50351.

[35] Roy Clark, My Life (New York: Simon and Schuster, 1994):13-28.

[36] H&F, 1 May 1956.

[37] H&F, 18 April 1956; WS, 21 April 1956: 1.

[38] GAY-CMA, Box 3.

[39] CMA-GAY, Box 12.

[40] H&F, 1 May 1956; Liner notes on MCA's "LIVE at the Opry – Volume 1."

[41] Liner notes on MCA's "LIVE, Volume 2."

[42] The Frederick [MD] Post, 30 June 1956: 5; The Frederick [MD] Post, 3 July 1956: 1.

[43] CMA-GAY, Box 11.

[44] TV Guide, 8 September 1956: A4; Armond Fields, Sophie Tucker (Jefferson, NC: McFarland Publishers, 2003).

[45] CMA-GAY, Box 1; TV Guide, 15 September 1956: A7-A8.

[46] CMA-GAY, Box 12.

[47] LA Times, 12 October 1956: 33.

[48] TV Guide, 27 October 1956: A8.

[49] The Morning [Hagerstown] Herald, 31 October 1956: 1.

[50] TV Guide, 17 November 1956: A1; TV Guide, 24 November 1956: A1.

[51] The Fauquier Democrat, 1 July 1955:1.

[52] CMA-GAY, Box 1; WashStar, 2 November 1955:A15.

[53] H&F, 21 October 1956; ORAL HISTORY – George Hamilton IV – 13 September 1997.

[54] TRIAL.

55 CMA-GAY, Box 12; Arthur Godfrey Collection, Library of American Broadcasting, Box 43; NYT, 4 March 1960: 22; NYT, 5 September 1961: 71.

Chapter 5

Patsy Cline Becomes a Star and a Mother

At precisely 8:59 p.m. eastern time on Monday, January 21, 1957, Patsy Cline's career took off with her win on *Arthur Godfrey's Talent Scouts*. At the end of each half-hour show of *Talent Scouts,* the audience voted by way of Godfrey's famous "applause meter" (really a simple volume-units sound-measuring device left over from World War II). Patsy Cline "buried the needle." Backed by Godfrey's in-house Big Band, she had sung "Walkin' After Midnight" in a pop fashion. Patsy broke down when Arthur Godfrey declared her the winner: "Don't go away Patsy honey," he said, "you just done won this. . . . Bless your little heart; sit down before you have a heart attack."[1]

The CBS show *Arthur Godfrey's Talent Scouts* had defined a new TV genre—discovering young professionals on their way up. It was not an amateur contest, like those Virginia Hensley had participated in back in Winchester. In fact, Godfrey differentiated his show from *Ted Mack's Amateur Hour* by continually announcing that his show presented no amateurs. He had been successful with this strategy, first tendering a hit network radio show and then, in 1949, beginning a decade-long run among TV's top ten most popular shows.

Godfrey had valuable help, especially from his producer, Janette Davis, a former singer and a rare woman in the television industry, holding as she did a position as important as producer of a national show. Davis conducted the auditions, chose the musical arrangements, selected the costumes and also the scouts, and ran such an efficient show that Godfrey himself could arrive at 8:25 p.m., start the live show at 8:30, finish at 9:00, and leave at 9:05. He had the formula down to a science. He only needed to ad lib the commercials, wholly ignoring the written advertising copy. All TV fans across the United States knew that Godfrey had discovered Tony Bennett, Connie Francis, and Rosemary Clooney. So who would be next? On January 21, 1957 — Patsy Cline.[2]

How did Patsy prepare? She had gotten the call from the Godfrey people just after New Year's Day, and she cut down her local appearances and practiced. On Friday, January 18, 1957, three days before her Monday night appearance, Patsy and her mother, Hilda Hensley, flew to New York City; for Hilda, age forty-one, it was the first airplane flight. Patsy, of course, had to miss *Town and Country Jamboree* that Saturday night. Connie B. Gay must have had mixed emotions, as her appearance on Godfrey's show would bring publicity to his own, but he knew that Patsy—unlike George Hamilton IV, who had won on *Talent Scouts* in October 1956—would jump ship and head to Nashville if she won. Indeed, after her triumph on that show, Patsy Cline would never again appear on *Town and Country Jamboree*.

Patsy went to New York expecting to wear her cowgirl costume, but producer Janette Davis literally took her down Broadway, bought her a cocktail dress, and dressed her like a New York nightclub singer. Davis also knocked down Patsy Cline's request to sing "A Poor Man's Roses (or a Rich Man's Gold)," and instead arranged for "Walkin' After Midnight." Davis preferred the bluesier pop tune.

On Monday night, Patsy grew more and more nervous as Godfrey's 53rd and Broadway studio filled up. Godfrey arrived five minutes before the show was to start, was handed notes on guests and commercials, and anticipated meeting Patsy and her scout, Hilda Hensley, for the first time. Godfrey liked the spontaneity of interacting with guests (both scouts and talent) without rehearsal.

At precisely 8:30 p.m. eastern time, *Talent Scouts* began with a prerecorded advertisement by Toni, a maker of women's hair and skin products. Then, live, announcer Tony Marvin intoned, with the Godfrey theme song behind him, "*Arthur Godfrey's Talent Scouts,* brought to you by Deep Magic Creme and long-lasting Toni home permanents." Godfrey did a little patter and reminded the studio audience, "You are going to predict the winner, and then we can see what doors we can open."

The first scout, Mrs. Ronald Smith, from Toronto, introduced light opera singer Margo McKinnon, from Windsor, Ontario, who sang "The Italian Street Song." Margo McKinnon's performance lasted from five minutes into the show to seven minutes—a typical two-minute presentation. Then Godfrey did a spontaneous-sounding Toni advertisement, in which he somehow mocked Elvis Presley's then hit "Hound Dog," as not fair to singers as good as Margo McKinnon, and plugged Toni for an astonishing three minutes and thirty seconds!

The second scout was Mrs. James Sonnenberg, whose husband was a ticket broker for Broadway shows. She and Godfrey talked about the hit "My Fair Lady." Janette Davis had recruited Sonnenberg to be a scout, as singer Jerry Antes lived and performed in Los Angeles, and needed someone from New York to introduce him. He had sung all over the United States and was the same age as Patsy Cline. In the singing style of a Tony Bennett tribute artist, Antes sang a well-known pop standard, "You Make Me Feel So Young." He was well rehearsed with the band, as there was a planned instrumental break in the middle.

During Antes' performance, Janette Davis called Patsy and Hilda to position them for Godfrey's introduction. Eighteen and a half minutes into the thirty-minute show, Hilda Hensley came out on stage as Patsy's scout, and sat next to Godfrey, who questioned her from cue sheets he had been handed as he walked in. Hilda stated she was a Virginian, a dressmaker, not a farmer, and became very embarrassed when Godfrey pressed her about her birth "in the mountains near Winchester." Hilda replied hesitatingly: "The town? Really small. Opequon. My people always lived there." All this time she sounded as if she wished Godfrey would stop—he had been going on for five minutes—because she wanted to do her rehearsed introduction: "I have brought a young girl from Virginia to do her next release on the 26th [of January 1957] on Decca. Patsy Cline. I have known her almost all her life," Hilda said, fudging with *almost.* She then told the national audience that Patsy Cline had just finished an appearance at Casino Royal in Washington, DC, and the year before had entertained at the Apple Blossom Festival. Godfrey picked up caught the reference, as he had been the national guest star at the 1953 Apple Blossom Festival.

"Hilda makes costume for Patsy"

Then Godfrey made his introduction: "And now in the Toni spotlight, Patsy Cline," who then started singing "Walkin' After Midnight" at 23 ½ minutes into the 30 minute show. Patsy sang a slower version than the one most fans are used to, sounding like a Big Band singer in front of Godfrey's house band. With trumpets and trombones supplying a final crescendo, this new song seemed like a Big Band pop number. Patsy sang for 2 ½ minutes. Arthur Godfrey commented, "Cute song; a wam-doodler."

Then Godfrey did a live pitch for Toni Deep Magic Lotion: "Deep softens as it deep cleans." And then he went into his finale:

"Now, bring them out in [the] order [in which] they appeared," Godfrey said, starting at twenty-eight minutes into the thirty minute show. Each did a ten-second reprise. Clearly, Patsy gained the loudest applause, and Godfrey did not hesitate as he intoned, "Don't go away, Patsy honey, you done won this." At twenty-eight minutes and fifty seconds, Godfrey interviewed Patsy, plugging her song: "I got a hunch this [will be a hit.] Well, neighbor [to Patsy], we start in the morning." Fade out with Pasty saying through her tears, "Oh thank you."[3]

At ten a.m. Tuesday morning, Patsy Cline joined Arthur Godfrey for his national morning show, and that evening, the front page of the *Washington Evening Star* told the newspaper readers of the U.S. capital, "Patsy Cline walked off with top honors on Godfrey's Talent Scouts Monday night, singing her new Decca recording." On the night after the second inauguration of President Dwight David Eisenhower, the leading paper of the nation's capital congratulated one of its own.[4]

On January 22 through 25, Tuesday through Friday, Patsy Cline appeared on Godfrey's simulcast morning show, a 10:00 a.m. to 11:30 a.m. variety show. This was broken into fifteen-minute segments, with a different Godfrey regular filling nine of the ten slots and the *Talent Scouts* winner performing in one 15-minute segment. For Patsy's fifteen minutes, she and Godfrey would talk at his desk, and then announcer Tony Marvin would introduce Patsy to sing. Godfrey continually complimented her and did his soft-selling advertisements, principally for Lipton Tea. (Indeed, all the New York–based advertising agencies recognized that Godfrey had used his TV shows to make Lipton the number-one-selling tea in the United States by converting a whole nation to iced tea.)

On Wednesday morning, the *Washington Post* reported the immediate effects of Patsy Cline's win. An unnamed reporter interviewed Hirsh de la Viez, president of Coin Machine Corporation, operator of 750 juke boxes in the Washington area, who said, "Within an hour after Patsy sang that song on TV, we had over 50 calls from juke box operators. All of them wanted to know when we would put the record on the boxes." The *Washington Post* correctly predicted the effect on Patsy Cline's career: "The record may also lift Miss Cline right out of the country and western music field. 'Walking [sic] After Midnight' is not a hillbilly tune. It falls into the 'popular' category." Newspaper commentators across the United States came to the same conclusion and printed the same prediction.[5]

In the February 2 issue of *Billboard,* Decca placed a full-page ad for the "Winner of the Arthur Godfrey Talent TV Show; A Winner All the Way with 'Walkin' After Midnight.'" The next *Billboard* issue, dated February 9, reviewed five new pop records: crooner Perry Como latest came first, followed by the Chordettes [another Arthur Godfrey discovery], the DeJohn Sisters, Roy Hamilton, and Patsy Cline. "With the 'Walkin' After Midnight' release, Miss Cline, heretofore identified mainly with the country field, makes a strong bid to break pop-wise. 'Walkin'' has a fine bluesy flavor."[6]

By March 2, *Billboard* had Sonny James's "Young Love" atop its pop charts, with "Walkin' After Midnight" in the twelfth spot. On its country charts, "Walkin' After Midnight" rose to number 2, just after "Young Love." Owen Bradley was right in summarizing the success of "Walkin' After Midnight:" "We'd try anything to see what would stick. In [looking back from 1979], we had a girl with a good strong voice. [But she] was not like some other girl [country] singers. We sort of lucked onto [Walkin' After Midnight]." Luck, indeed—Owen Bradley finally had a potential star in Patsy Cline, a pupil he could instruct and work with.[7]

Following her win on national television and soaring record sales, Patsy Cline began to tour, to make money from her win, knowing that she would receive no royalty checks from 4-Star's Bill McCall anytime soon. She worked furiously to gain live bookings to milk her new fame. On February 8, the *Winchester Evening Star* noted, "Patsy Cline leaves today by air for Springfield, Missouri, where she will make a guest appearance on the *Ozark Jubilee*." On February 10, Patsy Cline wrote her fan club president - Teva Miller - from an airplane on her way to Nashville for appearances on February 13 and 14. She listed her schedule: the *Town Hall* TV program from Los Angeles on February 22 and 23; *Ozark Jubilee* on March 2; Ed Sullivan's Sunday night variety show in five weeks; then back to Godfrey when he gets back from Africa [in April]. Patsy also reported to the fan club president that, just twenty days after her appearance on *Talent Scouts*, "Walkin' After Midnight" had sold more than 200,000 copies as a single.[8]

On February 16, *Billboard* told its national readership that Patsy Cline was touring the United States, and that "Walkin' After Midnight" was the most recent example of a country artist "coming into the pop market and cleaning up. Miss Cline has cracked New York, Philadelphia, Baltimore, Washington and other East Coast cities—as well as Southern and Midwestern markets—in both country and pop." Agent Hubert Long, of Nashville, booked her across the United States, according to Paul Cohen's instructions.[9]

On March 2, Patsy played Moline, Illinois, in a live show, then flew to California to appear on Tennessee Ernie Ford's afternoon TV show, then on Art Linkletter's TV show, Bob Crosby's [Bing's brother] TV show, and while still in Los Angeles, the *Town Hall Party* TV show. On March 15, she appeared at the Grand Ole Opry, and after that, journeyed to Knoxville for *The Tennessee Barn Dance* TV program. She anticipated that Godfrey would book her one week of every six, and that she would also appear on the Steve Allen and Perry Como TV shows. These last appearances, however, did not take place.

On March 7, Patsy Cline wrote her fan club president that she was lonely: "My Charlie left Monday [March 4]" to journey to Ft. Benning [Georgia]. "I've never loved a man so much in my life."

Paul Cohen told her she was the hottest-selling artist on the Decca label, as she had leapt past Jerry Lee Lewis, the Platters, and Bill Haley and the Comets. On April 4, 1957, the *Winchester Evening Star* gave its front page to Patsy Cline, headlining that she was currently on a personal appearance tour through Florida, Georgia, South Carolina, and South Carolina. Her tour with Ferlin Husky and Faron Young included Pensacola, Florida; Swainsboro, Macon, and Augusta, Georgia; and Columbia, South Carolina. The *Star* added that she would then travel to New York City to do two recording sessions. Her latest record, "Walking [sic] After Midnight," had already sold more than 750,000 copies. The *Star* also reported that Patsy Cline had been scheduled to be on the Ed Sullivan variety show on April 7, but at the last minute Sullivan cancelled.

For April 18 through 28, Hubert Long tentatively booked her for two weeks in a "rock & roll" event at the Paramount on Times Square, but Long backed off and deleted Patsy. Still, her booking schedule was full, and she was earning about $1,000 a week (before expenses). She was beginning to abandon her cowgirl look for the cocktail dresses similar to the one Janette Davis had bought her for her appearance on *Talent Scouts.*

On April 6, *Billboard* reported that the "Best Sellers in Stores for C&W" had "Walkin' After Midnight" at number 4, and a city-by-city placed "Walkin' After Midnight" at number 2 in Birmingham, Alabama; number 3 in Nashville; and number 10 in Houston.

The April 6 issue of *Cash Box* magazine also placed "Walkin' After Midnight" at number 4 nationally on its C&W chart.[10]

On 22 April, the *Winchester Evening Star* reported that Patsy Cline would do the Godfrey morning show on April 23, 24, 25, and 26. (After that, she planned (and did) leave on another tour—with Brenda Lee and Porter Wagoner—through Wyoming, Idaho, Utah, and Colorado.)

On Tuesday, April 23, Patsy Cline sang "Try Again" on Godfrey's morning show; on April 24, she sang "Three Cigarettes (in an Ashtray);" waited on the April 25, but was never called to sing; and on the April 26, she reprised "Walkin' After Midnight." Paul Cohen wanted to showcase these tunes, which were examples of her innovative pop-country style, and she would record "Try Again," and "Three Cigarettes (in an Ashtray)" as part of two sessions Cohen produced in New York City in the afternoons after she performed on the Godfrey morning shows.[11]

On Wednesday April 24, Patsy recorded for Cohen with a full New York pop treatment. Gone were Owen Bradley on piano and the Nashville session men. Instead she sang with the top New York pop players that Paul Cohen could hire. There was no steel guitar or fiddle; Cohen added brass and reeds, and the Anita Kerr singers for backup. We can easily pick these recordings, with their brass-laden, Big Band backings, out of Patsy Cline's body of work. Cohen used the main Decca recording facility, housed in the Pythian Temple, a vast space located at 135 West 70th street, near Broadway, in New York City, and all the recordings contained an echo because of the huge area.[12]

These sessions, Patsy Cline's fifth and sixth, turned out to be the only ones held in New York City. They demonstrated that even the skilled Paul Cohen could not find a hit in the 4-Star songs Bill McCall sent. "Today, Tomorrow and Forever" sought, but failed, to match

"Walkin' After Midnight." The ballad "Fingerprints" did no better. These New York sessions exacerbated a lack of stylistic continuity that marked Patsy's early recordings. Cohen did record one gem, "Three Cigarettes in an Ashtray," but it would take thirty years after Decca's August 12, 1957, release for the public to discover it, when k.d. lang made it her signature Patsy Cline cover.[13]

On May 3, 1957, Patsy Cline headlined a sold-out concert in Dubuque, Iowa, singing with what remained of saxophone-playing pop bandleader Tony Pastor's band. No group was more pop than Pastor's. He was active on the Big Band nostalgia circuit after the World War II. To Patsy, it must have seemed that she was back at W&L—not listening from her bedroom but singing on stage.[14]

On May 23, Patsy was back in Nashville in Owen Bradley's studio, to record with the top Nashville sidemen. At 9:30 a.m., she began recording six tunes: "I Don't Wanna," "Ain't No Wheels on this Ship," "That Wonderful Someone," "I Can't Forget," "Hungry for Love," and "(Write Me) in Care of the Blues." On Paul Cohen's orders, Owen Bradley used the Anita Kerr Singers—Anita Kerr, Dottie Dillard, Louis Nunley, and Gil Wright. Bradley also used Grady Martin on electric guitar, Bob Moore on acoustic bass, Farris Cousey on drums, and himself on piano, as he had on her first four Nashville sessions. But this time Bradley added three new touches: his brother Harold on electric bass guitar, Hank Garland on electric guitar, and Jack Shook on acoustic guitar; he jettisoned the steel guitar and fiddle. Cohen was still convinced Patsy Cline could be a breakthrough pop act, and did not want any fiddle or steel guitar sounds to confuse radio listeners or potential record buyers.[15]

In late May, Decca released the single "Today, Tomorrow and Forever," and "Try Again" from the Cohen-produced New York City sessions. Cohen had Decca PR herald this single with a full-page advertisement in *Billboard*, but neither side charted. Cohen had Decca's PR department back this single with an all-out effort—but to no avail. Cohen had intended one of these to be her followup hit to "Walkin' After Midnight."[246]

On May 25, Patsy appeared in Amarillo, Texas's, City Auditorium in a Saturday night show headed by fellow Decca pop artist (and also Bradley-produced) Brenda Lee. Country singer George Jones was billed third, and rockers the Everly Brothers were fifth on the pop–country bill.[16]

Thus, from late January to early June 1957, Patsy Cline toured the United States and earned the most money of her life up to that point. The first item on her agenda was to do something that even her marriage to Gerald Cline could not accomplish—buy her mother a new home.

On June 21, in Winchester, Clarica and Dorman Affleck sold Hilda Hensley the house at 608 South Kent, which Hilda had been renting since November 1948. Patsy Cline had given her mother $2,500 for the down payment. In a second transaction, Dorothy and Allen Hawthorne sold 720 South Kent Street to Hilda. This was a far nicer house, a modern brick bungalow, one hundred feet down the street. Patsy gave her mother $7,500 for that down payment. She finally got her mother (and brother and sister) out of the cramped 608 South Kent Street home, and bought them the nicest house on the block. The very next day Patsy Cline was back on the road for a Saturday night appearance with Brenda Lee on *Ozark Jubilee*.[17]

Through July, Patsy made more money touring throughout the western United States. For example, on Saturday, July 13, she appeared in Albuquerque, New Mexico, for two shows with Johnny Cash in the new Civic Auditorium. The two shows, at eight p.m. and ten p.m., filled the hall. Two days later Cline and Cash did the same show in Salt Lake City, Utah.[18]

On July 26, Patsy appeared on Alan Freed's *Big Beat* TV Show, in New York City. For Freed's show, Patsy dressed pop in a full, cocktail-length dress, and lip-synched "Walkin' After Midnight." On August 10, she appeared again on *Ozark Jubilee*. And her first album, called simply Patsy Cline, was issued in late August. But by that time, Patsy wrote her fan club president with a note of disappointment, "The [live gigs are] really slowing down."[19]

Patsy Cline's first LP

Patsy's first album contains twelve tracks, featuring "Walkin' After Midnight," with a color image of Patsy Cline dressed not in her once standard cowgirl outfit but in a colorful sweater. The LP liner notes outline the PR campaign that Decca was using: "Patsy Cline waited two rather long years to appear on the Arthur Godfrey 'Talent Scout' [sic] television program . . . the result was overwhelming. Her Decca recording of the song became a top hit, and Patsy Cline became a singing sensation almost instantly." Decca PR also noted, "In this album Patsy Cline displays her wonderful talent for singing 'pops,' and does a bang-up job on a group of brand new, delightful tunes." This LP proved the climax to winning the Godfrey show eight months earlier.[20]

Patsy Cline focused on her personal life. On August 16, 1957, the *Winchester Evening Star* printed, "Mrs. Hilda Hensley of this city announces the engagement and approaching marriage of her daughter, Virginia Hensley Cline, known professionally as Patsy Cline, to Pvt. Charles A. Dick, son of Mrs. Mary Dick of 331 National Ave. and the late Mr. L.E. Dick." The wedding took place on Sunday, September 15 of that year at four p.m., at 720 South Kent Street, with the Rev. S. J. Goode performing the ceremony. A reception followed at eight p.m. at the Mountainside Inn, west of Winchester, near Gore. Then the couple moved to Fayetteville, North Carolina, where Charles was stationed at Ft. Bragg.

Charles and Patsy's home
in Fayetteville, North Carolina

Patsy Cline had failed at her first marriage and felt the social-cultural pressure to try again. In the United States, marriages were being performed at a record rate. Scholar Jessica Weiss has argued in *To Have and to Hold* (University of Chicago Press, 2000) that the seeds of feminist change were sown in the 1950s, with these seemingly conforming marriages placing pioneering professional women in a constant struggle to deal properly with marriage, child rearing, and career. Patsy Cline wanted to be a proper mother, to overcome the stigma of divorce, and to retain her star status. But this last goal required her to be away from home—on the road to earn money. There is no better example of the contradictory pressures that Weiss describes than Patsy Cline Dick.

Charles Dick was a skilled working man. Born on May 25, 1934, he had dropped out of Handley High School at age sixteen and gone to work for the *Winchester Evening Star*, first in its distribution department and then, later, as a skilled Linotype operator, setting type. He met Patsy on Friday the 13th of April, 1956, at her regular gig in Berryville. But Patsy was still married to Gerald Cline, and so had to divorce Gerald (in March 1957) before she could marry Dick.[21]

At Fort Bragg, Charles was assigned to the First L&L (loudspeakers and leaflets) unit. The U.S. Army used his experience as a Linotype operator to produce materials for the Army's effort to print propaganda leaflets and drop them into Communist nations. Despite the myth that mother and daughter sang in church, when it came to getting married, Hilda and her daughter had no church affiliation. (Hilda had been a Baptist in Gore only because of her mother.) So Hilda Hensley turned to a neighbor, the retired Rev. Sewell Jackson Goode, who married couples in fifteen minutes for a few dollars.[22]

On September 12, 1957, with Patsy's divorce from Cline having become final in March, she and Charles applied to the Clerk of the Court for Winchester for a marriage license. They supplied the following information: Groom: Charles A. Dick, bride: Virginia P[atterson] H[ensley] Cline; Groom: 23, single; bride: 25, divorced. On Sunday afternoon, September 15, Patsy became Mrs. Virginia H[ensley] Dick—but to fans she was still Patsy Cline.

At the marriage ceremony, she wore a light blue two-piece knit suit, high heels, pearl earrings, a wide inverted bowl hat with sheaves of ostrich feathers, and a large orchid corsage. Charles wore a beige suit. William L. Dick was his brother's best man, while Patsy's brother, Sam, Jr., gave her away, as he had done at the Cline wedding 4 ½ years earlier. With Charles on leave from Ft. Bragg, there was only a one-night honeymoon in Capon Bridge, West Virginia, 20 miles west of Winchester. The next day, the couple drove to Fayetteville, North Carolina, 350 miles away,- to live in a small house off base.[23]

On Monday, September 16, the *Winchester Evening Star* added more details: The bride's attendants were Miss Patsy Lillis, a neighbor, and Patsy's sister. They wore dresses of dark blue cotton and silk with blue hats and white carnations. The flower girl, Nancy Conner, wore a pink dress with a matching hat and white accessories. Hilda Hensley wore a royal blue velvet dress with black accessories; Mary Dick wore a navy blue dress with pink accessories. The most telling line printed in the *Winchester Evening Star:* "[The bride] plans to continue with her singing career."[24]

In Fayetteville, the couple rented a small house at 758 Poole Drive, about two miles from the base, with five rooms in nine hundred square feet, all on one floor. It had been built in 1952 as a rental unit in a community that had started as an officer's off-base housing and then was filled in with smaller rental properties. It was four blocks from the Fayetteville's first shopping center, with a large grocery store, the first branch of the local department store outside downtown, and about thirty more specialty stores, all to serve the expanding off-base population. Patsy could easily walk to shop or purchase anything she needed.[25]

Patsy was soon pregnant. This did not stop her from going on the road. Patsy's touring brought them necessary money; she was a very hard working performer.[26]

Five weeks after her marriage, on Monday, October 21, the *Winchester Evening Star* printed, "Patsy Cline will appear on Arthur Godfrey's morning show tomorrow and the rest of the week." On Tuesday, October 22, Godfrey's morning show, Patsy sang "Three Cigarettes (in an Ashtray);" on Wednesday she was ready but did not appear; on Thursday she sang "Then You'll Know;" on Friday 25 October 1957 she sang "Too Many Secrets." These were recordings that never charted for her.

She toured continuously. On November 2, Patsy appeared on *The Old Dominion Barn Dance,* in Richmond, Virginia. On November 15 and 16, she attended the Disc Jockey Convention in Nashville, where she won *Cash Box* magazine's Most Promising Female Country Vocalist; *Cash Box*'s Most Programmed Up and Coming Female C&W Artist; *Billboard*'s Most Promising Female Artist; *Billboard*'s C&W Disc Jockey Poll; *Country Western Jamboree* magazine's Best New Singer of 1957; *Country and Western Jamboree* magazine's Best New Female Singer of 1957; and *Music Vendor* magazine's award for Greatest Achievement in Records in 1957. She was still being honored for the success of "Walkin' After Midnight."

Immediately, on November 17, Patsy left with Porter Wagoner, Bobby Helms, and Jimmy C. Newman on a ten-day tour through the Southwest, which included stops at the Civic Auditoriums in El Paso, Tucson, and Albuquerque. At each stop, she promoted her new single "Then You'll Never Know," and "I Don't Wanna." On November 21, Patsy wrote her fan club president: "Still one more week on tour. "I Don't Wanna" is moving slowly. I am out of money with too little work. Bill McCall has not paid anything." She returned to Fayetteville, and not until December 7 did she have more work, when she journeyed to Springfield, Missouri, to appear on *The Ozark Jubilee* TV show.[27]

On December 13, Patsy flew to Nashville to record. Backed by the Anita Kerr singers, whom Paul Cohen insisted on, Owen Bradley was still searching for a follow up hit to "Walkin' After Midnight" in this, her eighth, recording session. Another batch of 4-Star songs included "Stop the World (and Let Me Off)," "Walking Dream," "Cry Not for Me," and "If I Could See the World (through the Eyes of a

Child)." Bradley's team assembled for the seventh recording session (seven months earlier) added masterful guitarist Hank Garland and an unknown vibraphone player; Bradley knew this percussive instrument from his Big Band experience and thought it would offer a new sound for Patsy. Bradley was seriously experimenting for a pop-crossover sound. The next day, Patsy appeared on the Grand Ole Opry to sing "Walkin' After Midnight" on the *Prince Albert Show* portion of the Opry, broadcast over the NBC radio network.[28]

On December 21, Patsy traveled to Chicago and appeared on the *Howard Miller Show* for dancing teens, a Chicago-based *American Bandstand*–style show that lasted only a year. The ABC television network was feeding *American Bandstand* to affiliates across the United States, and to mimic ABC's success, CBS tried to counter with the *Howard Miller Show*. WBBM-TV fed it from the stage of the Chicago Lyric Opera house. Prior to Patsy, the Everly Brothers, who also recorded in Nashville, appeared on the *Miller Show,* plugging "Bye Bye Love," and "Wake Up Little Susie."

But by the close of 1957, Patsy was back to playing the same small venues where she had performed with Bill Peer. On New Year's Eve, she (and Charles) journeyed to Lorton, Virginia. Her final major gig came on January 6, 1958, when she appeared on the Arthur Godfrey morning show to sing "Come On In (and Make Yourself at Home)," "Walkin' After Midnight," "I Don't Wanna," and cover "Your Cheatin' Heart," "Walkin' Dream," "Don't Ever Leave Me Again," "The Man Upstairs (which she never recorded), "Stop the World (and Let Me Off)," "Down by the Riverside," (never recorded), "(Write Me) in Care of the Blues" (never recorded), "Ain't No Wheels on This Ship," "Hungry for Love," and "Walking Dream." The Godfrey effect was no longer in place nationally, and Owen Bradley, Bill McCall and Paul Cohen went looking for another hit.[29]

On January 26, Patsy wrote her fan club president from Fayetteville, complaining of feeling sick from her pregnancy. She planned to work until May. On 13 February 1958, Bradley called Patsy in for a ninth session and recorded six songs: "Just out of Reach," "I Can See an Angel," "Come On In (and Make Yourself at Home)," "Let the Teardrops Fall," "Never No More," and "If I Could Only Stay Asleep." Owen Bradley had taken full charge of the Decca Nashville operation when Paul Cohen moved to head the Coral label. For this ninth (of twenty-nine) session, Bradley was able to book Floyd Cramer at piano (replacing himself) and Buddy Harman on drums (replacing Farris Coursey). Cramer, two years away from stardom, was a session player Bradley admired, and this hire freed Bradley to be a full-time producer. Harman was a professional drummer of the top order. These additions were crucial in the long-term sound Bradley would develop. Later, for example, fans would hear Cramer and Harman open "Crazy," fashioning the complexity of the iconic Patsy Cline sound. But because of her pregnancy, Bradley did not schedule her next recording session until almost a year later.[30]

With few bookings on the U.S. mainland, Patsy, three months pregnant, left on the final day of February to perform from March 1 through 10 in Honolulu.[31]

"Patsy on her way to Hawaii"

Instead of enjoying a vacation, Patsy wrote her fan club president of loneliness: "Been here 8 days and not one piece of mail from Charlie or Mom." She was beginning to show, so she could not wear tight cocktail dresses. To save time, she had gotten her hair cut short and curled with a permanent wave.

The March 24 front page of *Billboard* headlined Patsy's career problem: "Charts Point High Mortality Rate for Disk Artists." *Billboard's* editors had checked its charts, and found that Patsy Cline had been on them a year earlier, and had not charted since March of the previous year. It was not that Decca and 4-Star had not tried. Decca had released four new singles, an extended-play record (the size of a 45-rpm record, but actually at 33 1/3 rpm was meant to be played on small-stemmed record player), and an LP. But they were all based on one hit, "Walkin' After Midnight." And so *Billboard* labeled her a "one hit wonder."

The April 1958 issue of the C&W fan magazine *Trail* printed Decca's PR department's reconfiguring of her image: "Patsy has an extremely fine wardrobe which includes quality rather than quantity, because according to her views, one good dress makes more of an impression, and lasts longer, than three of lesser value." *Trail* noted that she preferred sleek dresses with an eye to colors best suited to her skin tone, light blue cocktail frocks. She did love to accessorize with elbow-length gloves, often with a bracelet, which she wore over the gloves. She loved earrings that matched her bracelets and high heels—not cowboy boots. This sophisticated image would define Patsy Cline for the rest of her career.[32]

On June 15, 1958, she wrote her fan club president from home in Fayetteville. The issue was money, and Patsy complained that she owed $1,050 that had to be paid before the end of the month. Patsy worried that she and Charles would lose everything. Two months from delivery, Patsy complained to her fan club president that the baby kicked "like crazy all the time," and it was so hot in North Carolina that she was frying. Sylvia, her sister, had come down for the summer, and Patsy appreciated the extra help. In surprising news, never revealed in her lifetime, Patsy noted: "Mom is going to sell the brick house and move to Florida. She can get $12,000 out of the big house and can buy one in Florida for $8,500. One that has the landscaping, big picture windows, a car port, colored bath room, glass sliding doors to the patio and 5 rooms, and hardwood floors and tile in bath and kitchen. They only ask $2,000 down and $66.00 per month." Here is Patsy Cline expressing her admiration of the 1950s suburban life style.

She went on to state that she had told Charles she would like to live in Florida, once he got discharged from the Army. However—here she revealed a hint of her second husband's ambition—Charles had expressed that he wanted, instead, to move to Nashville. He had been working at newspapers since age 9, and he reasoned that he could get a Linotype operator's job in Nashville, and they could live oin two steady incomes.

"Patsy on a visit to Florida"

On July 14, she appeared riding atop a convertible as the Grand Marshal of Elkton's Golden Jubilee parade, cheered by a crowd of 12,000. This was her return as a star to the place where she and her mother had struggled to feed and clothe themselves a quarter-century before. She was greeted by round after round of applause. Eight months pregnant, Patsy Cline wore a flowered sun dress that flowed across her expanded body. She was not paid for this appearance.[33]

Patsy sought help to have her baby, and she alone went to Winchester to give birth with her mother's guidance and help.[34]

On August 18 1958, Patsy wrote her fan club president from 720 South Kent, revealing that pressing money problems had forced her to play the Dixie Pig Club, in Prince George's County, Maryland, from Friday, August 15, through Sunday, August 18. She did this out of desperation, as she was scheduled to enter the Winchester Memorial Hospital the following Sunday, the 25th. On August 25, 1958, the doctor induced labor, and she became a full-time Mom, living in Winchester.

Julia Simadore Dick was born in the Winchester Memorial Hospital, in what Patsy's cousin recalled as a relatively easy birth. Patsy doted on her baby, according to her mother's memory. On August 27, Patsy wrote her fan club president from the Winchester Memorial Hospital, while waiting for Julie (as Patsy called her baby) to come to be fed. Patsy confessed, "I feel like a real woman now."[35]

"Patsy Cline holding her baby daughter, Julie"

The "Women's Page" of the August 27 *Winchester Evening Star*, printed a photo of Patsy Cline and baby Julie with the caption: "Mrs. Charles Allen Dick (singer Patsy Cline) sings a lullaby to baby daughter, Julia Simadore, at Winchester Memorial Hospital where [the] baby was born Monday."[36]

Patsy looked forward to going back to work, but with no recent hits, bookings were hard for her to get. Nevertheless, not quite two months after Julie's birth, with Hilda happy to care for her first grandchild, Patsy began singing every Saturday night with Don Owens on WTTG-TV, the sole independent non-network TV station in Washington, DC. Owens had inherited Connie B. Gay's position at WARL-AM, but all he could do was secure poorly paid gigs for

Patsy. On October 31, Patsy Cline sang in Norfolk, Virginia, with the Texas Wildcats (sans Jimmy Dean). This helped, as Patsy Cline owed creditors $1,600. "If I Could See the World," just released, on September 9, was selling well in Washington, DC, stores, but Patsy doubted—correctly—that it would chart. "Things are so rough here; Mom and my brother don't like Charlie and I've been so upset lately I couldn't write anyone." Bill McCall helped with bills, advancing her some money, picking up the final option of the 4-Star contract. But Patsy had been reduced to doing small-time gigs for Don Owens. On December 20 and 21, for example, she sang at the Villa movie theater in small town Rockville, Maryland, at 1:55 p.m., 5:10 p.m., and 8:30 p.m., along with Owens's discoveries Vernon Taylor and Luke Gordon, for twenty-five dollars each.[37]

Even with her hit "Walkin' After Midnight," she did not make a large sum for any single appearance; hence she had to work frequently. If some of these modest gigs were adjusted for inflation, she would be making one hundred dollars in today's dollars. That was hardly enough to support a family when Charles was living on Army pay and Patsy was trying to help out her husband and daughter, as well as her mother, sister, and brother.

The U.S. Army honorably discharged Charles Dick, and he arrived back in Winchester on February 23, 1959. Charles and Patsy rented a small bungalow on the north side of Winchester, and Charles began looking for a job. Then the couple caught a break: "When I got out of the Army, Patsy was getting an allotment check of $137 a month; and they didn't stop. In all [she] got seven checks." That $959 collected through September enabled the couple to move to Nashville in October.[38]

Owen Bradley wooed Patsy. In the January 1959 issue of *Cowboy Songs* magazine, he offered her an olive branch: "We recently had a chat with Harry Silverstein (Owen Bradley's assistant) [who stated that] Patsy has all the natural ability in the world, and she sings her songs right from the heart." Patsy was the type of singer Bradley enjoyed working with. Silverstein praised her as a credit to the music business and a rare treat for all who love listening to good music.

Indeed, on January 8, 1959, despite his—and Patsy's— dislike of the songs Bill McCall was sending, Bradley booked Patsy for her tenth recording session in his Nashville studio, and they created "I'm Moving Along," "I'm Blue Again," and "Love, Love, Love Me Honey Do." Bradley again made a profound change that eventually would help sell millions of records. With Paul Cohen no longer his boss, Bradley hired backup singers the Jordanaires, famous for their work with Elvis. The all-male Jordanaires had helped Elvis make hits; perhaps, Bradley reasoned, they could do the same for Patsy Cline. The Jordanaires would sing backup in all but one of the rest of her sessions.

For this tenth recording session, Bradley used the new recording equipment he had acquired from Ampex: three-track stereo. The next day, January 9, for session number 11, Patsy and the Jordanaires created "Yes, I Understand," and "Gotta Lot of Rhythm in My Soul." But Bradley could only do so much, as they had not recorded a hit in two years. Patsy waited for her 4-Star contract to end.[39]

Patsy was happy to be recording again, and hoped she could later sign with Decca for a royalty of 6 percent and take Bradley up on his promise to record "St. Louis Blues," "A Good Man Is Hard to Find," and other pop standards. (She would not record these, but would later cover many other pop classics with Bradley.) Charles was anxious to move to Nashville, and she hoped Bradley would help her become a regular on the Grand Ole Opry (he did), and that Hubert Long would get his protégé, Randy Hughes, to manage her (Long did).

On February 23 came some more good news: While most accounts of Patsy Cline's inability to chart used *Billboard* numbers, *Cash Box* magazine also offered charts. Decca had released "Cry Not for Me" and "Yes, I Understand" on February 23, and while *Billboard* did not chart this single, it made it onto the *Cash Box* Top 100 Country at number 59 a month later. This hardly represented a hit, but at least her fans were not deserting her altogether.

Through the spring and summer of 1959, before moving to Nashville, Patsy continued to take on gigs that Don Owens booked in Maryland and Virginia. For example, on February 25, a Wednesday night, she appeared at the Starlite Room, in Salisbury, Maryland (some two hundred miles from Winchester), from nine p.m. to twelve midnight. Patsy only earned fifty dollars per night at spots such as Washington, DC's (at that time, still segregated) Glen Echo Amusement Park, Berryville's Watermelon Park, and the Rockville (Maryland) Carnival.[40]

Owens was even able to get her the occasional national gig. On April 4, she again traveled to Springfield, Missouri, to appear with Ferlin Husky and Red Foley on TV's *Jubilee USA,* the former *Ozark Jubilee.* On the 12th of that month, Patsy traveled to Winona, Minnesota, to appear in the Sunday-evening Country Round-up package show held at the Red Man's Fraternal Organization benefit—with a top ticket price of ninety cents. This thousand-mile trip, to the banks of a small town on the Mississippi River, would hardly have seemed worth it. But the gig paid her way and she was even able to save a little.[41]

Typically, as on April 19, Owens booked Patsy Cline at the annual opening of New River Ranch, in Rising Sun, Maryland, where she was billed as "Patsy Cline and Hank Rector and the Rambling Rangers." On May 31, she performed at Playland Park (located ninety miles northeast of the Rising Sun Ranch), in Coopersburg, Pennsylvania as "Patsy Cline Decca – Recording Star." Many of these small towns were located behind mountains and thus had early cable TV service. Fans saw Patsy Cline on Don Owens' shows on WTTG-TV, via cable TV from Washington.[42]

Owens booked Patsy Cline to perform on a Saturday afternoon with Don Reno and Red Smiley and the Tennessee Cut-Ups on Harrisonburg, Virginia's, single TV channel, and then drive back to the DC, a total of some three hundred miles of driving in one day—all for fifty dollars net. She sang at the Adamstown, Maryland, Fire Department Carnival as "Patsy Kline." And she sang for dances at Rockwood Hall, in Warrenton, Virginia, for twenty-five dollars an appearance. On July 1, she sang at the New Market, Maryland, District Volunteer Fire Company Carnival, and on July 11, she sang at Hagerstown Fairplay Fireman's Carnival. But she was not invited to the 1959 Apple Blossom Festival, as Owens could not come up with a sponsor.[43]

Owen Bradley still pursued Patsy Cline, and on July 3, 1959, he brought her back to his Nashville studio for her twelfth recording session. Desperate for material, Bradley made a deal with Bill McCall to re-arrange two gospel songs, and then McCall could claim two more copyrights—on "Life's Railway to Heaven," and "Just a Closer Walk with Thee." Bradley figured, why not try these songs to sell to the gospel market? Bradley continued to offer up his best session players: Floyd Cramer on piano, guitarists Grady Martin and Hank Garland, acoustic bass player Bob Moore, drummer Buddy Harman, and the Jordanaires. Bradley ignored what McCall sent him and arranged these public-domain works for Patsy Cline's voice. Owen Bradley recalled Patsy's saying that she was so broke that all she would return to Winchester with was twenty dollars that she would receive for two appearances on the Grand Ole Opry, after paying for gas for the trip. Bradley promised that, if she moved to Nashville, he could get her on the Opry as a regular, but legally he could not force McCall to sell her contract. In late September 1959, Patsy, Charles, and baby Julie moved to Nashville.[44]

After cashing one final U.S. Army check, Charles and Patsy rented a small house at 213 East Marthona Drive, in the suburbs northeast of Nashville. Charles quickly got work in the composing room of the Newspaper Printing Corporation, the company that printed both of Nashville's newspapers, the *Tennessean* and the *Banner*.[45]

Bradley came through, and Patsy received an invitation to become a member of the Grand Ole Opry, which guaranteed her regular earnings and gigs. Hubert Long took her on as a client and assigned her to his thirty-year-old protégé, Ramsey "Randy" Hughes. Hughes booked her for Saturday, October 3, on KWKH's *Louisiana Hayride* in Shreveport's Municipal Auditorium. On November 7, she went to Springfield, Missouri, to sing "Walkin' After Midnight," and "Come On In" as solos, and "Let's Go to Church" on *Jubilee USA*.[46]

Billboard ranked her the number 9 favorite C&W DJ-voted female artist. Her new agent, Randy Hughes, booked her gigs until late in 1960, since Patsy was again pregnant and due in January 1961. Now the family was a traditional one, with Charles as full-time earner and Patsy as part-time earner and mother.[47]

On January 27, 1960, Owen Bradley scheduled one last 4-Star session, their thirteenth, and even persuaded Bill McCall to let Patsy cover Hank Williams' "Lovesick Blues." Decca released this recording on March 7, backed by "How Can I Face Tomorrow?" This same session created "There He Goes" (released August 1) and "Crazy

Dreams" (also released on August 1)—her fifty-first and last recording under the 4-Star contract. Bradley planned to make a hit covering Hank Williams, but it did not chart. Again Bradley experimented, again adding a steel guitar, but as part of the rhythm section. This was done in stereo, as would be the remainder of Patsy Cline recordings.[48]

Randy Hughes booked Patsy for an appearance, on March 22, in Sioux City, Iowa, as part of the WSM (radio Nashville) Presents tour with Faron Young, Roy Drusky, and Leon McAuliff. This was a far larger venue than any she had been playing, as it held 3,500 fans. When not on the road, Patsy regularly appeared on the Grand Ole Opry. On April 2, she sang "Lovesick Blues;" on April 29, she sang "How Can I Face Tomorrow?"— both current releases. Then, on May 1, Patsy started another WSM tour, including stops in Abilene, Texas, and Springfield, Missouri, followed by forty-two straight days traveling from venue to venue around the western United States. Thus, for example, on May 1960, the *Idaho Journal* advertised the Grand Ole Opry, starring Faron Young, Patsy Cline, and Jimmy C. Newman, sponsored by the local Kiwanis Club. Later that summer, she appeared at the Wisconsin State Fair in Milwaukee.[49]

In between these appearances, Owen Bradley arranged for Patsy to return to Nashville on June 7, and again of June 14 and 15, to film a series of recruiting shows for the U.S. Army. These thirteen-minute shows were part of a series called *Country Style USA*, complete with ads for recruiting, and the U.S. Army sent them free to TV stations across the country. These shows included Army recruiting advertisements, and the station was free to sell the remaining two minutes to local sponsors.[50]

"Patsy after a doing a show for the U.S. military"

As Patsy was touring and Charles was working, family finances improved—temporarily. But then serious health issues, aside from Patsy's pregnancy, came up. Charles injured his pelvic bone and was confined to a wheel chair. So, pregnant Patsy Cline toured as much as she physically could. Her cousin remembered this new dark period: "Aunt Hilda got letters stating 'Mom it's been hell today; the worst part of my life.'" It certainly must have been stressful and chaotic. Much has been made of the June 1961 auto accident that almost took the life of Patsy Cline, but the latter part of 1960 was almost as bad, since Patsy Cline duly had to balance remaining healthy as her pregnancy progressed, making money on tour, tending to an immobile husband, and caring for a daughter going through the terrible twos.[51]

The family finances suffered. Later, in 1979, Charles Dick told scholar Joli Jensen, "Henry and Joyce Blair helped. We were in bad shape. We were flat busted." The Blairs, the Sam Holt family, Tommy Parker and his brother, the Kinkaid family, and the Lasiter family solicited the neighbors and handed Patsy and Charlie four hundred dollars to tide them over. And Patsy found reliable baby sitters Sophie and Anita. In 2003, Anita, who lived next door, remembered on the www.patsy.nu Web site that during this bleak period, Patsy's mom used to call her to reach Patsy, as Charles and Patsy could not afford a telephone. According to Anita, "Patsy used to wash her 'stage' clothes and hang them on her clothes line." Patsy Cline went back to making her own clothes and strove to cut corners until Charles could go back to work.[52]

Then, on July 27, Patsy experienced her own health issue. On tour, she entered Los Angeles' Cedars of Lebanon Hospital at four a.m. and stayed for two days. Although the newspapers didn't report the nature of her problem, her cousin later revealed that Patsy seemed to be having a miscarriage. It started with lower back pain, and then when vaginal bleeding began, Patsy was rushed to the hospital. For the next six months, she lived in constant fear that she would lose her child.[53]

Patsy temporarily restricted her appearances solely to the Grand Ole Opry, as on August 12, when she sang "Loose Talk" and "Crazy Dreams." But, short of money, she journeyed eight hundred miles round-trip by car to appear in an August 13 Grand Ole Opry Show at the Illinois State Fair, in Springfield, Illinois, with Opry stars Roy Acuff, Ray Price, and Lester Flatt and Earl Scruggs and the Foggy Mountain Boys. The Opry gig played the first Saturday night of fair week, and Bob Hope did the final night with Brenda Lee. Patsy was just two weeks out of the hospital.[54]

Due to financial difficulties, Patsy never stopped working as her pregnancy progressed. For example, when she was five months pregnant, on Saturday night, September 17, she appeared at the Greater Allentown (Pennsylvania) Fair in an Opry package show including Minnie Pearl, Mother Maybelle and the Carter Sisters, Kitty Wells, and Jim Reeves. She looked forward to the end of the month, since she could ask Owen Bradley for an advance when she signed with Decca, and to Charles' returning to work. Patsy Cline had memories of abject poverty, and she did not want to repeat that experience.[55]

When Patsy Cline's 4-Star contract expired on September 30, 1960, Patsy immediately signed with Bradley. Since she was broke, Bradley authorized Decca to advance her the money she needed to pay all bills. Owen Bradley had come through on the promise that had originally lured the family to Nashville.[56]

On September 30, Patsy wrote her mother: "Of course things aren't the very best around me, but we are all improving in health and we are eating. When Charlie got his insurance check it was $17 and paid a few bills, and got Julie some clothes. He gets about $40 a week from insurance until he goes back to work in October." Joyce Blair kindly lent Patsy her car until the Decca advance check arrived, and Bradley found her local work: In October 1960, she filmed another *Country Style USA*.[57]

On October 31, *Billboard* previewed the Country Music Association (CMA) convention which would take place on November 3 through 5. With no hit in nearly four years, Patsy Cline was still voted the sixth-favorite female artist by C&W DJs. In its *Billboard* advertisement, Decca promoted 27 artists—including Patsy. Owen

Bradley was looking forward to creating a hit with Patsy Cline to entice teen-oriented record buyers and match the success of his new rocker, Brenda Lee, who was then atop the pop charts and making Decca millions.[58]

On November 16, in her first Decca session (her fourteenth overall), Patsy recorded "I Fall to Pieces" (written by Hank Cochran and Harlan Howard), "Shoes" (by Hank Cochran and Velma Smith), and "Lovin' In Vain" (by Freddie Hart)—all between 2:30 and 5:30 p.m. Bradley, showing how much he wanted Patsy, added her manager, Randy Hughes, on acoustic guitar, to his A team. But if we listen closely, we rarely hear any chords by Hughes. Patsy sat in the middle of the Bradley studio on a stool with a microphone and a music stand, with the Jordanaires on her left. Bradley reasoned that "I Fall to Pieces" would introduce a "new" Patsy Cline, and so Decca released "I Fall to Pieces" on January 30, 1961, on a 45 in mono, despite having recorded it in stereo.[60]

If Patsy Cline saw a rebirth with "I Fall to Pieces," it happened in part because guitarist Hank Garland was at the top of his game. Bradley gave the legendary guitarist his freedom on this session, and thus created its distinctive sound. Sadly, this proved to be Garland's last Patsy Cline session, as he was involved in a crippling auto accident that ended his career a few months later. More famous than Grady Martin because of his solo work, Garland epitomized the image of the Nashville session player: a skilled guitarist, able to walk into a studio, tune up, hear a run-through of the songs to be recorded (as played on piano by Owen Bradley), and provide a creative and sympathetic backing.[61]

On November 19, three days after recording, Patsy performed on the Grand Ole Opry, but found time to write her Mother: "I am wearing dresses to hide my pregnancy. Julie is sick in throat and ears. Randy [Hughes] is trying to get me on tour beginning at the end of

February for 8 weeks in Iceland and Greenland." As Patsy Cline had done with the birth of her daughter, she planned her touring schedule to begin a month after she was scheduled to give birth, and she was counting on her mother to help.[62]

On November 27, Patsy wrote her mother again reporting that she was worried because she was not working, as she had grown too large. "This baby wakes me up at night. I could scream from the pain. Because of pains, I just pray that it's normal and healthy. I've never had anything before take my energy like this has." Tellingly, she revealed to her mother: "I sure hope this is the last one. Besides, two is enough for us and we'll be doing good if we feed these 2. I did the Pet Milk [portion of the Grand Ole Opry] show again on Fri. Night [the 25th] so that means $48.00, but I've still got a milk bill. I hope to get my check from Army films I've made, before X-mas comes. It will be $100." She apologized that she could not afford to come to Winchester for Christmas. She ended, sounding like a typical mother: "Well Julie & Charlie want me to fix something to eat. They had their supper, but it's snack time again."

This letter, and the others to her mother, revealed a side of Patsy Cline that fans never got to see: continual economic struggle and balancing obligations as a mother and a working woman. Later fans would claim to hear her pain in the lyrics of the songs Owen Bradley had chosen.[63]

On January 22, 1961, at seven a.m., Patsy woke up neighbor Joyce Blair to take her to the St. Thomas Hospital where Allen (Charles' middle name) Randolph (Patsy's stepbrother's name) Dick was born. Blair took Patsy to the hospital and left Julie with neighbors. Blair later remembered, "Charlie had been out all night havin' him a ball, I guess. Well we took off to St. Thomas Hospital and they rushed her right upstairs at 5 a.m."[64]

It had been a far more difficult pregnancy for Patsy than her first, with Julie, in 1958, and a very difficult year in terms of other health concerns and constantly pressing economic difficulties. However, Patsy's mother arrived to help take care of two-year-old Julie and baby Randy.[65]

On January 30, eight days after her son's birth, Patsy Cline learned that Decca had released "I Fall to Pieces" and "Lovin' in Vain." The latter, her eighteenth single, initially created no mark on the *Billboard* or *Cash Box* charts. Frustratingly, Patsy would have to wait until April 3 for "I Fall to Pieces" to enter the *Billboard* charts. No one had any idea that, by July, "I Fall to Pieces" would chart C&W number 1, Pop number 12, and Easy Listening (a new *Billboard* category) number 6.

It proved an agonizing spring. Indeed, Patsy could do nothing but sit by as her mother sold 720 South Kent Street, and purchased the far less elegant 605 South Kent Street, across the street. Hilda would remain there for nearly thirty-nine years, the rest of her life, continuing to rent out 608 South Kent Street for income.[66]

Her difficult pregnancy forced Patsy Cline to say home—and off the road—through February and March 1961. But then her songwriter helped her; Hank Cochran, who co-wrote "I Fall to Pieces," posted on his MySpace Web page in 2007, "Patsy and I went up to Cincinnati to see Pat Nelson, who worked plugging songs for my publisher, Pamper Music." Cochran, Pat Nelson, and Cline convinced WLW, the biggest radio station in Cincinnati to play "I Fall to Pieces." With the additional play, a local distributor placed a new order for 5,000 singles. And so, on April 3, "I Fall to Pieces" finally charted.[67]

By April, as Patsy was feeling better (and had dropped thirty Pounds), she was able to go back on the road to earn money. But on April 22, while on an airline flight, having pushed herself too fast, she penned the following remarkable document on Delta Air Lines stationery: "To WHOM IT MAY CONCERN: I, Virginia Hensley Dick (known in my profession as singer Patsy Cline), being of a sound mind and body, leave (and it is my wish) to Hilda Virginia Hensley my mother, my children Julia Simadore Dick and Allen Randolph Dick to be cared for, and raised to the best of her ability until they are eighteen years of age." This twenty-eight year-old mother two left all her royalties to her own mother, to use to care for her children. (Patsy revealed that Decca was paying her royalties of 5 percent, double what 4-Star had.) Patsy then wrote that her children's father, "also of sound mind and body and good income, can visit, help in raising, clothing and educating the children . . . [but] the children [must] remain [emphasis in the original] in the home of my mother Hilda V. Hensley."

The rest of this document dealt in detail with ownership of their home and her awards, which she left to her children. She was so careful that she prescribed, "One oil painting of mylsef I leave to my mother, Hilda V. Hensley, until her death and then to be passed on" to Julia and Randy. After specific bequests to her mother, sister, and brother, she wrote: "To my husband Charles A. Dick I leave my western designed den furniture, a hi-fi stereo record player and radio, records and albums and tape recorder and blond floor model television set." She even described her desired burial outfit: "I wish to be put away in a white western dress I designed with my daughter's little gold cross necklace and my son's small white testament in my hands.[68]

This will was never legally filed, but that a twenty-eight-year-old would even think about writing a will is nothing short of astonishing. With a newly charted record, this seems to represent a document of a clinically depressed woman.[69]

Could this will have been an expression of an undiagnosed case of postpartum depression (PPD)? Having a new child can be hard and stressful, leaving new mothers feeling sad, anxious, afraid, and/or confused. PPD is a serious condition that, in the late twentieth and early twenty-first century, physicians would treat quickly, but as far as we know, Patsy Cline never sought help. PPD can happen a few days or even months after childbirth, and if a woman does not get treatment, symptoms can get worse and she can lose touch with reality. We now know that PPD affects women of all ages, economic levels, and racial/ethnic backgrounds. Still, researchers do not know what causes PPD. In Patsy Cline's case, it may have been a case aggravated by going back on the road with its irregular schedules and time away from her children. She seemed not to have regained her full strength for weeks. Patsy Cline went on the road, alone, and untreated.[70]

She penned her will on the way to an April 23 Grand Ole Opry Spectacular in Kansas City, Kansas, with Carl Smith, the duo of Homer and Jethro, and the Carter Family. Patsy's depression did seem to ameliorate when, on May 27, she met fan Louise Seger on the road in Houston. Seger remembered that she and her friends arrived so early that they were the only people there. Louise Seger later explained, "I saw a woman walk in and sit down at a table alone. I knew it was Patsy. I decided to get real brave and introduce myself. She turned to me with that open smile and we just clicked." Louise Seger invited Patsy to her home for a late-night breakfast. But most important, Seger served as a sympathetic sounding board. Seger remembered, "She told me about her life, her hopes, her dreams. We discussed loves lost, loves found, loves yet to be. We talked about her troubled marriage and the pain she endured being away from her children."

Soon thereafter, still on the road, Patsy Cline mailed Seger the first of many letters. "I often would receive calls at 1:00 in the morning. She'd be singing in some town wanting a friend to talk to." Louise Seger Zurbuchen (1932–2004) was three months older than

Patsy Cline, and a divorced mother of two. She and Cline had much in common, and she helped Patsy Cline with an informal version of "talk" therapy.[71]

In one of the first of those correspondences, sent on May 29, Patsy said again that her husband was proving hard to live with, but that she stayed "for the sake of the children." On June 6, Patsy wrote again, saying that she was scheduled to go back to Winchester to attend her sister Sylvia's June 8 graduation from high school—a family first.

Graduation activities took place in the Handley High Auditorium, where a decade earlier, Virginia Hensley had performed in amateur contests. High school dropout Patsy Cline was proud of her little sister. After working a gig to pay for the trip, on Tuesday, June 13, Patsy, her two babies, Sylvia, Sam, Jr., and Hilda left Winchester early to drive the six hundred miles to Nashville. Charles had remained in Nashville, working at his Linotype job.[72]

The next day, still exhausted from the long trip, she and her brother were involved in a serious automobile accident, and both were taken to the hospital in suburban Nashville. Sam, Jr., (age 21) had driven Patsy to the Madison Square Shopping Center, where she bought her mother cloth to make some dresses. At about 4:30 p.m., Patsy saw a rainstorm brewing, and she and Sam started driving home. At 4:43 p.m., Sam drove up a hill, started down, and sought to avoid an oncoming car in his lane. Sam swerved but had little room to maneuver, since children were playing next to the road. Thus, he hit the oncoming car, and Patsy went through the auto's windshield. The glass cut her face but missed her eyes by a quarter-inch; her right hip was knocked out of its socket, and her right wrist was fractured.

But it was her brother who faced death. Sam had a hole punched in his chest as big as a dime and about three inches deep, plus a few cuts and bruises. At nearby Madison Hospital, Dr. Hillis

Evans immediately began operating on Patsy Cline, while another emergency room physician stabilized Sam. Evans repaired a gash across her forehead and also put her hip back in place, repairing her broken right wrist and filling her with pints of blood to replace what she had lost. The other physician repaired Sam's breastbone and cracked ribs. At one point, since he had lost so much blood, the physicians called for a priest. Hilda and Sylvia stayed in Nashville to help tend Randy and Julie. Patsy would be in the hospital for more than month, which cost $1,200, eventually paid by Sam's insurance company.[73]

The accident left Patsy Cline temporality immobilized and scarred -- which she stated would have to be repaired by plastic surgery, but never was. (She would wear wigs for the rest of her life.) It was only by the end of July, that Patsy was able to leave the hospital on crutches, ready to work again. "We needed [money]," Charles later recounted. Ironically, Patsy Cline was dependent on her husband's assistance day and night—only three months after she expressed her complete distrust of him.[74]

On June 23, from the hospital, Patsy wrote Louise Seger, "I was sure glad to get the two cards and letters and even tho I'm in bed and in traction [Patsy's underlining]. Honestly I've gotten so many calls, telegrams, cards & letters that I'm just stunned. . . . I just thank God above that I can see perfect and my babies weren't with me." Her doctor anticipated two months of recovery, but had never dealt with the determination and work ethic of Patsy Cline. She would do play her first engagement in Tulsa, Oklahoma, before July was over.[75]

Patsy did, however, miss several high-paying dates. For example, on Saturday night, July 1, she was billed on an Everly Brothers show at the Gator Bowl football stadium in Jacksonville, Florida. The Everlys were the stars, but the bill included early 1960s pop stars Jack Scott, Bobby Vee, Del

Shannon, Gene Pitney, Jerry Lee Lewis, and Bobby Vinton. This pop/country show went on without her, and she lost a $1,000 payday.[76]

Fortunately, all Patsy Cline's immediate economic woes were resolved by a royalty check from Decca. Hank Cochran later recalled, "When ["I Fall to Pieces"] really hit strong, Patsy was in the hospital with her head wrapped with bandages. I came in to see her with the [Decca company] reports. I told her, 'You got yourself a pop hit, girl.' She couldn't believe it. I think she thought I was just fooling around." According to Cochran, she had but a single word response: "Damn!" On July 20, Patsy wrote Louise Seger: "How about that 'I Fall to Pieces'? No. 1 in 3 trade magazines. I still can't hardly believe it's no. 1 Louise." Patsy Cline asserted that she would never be poor again: "I go to Tulsa & Enid, Oklahoma, 29 & 30th of this month. They say I won't make it but I'm gonna show them. [underscoring in the original]"[77]

NOTES

Chapter 5

1   "The Arthur Godfrey Collection, held at the Library of American Broadcasting, University of Maryland-College Park, contains 300 boxes covering Godfrey's career [hereafter LAB].

2   TV Guide May 11, 1957: 8-11.

3   LAB.

4   TV Guide, January 19, 1957, A-18; WashStar, January 22, 1957: A-31.

5   Wpost, February 2, 1957: B11.

6   Billboard, February 2, 1957: 51; Billboard, February 9, 1957: 46.

7   Billboard, March 2, 1957: 23; ORAL HISTORY - Owen Bradley by Joli Jensen – June 26, 1979.

8   H&F March 16, 1957; H&F, February 27, 1957; H&F, February 9, 1957 & February 10, 1957; WS, February 8, 1957: 7.

9   Billboard, February 16, 1957: 52, 59; ORAL HISTORY – Charles Dick by Joli Jensen, June 21, 1979.

10   Joel Whitburn, Top Country Singles: 1944-1993 (Menomonee Falls, Wisconsin: Record Research, Inc., 1994): 57.

11   WS, April 22, 1957: 8; Liner notes on CD released By Razor & Tie as "The Birth of A Star," of recordings made on The Arthur Godfrey shows released August 18, 1997.

12   Norval White and Elliott Willensky (editors), The AIA Guide to New York City, 4th edition (New York: Three Rivers Press, 2000): 323.

13   countrydiscography.

14   WS, May 4, 1957:6; The Pittsburgh Gazette, May 5, 1957: 12.

15   countrydiscography.

16   countrydiscography.

17 The Amarillo (Texas) Globe Times, May 25, 1957: 24.

18 Winchester City Clerk's Deed Books: 64/320, 69/34, and 88/319-323.

19 The Albuquerque (NM) Tribute, July 13, 1957: 8; The Salt Lake City (UT) Tribune, July 15, 1957: 30.

20 Copy at CMA.

21 Web site www.patsycline.info – accessed April 5, 2006; Liner notes from album.

22 WS, September 1, 2001: A1; WS, July 11, 2002; WS, April 23, 2003: B1; ORAL HISTORY – July 31, 2007.

23 WS, May 2, 2001: B1.

24 Clerk of the Court, City of Winchester, marriage license files; Brown Archives; WS, September 1, 2001: A7.

25 WS, September 16, 1957: 6.

26 Author's tour of house and neighborhood on 4 February 2009.

27 Nancy F. Cott, Public Vows: A History of Marriage and the Nation (Cambridge: Harvard University Press, 2002).

28 The El Paso [Texas] Herald-Post, November 7, 1957: 23; The Tucson [AZ] Daily Citizen, November 22, 1957: 22; The Albuquerque [NM] Tribune, November 23, 1957: 7.

29 Liner notes, MCA Records, "Live At The Opry" [hereafter LIVE]

30 WS, January 4, 1958: 2; WS, January 11, 1958: 6.

31 TRIAL.

32 The Frederick (MD) News, February 25, 1958:1; Billboard, March 3, 1958: 44.

33 Trail, February 1958: 37; Trail, April 1958: 34.

34 The Harrisonburg [VA] News-Record, March 28, 1985, 9-10; Welty H. Hensley, History of Elkton (Elkton: Privately Printed, 2004): 9.

[35] E. Mark Cummings, and Patrick T. Davies, <u>Children and Marital Conflict</u> (New York: Guilford, 1994); Kathryn Edin, and Maria Kefalas, <u>Promises I Can Keep: Why Poor Women Put Motherhood Before Marriage</u> (Berkeley: University of California Press, 2004).

[36] TRIAL.

[37] TRIAL; WS, August 27, 1958: 8.

[38] <u>Billboard</u>, November 17, 1958: 20; Wpost, December 20, 1958: B18.

[39] "The Real Patsy Cline," video, 1986; THE TRIAL.

[40] TRIAL.

[41] <u>The Salisbury (MD) Times</u>, February 23, 1959:14; Wpost, February 24, 1959: B11; <u>Broadcasting</u>, March 2, 1959: 83.

[42] <u>The Cedar Rapids [Iowa] Gazette</u>, April 4, 1959: 22; <u>The Winona [MN] Daily News</u>, April 12, 1959: B12.

[43] TRIAL; WS, September 1, 2001: A7; Eddie Dean, <u>Pure Country</u> (Port Townsend, WA: Process Media, 2008): 34-35.

[44] <u>The Frederick [MD] News</u>, June 29, 1959: 12; <u>The Hagerstown Morning Herald</u>, July 11, 1959: 13.

[45] TRIAL.

[46] <u>Country Music</u>, October 1979: 64-66.

[47] Robert Gentry, (compiler), <u>The Louisiana Hayride -- The Glory Years--1948-1960</u> (Many, Louisiana: published by author, 1998), Volume 2: 314.

[48] <u>Billboard</u>, November 9, 1959: 33; <u>Billboard</u>, November 16,1959; Paul Kingsbury notes in booklet for "The Pasty Cline Collection" – from files of the CMA.

[49] TRIAL.

[50] <u>The Sioux City [Iowa] Journal</u>, March 22, 1960:15; 9 May 1960, <u>The Idaho [Boise] Journal</u>, May 9, 1960:15; Liner notes for MCA's

"LIVE At The Opry;" The Springfield [Illinois] Leader & Press, September 18, 1960: D4.

[51] Released as "LIVE, Volume 2."

[52] ORAL HISTORY – July 31, 2007.

[53] ORAL HISTORY – Charles Dick – by Joli Jensen - June 21, 1979.

[54] ORAL HISTORY – July 31, 2007.

[55] Author's copy of Fair Program.

[56] TRIAL; "LIVE At The Opry;" program in possession of the author.

[57] TRIAL.

[58] Paul Kingsbury, The Patsy Cline Collection (1991).

[59] Billboard, October 31, 1960: 1, 22, 24..

[60] TRIAL.

[61] James Sallis, The Guitar Players (New York: Quill, 1982); web site: www.billboard.com – accessed 28 December 2004.

[62] TRIAL.

[63] TRIAL.

[64] "The Real Patsy Cline,"video.

[65] TRIAL.

[66] Winchester City Clerk's office, Deed Book 64/328.

[67] Web site www.myspace.com/songwritersingerhankcochran – accessed 16 May 2005.

[68] TRIAL.

[69] TRIAL; Dissent from Will, Motion filed by Charles A. Dick, May 14, 1965.

[70] Linda Sebastain, Overcoming Postpartum Depression and Anxiety (New York: Addicus Books, 1998); Katharina Dalton, Depression After Childbirth (New York: Oxford University Press, 1996).

[71] The Houston Chronicle, November 7, 2004: B12.

72   CMA, Louise Seger collection; WS, June 9, 1961: 1; TRIAL.

73   ORAL HISTORY – June 12 2007; WS, June 15, 1961: 1; <u>The Nashville Banner</u>, June 16, 1961: 1; <u>The [Nashville] Tennessean</u>, June 17, 1961: 7; WS, September 1, 2001:A1.

74   WS, May 5, 2001: B1.

75   CMA - Louise Seger Collection.

76   Ticket stub – accessed on <u>www.ebay.com</u> on 2 April 2007.

77   Web site www.myspace.com/songwritersingerhankcochran – accessed 7 September 2005; CMA– Louise Seger Collection.

Chapter 6

Patsy Cline Triumphs

On the evening of July 29, 1961, Patsy Cline appeared at Tulsa, Oklahoma's, Cimarron Ballroom, backed by Leon McAuliffe and His Cimarron Boys. This was the first gig after her auto accident—and after "I Fall to Pieces" had risen to the top of the charts. What was even more special about this live performance was that part of it was recorded. Someone preserved Patsy singing fifteen songs and speaking to the crowd. Patsy spoke casually to her audience, sitting because of the effects of her auto injuries just six weeks earlier. She even took a moment to explain her situation to Cimarron crowd: "You know folks have been askin'—well what happened to you? You look kinda beat up. Another woman tried to pass another car in front of my brother and it and hit us head on." Patsy explained the extent of her injuries, and her plans for plastic surgery. She thanked her fans. "I just want to thank each and every one of ya. I received over 1,200 cards. Boy you'll never know what it meant to this ol' gal to know that there was that many people left on this good ole earth that still think of me once in a while."

Patsy even managed to issue a challenge to the Soviet Union Premier Nikita Khrushchev—4 months after the Kennedy administration's failed invasion of Cuba—more popularly known as the Bay of Pigs. She proved she kept up with current events, but also while singing her past hits, she offered up three songs that she had never recorded commercially: "Shake, Rattle and Roll," "Stupid Cupid," and "When My Dreamboat Comes Home." While she pleased the dancers with "Shake, Rattle and Roll," Patsy seemed more at home with the Connie Francis' pop hit—"Stupid Cupid." And she showed her familiarity with Big Band hits of the past as she covered Bing Crosby's 1942 "When My Deamboat Comes Home." She knew these songs from her continual self-training—listening to the radio and taking notes. By July 1961 she was a quick learner.

Since Patsy never had her own band, she had worked with many a local outfit. She coordinated the keys ["gears" in her stage slang], and praised this house band—led by steel guitar great, Leon McAuliffe. Three weeks before Patsy's appearance, McAuliffe had released a single of Harlan Howard's song "Cozy Inn"—that peaked at number 16 on *Billboard*'s C&W chart. In 1961 McAuliffe had assembled a band that consisted of eight members: Billy Dozier on electric guitar, his brother Richard on drums, Pee Wee Calhoun on piano, Bob White and Curly Lewis on fiddles, Jack Lloyd on saxophone and clarinet, and Joe Allen on acoustic bass. McAuliffe led and played steel guitar. Here was a Texas swing band—following the model that Bob Wills had set.[1]

McAuliffe hated the road, and so he had settled in Tulsa. The Cimarron Ballroom was a beautiful three-story Moorish-style structure, opened in 1925, which became McAuliffe's home base in 1950. It held two thousand people and had a twenty-five-foot-wide, raised, crescent-shaped band-shell stage. McAuliffe acted as his own master of ceremonies. At one point in this show, Patsy makes a point of saying of McAuliffe (and for the crowd's benefit), "I'd like to work for him all the time. As I've told you before, this is the sweetest music this side of heaven."

We hear Patsy the self-promoter, pushing her hits: "Walkin' After Midnight," "A Poor Man's Roses," and twice singing "I Fall to Pieces." We do not hear McAuliffe introduce Patsy, but as the show ends, we hear the forty-four-year-old McAuliffe announce her way off the stage (helped by her husband): "On behalf of all the folks here at the Cimarron, all the staff, all the Cimarron Boys and myself. . . . Really I think this is the greatest entertainer we've ever had." High praise from one the greatest steel guitar players in music history—who could appreciate the complex way Patsy used her voice—sliding up and down scales, just as McAuliffe did on his steel guitar. While many danced, hundreds stood in front of the stage and simply listened.[2]

Charles Dick helped his wife with her six-hundred-mile journey—completed by commercial airliner and rental car. He had taken a "temporary" leave of absence from his Linotype job—to which he would never return. Patsy, as determined as she had been all through her professional life, drove with Charles the very next day to Enid, Oklahoma (120 miles west of Tulsa) for a follow up date that night. Unfortunately, however, this gig, like all her others, was not recorded. Despite her auto accident, Patsy Cline had full mastery of her voice, and again demonstrated she was a powerful, appealing singer. Even in Oklahoma, she refrained from wearing to wear a cowgirl outfit, donning instead a white dress and a brown wig to cover her scars, with her classic, glowing red lipstick. In the Tulsa performance, she routinely used the language of the crowd: "honey child," and "lawda mercy," and was even a bit bawdy on stage. "Shake a leg—we don't care which one it is!" She knew how to please a crowd. And get them to dance.

Her recordings—produced so well by Owen Bradley—established her sound and created her record sales. As of August 1961, she and Owen Bradley had not been in a studio in nine months; so starting on August 17 and working until the month ran out, they recorded fourteen songs—about one-sixth of her entire body of work—including what later came to be considered by critics her masterwork, "Crazy." Then came another recording session in December, which created another number 1 hit: "She's Got You."

"Grady Martin (left) and Harold Bradley (right)
practice their guitars for a session"

To follow that up she did four sessions in February 1962, creating fourteen more cuts. There were another two sessions in September of that year, and then Owen Bradley spent the next four months looking for more hits. She did her four final sessions in February 1963, creating her final dozen cuts. In all, this blitz of recording between August 1961 and February 1963 constituted half Patsy Cline's recorded works.[3]

All the 1961 through 1963 sessions—which in the first decade of the twenty-first century are easily accessed on CD and through Internet downloading—were produced in stereo, in a quality that makes them sound as if they were just recorded yesterday. Owen Bradley later stated that he was careful in the recording sessions to get a clean sound. "We weren't digital, but we kept separation," he later reflected. "We kept the instruments from bleeding into each other. I was fanatical about it." So these later recordings lacked the one-mike bleeding of voice and instruments common with mono 4-Star recordings. As recordings, they sound modern.[4]

With songs of his choosing, Owen Bradley was able to bring out more and more complexity in Patsy's vocal phrasing. She seemed vocally at ease, able to express pain and job. But the pain of lost love became her defining style. She and Bradley had worked together long enough for Bradley to match more melodic and emotional material with her expressive, unique voice. The period from August 17, 1961, to her last session, on February 7, 1963 proved a Golden Age of creation for Owen Bradley, who encouraged Patsy to take risks—with distinctive pauses, elongation of notes, and sliding from phrase to phrase. She seemed equally at home covering pop standards and new compostions written just for her.

"The Bradley recording complex, the home in front
and the Quonset Hut behind"

What market these Decca sessions was the justaposition of new ballads with covers of past pop and country hits. Bradley had her cover country standards like Bob Wills' "Faded Love," and "San Antonio Rose," and Bill Monroe's "Blue Moon of Kentucky." But he added pop standards like Cole Porter's "True Love" and Irving Berlin's "Always." Her LPs centered on current hits (what she called her "hurting songs") but were filled with covers of country and pop standards.

Two good examples of Patsy's wider range and more expressive phrasing come from her twenty-third session (eleventh under the Decca contract), on February 28, 1962. "Imagine That" and "So Wrong" are ballads in which Patsy easily slips from a near speaking voice to full-throated singing, holding off on certain phrases, shaping and emphasizing others, and even giving a brave but hrut-filled laugh. This practiced and arranged expressiveness meant that the "hurting songs" did express *real hurt*, as in "Crazy" and "Sweet Dreams (of You)."

Patsy's power to interpret lyrics with new meaning became evident in her covers. Consider the way she begins "Bill Bailey, Won't You Please Come Home" as a slow, sorrowful ballad, turning the familiar lyrics into a poignant plea for forgiveness. She then segues into the more traditional rousing beat, and in the second half of the song, she sowcases her earlier complex, up-tempo singing style. Her interpretative skills demonstrated that she was in full command of her vocalization under Owen Bradley's direction.

With a new sound in mind, Owen Bradley looked for new musicians to complement Patsy Cline's vocals. He had already started process with the late 4-Star sessions, when he added Floyd Cramer on piano and Buddy Harman on drums. Then, for Patsy's last 4-Star session, Owen Bradley had asked his brother Harold to switch to a solid-body, six-string Fender electric bass and to work a more complex rhythm with Bob Moore's acoustic bass and Harman's drum kit. These session musicians gave the final 4-Star recordings—"Lovesick Blues," "How Can I Face Tomorrow?" "There He Goes," and "Crazy Dreams" a new and different beat, which served as a precursor to all the later Decca recordings. Harold Bradley, Bob Moore, and Buddy Harman provided Patsy with a strong and new-sounding beat—appealing to rock 'n' roll fans. who desired something to dance to.

Bradley hired the Jordanaires in January 1959, and they were on every other Patsy Cline cut thereafter, save those from a January 1960 session. The all-male quartet could have gone to Hollywood with Elvis but remained in Nashville to work sessions and live at home rather than on the road. Leader Gordon Stoker calculated that they could live a more stable lifestyle in Nashville session work than following Elvis around. While there have been many incarnations of the quartet, for Patsy Cline, Owen Bradley used tenor Gordon Stoker (b. 1924) tenor, second tenor Neal Matthews, Jr. (1929–2000), baritone Hoyt Hawkins (1927–82), and bass Ray Walker (b. 1934).[5]

Neal Matthews, Jr., was the member who could read music, so he devised their version of a "number system"—to denote the chords to sing with numbers, not musical notation. This was a version of traditional musical shorthand; he assigned each chord a number, and if the session leader, Owen Bradley, changed the key, it didn't matter, as Mathews simply changed the numbers. Mathews reflected, "Some singers like Willie Nelson don't sing with the beat and you have to allow for that with your 'oohs and aahs.' It was easy harmonizing with Patsy Cline." Leader Gordon Stoker often repeated a story told to him: "You know, Irving Berlin said, 'I don't even like country music, but there is no one who sings my song "Always" like Patsy Cline.'"[6]

Bradley kept experimenting. For the February 1962 sessions, he added Charlie McCoy's harmonica—most notably heard on "Half as Much," and "Lonely Street." Charles McCoy (b. 1941) was comfortable blending his harmonica with Owen Bradley's desire for a new sound. His first session in Nashville was Roy Orbison's "Candy Man," in 1961 (pay $49). He then became an A Team specialist on the harmonica—as this proved his comparative talent advantage, a skill that would later have him inducted into the Country Music Hall of Fame as a session player.[7]

Bradley picked up Ray Edenton on guitar—to replace Hank Garland—starting in December 1961. Edenton worked well as an all-around guitarist. Born six years before Patsy Cline, some hundred miles south of Winchester, Edenton had by 1957 moved to Nashville and helped define the distinctive Everly Brothers sound in "Wake Up Little Susie" and "Bye, Bye Love" with his hard-strumming rhythm guitar. He had begun working with new tunings and later remembered, "I had learned a lot of [jazz] chords and things that a lot of the country players didn't normally play." Edenton was part of what would make Patsy Cline's last ten sessions so special.[8]

Later, Edenton pointed out that working with Floyd Cramer, Buddy Harman, and Grady Martin—under Bradley's direction—was the high point of his career. "The group of us that worked so much together, we could adapt very quickly," Edenton remembered. "We might do a pop session in the morning, then a country session, then bluegrass, then jazz, all in one day." Edenton admired Owen Bradley because Edenton too had learned music from a piano teacher. Edenton then adapted his guitar skills to piano keys.[9]

On February 13, 1989, the Country Music Hall of Fame gathered Harold Bradley, Ray Edenton, Buddy Harman, and Bob Moore together to create an oral history. Rumble asserted that these four A Team players had helped fashion the "Nashville Sound"— rooted in drums (formerly shunned by the Grand Ole Opry) and all written in piano keys by Owen Bradley. Harold Bradley summed up his brother's accomplishments: "My brother had the ability to conceive the whole song in his head and then he asked us to help him create that sound." Indeed, Owen Bradley started these Decca sessions teaching Patsy, the Jordanaires, and the musicians what he wanted for each song—by demonstrating on the piano. Then the "A Team" members taught themselves their assigned parts, as none could read music. These were known as head sessions. Patsy sang from lyrics she placed in front of herself on a music stand, after she had committed the melody and phasing to memory.[10]

Then Owen Bradley boldly added a whole new section: orchestral strings for Patsy's final seven sessions. Bradley had had added strings first to Brenda Lee with "I'm Sorry," which she recorded on March 27, 1960. On August 17 of the following year (Patsy's fifteenth session), Bradley hired strings for covering a pop classic: Cole Porter's

"True Love." Bradley did not hire orchestral strings again until session 22, employing strings on all Patsy Cline's sessions thereafter. Bradley used various combinations of violins, violas, and cellos, but treated them as a single instrument. For this he needed a cooperative classically trained string player, and found him in African American Brenton Banks, who was then teaching at Nashville's traditionally black college, Tennessee State University. Banks played jazz on the side, as he was unable to get a spot in the Nashville Symphony because of race. Under Bradley's sponsorship, Banks became the de facto leader of a set of freelance string players.

Banks had gotten a different type of classical music training at the Cleveland Institute of Music, where he learned violin and piano. Bradley arranged the strings to back Patsy Cline, as the Jordanaires did. Banks later remembered, "We were [there] to fill in the gaps and blend. Our thing was to mesh on the spot. We learned to become one sound."[11]

Patsy Cline worked well with Brenton Banks (and his fellow sting players) because they reminded her of the "sweet" Big Band music she had learned to love at W&L. Banks had learned to love Big Band sounds at the Cleveland Institute of Music. Ernest Bloch, the esteemed composer, was named the first musical director of the institute, and he set the school's goal: "Musical education, in addition to the thorough study of technique, ought to above all else develop a love of all musics." Banks was motivated to do cooperative session work to earn extra money.[12]

With these musicians, Owen Bradley developed for Patsy Cline a new strain of country music—not a separate form but just another type of popular music. The piano and the electric guitar became the centerpieces, replacing country's acoustic guitars and banjos. String sections took the place of the fiddle sounds; tempered rhythm sections (including subdued steel guitars) added a different sound; the backing vocals of the Jordanaires reminded teen rock fans of Elvis. Bradley wanted to make popular music that would sell broadly. But he did this in a seemingly relaxed manner—resulting in relaxed but creative sessions. Tellingly, Bradley dressed casually in flannel sports shirts and khaki pants. "You can ask him to come to an important meeting," remembered agent Hubert Long, "and when he says, 'Do y'all really need me?' by which he means 'Oh, hell, I've got to put on a tie again.'" Owen Bradley became the leading producer in Nashville, seeking to convert country music into a branch of popular music that would sell as well as rock 'n' roll.[13]

Bradley knew how to organize and communicate from his experience as a longtime bandleader. He had learned from Paul Cohen the way to deal with Decca executives based in New York City, as they had been trained in the pop tradition. Like Patsy, Bradley grew up loving pop music played by Big Bands. Born in 1915 and raised in Nashville, he started his musical career playing piano in several local Big Bands. By 1940, WSM-AM, an NBC radio network affiliate, hired him as a player and then arranger and then leader for its in-house Big Band. While home to the Grand Ole Opry, which aired on Saturday nights, during the rest of week WSM played Big Band music.

In 1947, the thirty-two-year-old Bradley began to apprentice with Decca executive Paul Cohen. By 1950, Cohen appointed Bradley his onsite assistant in Nashville. Together they rapidly made Decca a major force in postwar music, producing Red Foley, Kitty Wells, Ernest Tubb, and Bill Monroe. Starting in 1958, Decca moved Cohen to head its ailing Coral label and appointed Bradley to be Decca's man in Nashville. Quickly Bradley took the hitless Brenda Lee and made her a national phenomenon—as a rocker. And he made Patsy Cline a major star, from her first number 1 hit, "I Fall to Pieces," in July

1961 to her last sessions in February 1963, which produced the likes of "Sweet Dreams."[14]

Bradley credited his apprenticeship with Cohen with teaching him how to make crossover hits: "Paul [Cohen] told me to take the Delmore Brothers country hit 'Blues Stay Away from Me,' and to put an organ on it and get a couple of background singers, and I could make a hit. We did just that, and it sold half a million copies." Bradley also arranged Red Foley's crossover hit "Chattanoogie Shoe Shine Boy" for Cohen. Harold Bradley recalled: "Owen asked Sap (drummer Farris Coursey's nickname) to think about the 'shoe shine' sound, and Farris came up with the idea of slapping the palm of his hand onto his leg." Foley's "Chattanoogie Shoe Shine Boy" made number 1 in C&W for thirteen weeks and number 1 pop for eight weeks. Owen Bradley told of his admiration for Cohen: "He had worked out of Paducah, Kentucky, and Chicago, and he was much more informed than I was about country music. [We all] enjoyed working with Paul because he was so enthusiastic. Paul would say, 'It's a smash,' and when it was, you remembered it and forgot about all the others."[15]

Cohen preached to Bradley the two Decca mantras: First, all songs had to have a beat. Maybe WSM would not permit drums on the Grand Ole Opry, but Paul Cohen insisted on drums. Second, all songs had to have a distinctive melody. If one listens to Patsy Cline recordings made from 1961 to 1963, all musical elements are meshed into a clear melody. These principles made Patsy Cline a crossover artist.

Cohen also backed Bradley's desire to own and control his own recording studio. While most accounts note the excellence of the Bradley studio, few realize that creating it took three tries. First, in 1952, the Bradley brothers, Owen and Harold, rented space in downtown Nashville, but went out of business. Next, in 1953, the brothers tried again and rented a building southwest of downtown. Owen Bradley later remembered, "We were there just two years [and] the sessions did not work well because we had a low ceiling and the sound would bounce off them." Paul Cohen recorded several top-selling country discs, including "It Wasn't God Who Made Honk Tonk Angels," at this second location.

Finally, in 1955, Owen and Harold Bradley opened their Film and Recording Studio at 804 16th Avenue South, in a nineteenth-century mansion. Paul Cohen made the commitment that all future Decca Nashville recordings sessions would take place there. Harold Bradley remembered, "We paid $7,500 for the house and then $7,500 [to add] a Quonset hut [behind the house], and we were still paying it off when we sold the studios" to Columbia for $2.5 million in late 1962.[16]

Owen Bradley's son, Nashville producer Jerry Bradley, recalled that the Decca backing proved so successful that Cohen struck deals with independents like 4-Star's Bill McCall to record singers like Patsy Cline in Nashville. Patsy was lucky that she recorded all but two of the 4-Star sessions in the converted mansion. For later Decca recordings, Bradley moved his ever growing ensemble of players and singers into the Quonset hut. Owen and Harold Bradley used old curtains, pieces of wood made into louvers, and raw insulation covered with burlap to create an ideal sound space. "My dad had a way of dealing with materials to acoustically fix a room," son Jerry Bradley recalled. Owen and Harold Bradley "tuned" the spaces by trial and error. By the time Patsy Cline started on her Decca contract, the Quonset hut had become the top recording space in Nashville.[17]

Owen Bradley and Patsy Cline had much in common. Like Patsy, Bradley was a radio child. In 1922, when he was seven, his father gave him a crystal radio, and young Owen listened to WSM's sign-on. Like the young Virginia Hensley, he grew up poor and listened to the radio to learn the latest Big Band hits. Also like her, Bradley could pick up emerging Big Bands from distant cities, which inspired him to learn the piano. In 1930, at age fifteen, he dropped out of school to help support his family (as did Virginia Hensely), playing pop music with drummer Farris Coursey's Blue Diamond Melody Boys at (illegal) gambling halls in Cheatham County, just outside Nashville. Bradley saw and heard all the Big Bands that came through Nashville. Even in the Merchant Marines (1943–45), Owen Bradley played with a San Francisco-based military Big Band led by Ted Weems, who taught Bradley arranging skills. Indeed, until producing Patsy Cline and Brenda Lee made him rich, he maintained his own Big Band, playing top Nashville nightclubs and private society functions.

When, in 1958, he was Decca's man in Nashville, Bradley's New York bosses encouraged him to broaden the appeal of country music. "I used to get a lot of great feedback from New York." For Patsy Cline, New York would encourage Bradley to make records that would sell to a broader audience than hard-core country fans. Bradley experimented and later remembered, "We did 'Crazy,' probably the finest [record] I've ever been involved with. It's country and a little bit pop—though it's not supposed to be either." Bradley tellingly reflected, "You'll even find steel guitar on 'Crazy.' It didn't sound like a steel . . . more like vibraphone. We were tryin' to do something different."[18]

Bradley's Decca sessions with Patsy Cline were rapidly paced and demanding. Bradley selected the songs, with some consultation with Patsy, hired the musicians, and in his studio, he selected the final take to be pressed onto a single or LP. All those at the session knew the schedule called for at least three potential final cuts to be created in a three-hour session. Bradley started all sessions by playing on the piano the songs as he had arranged them. He then taught the members of the ensemble their parts in the three-minute songs. Working from a piano, Bradley could demonstrate a considerably wider range than working from a guitar (as rival RCA producer Chet Atkins was doing down the street), since the piano ranged from three octaves below the A below middle C, to four octaves above middle C.

Bradley knew how to keep the music of all session components in his head, as he had when he was a working Big Band conductor. And he liked working with Patsy Cline. Owen Bradley recalled, "I never really saw that tough side people talk about. We'd sometimes fuss at each other but it was more like an old married couple than anything else." He strove to remake both Patsy Cline and Brenda Lee—and used the same musicians for both, save that to make Lee a rocker, he added a sax.[19]

Bradley convinced Patsy Cline to try for a smoother sound than that of her earlier work. For example, "She's Got You" (recorded December 17) ends with a mellow note —and became her second number 1 hit. Bradley crafted arrangements to surround Patsy's voice, not to dominate it. He built layered musical sessions—Patsy Cline on one track and all the rest on the other two tracks. He encouraged Patsy to take risks—with pauses, sighs, lingering over her words—that, he judged, added emotional power to the lyrics.[20]

Bradley reflected, "Patsy was way ahead of her times. She was the first country girl in the fifties with a smooth, polished voice; what she really had was a pop voice in a country music head. Until Patsy, no country female singer dared being smooth; they were all rough." He was referring to Decca's own Kitty Wells and his own later creation, Loretta Lynn. Owen Bradley best summed up Patsy's nineteen months of fame: "When Patsy and I first started workin' together, she didn't have her own style—sometimes she sounded like Kitty Wells, other times like Patti Page. But as she had more and more success, she grew into her style. She was one of the greatest interpretive voices in America, pop or country." Bradley continued, "I'm very proud of those records, I was proud of them then. I thought Patsy sung the hell out of 'True Love,' but at the time we did it, it didn't get all that attention."[21]

Bradley's session players loved working with him. These musicians enjoyed far more musical freedom in Nashville than their contemporaries in Los Angeles or New York. Bradley asked the musicians he trusted to improvise and interpret their parts. Instead of making all the music sound alike, Owen Bradley paid attention to each artist, and for the most part, they stayed true to their individual styles. Drummer Buddy Harman remembered, "He'd usually worked out an arrangement well ahead of time, but still left room for the musicians to improvise." Bradley told noted former DJ Ralph Emery that he often thought back to the day he attended a meeting in New York, just after Decca had moved from 57th Street to Park Avenue, in 1960. "[The executives] told me to go back to Nashville and make records that would last ten years," he said with a grin. He went back and recorded Patsy Cline.[22]

Legendary producer Billy Sherrill (who worked with Tammy Wynette and Tanya Tucker) looked back: "You can tell an Owen Bradley record. He was digital before there was digital. He had the cleanest-sounding records of any producer I ever heard." As revolutionary as the Bradley three-track stereo soundscape was his collaborative approach to the recording process. Gordon Stoker of the Jordanaires has stated: "Everyone whose life he touched, the thing we all share is that we're all from the University of Owen Bradley." Patsy Cline was at the top of the class.[23]

The October 30, 1961, *Billboard* highlighted Patsy Cline's new status, based on "I Fall to Pieces." A poll by *Billboard* of C&W DJs voted Patsy Cline the number 1 female country singer. *Billboard* also tapped—as its C&W man of the year—Owen Bradley. And "I Fall to Pieces" had been on the charts for an astonishing 31 weeks.

But favorable publicity did not pay Patsy's current bills. So she took to the road full time—starting after the four August 1961 recording sessions (which produced thirteen songs, most notably "Crazy"). While she would reach larger venues, no one expected that one of her first dates without a wheel chair would be at New York City's famed Carnegie Hall.

For her Carnegie Hall appearance, on Wednesday, November 29, Patsy Cline did not get paid—but the exposure relaunched her crossover career in the largest city in the United States. WSM manager Robert Cooper negotiated with executive director Dr. George D. Brooks, of the Musicians Aid Society of New York City, for a benefit. WSM underwrote transportation and lodging expenses for Patsy Cline, Jim Reeves, Marty Robbins, Faron Young, Grandpa Jones, Bill Monroe, Tommy Jackson, Minnie Pearl, the Jordanaires, and master of ceremonies T. Tommy Cutler (with whom Patsy had made military recruiting shows).[24]

"Patsy and Randy Hughes meeting
back stage at Carnegie Hall"

The New York City newspapers heralded the Carnegie Hall show. The November 8 *New York Times* headlined, "'Grand Ole Opry' To Perform Here," and told its readers that while some of the performers, well known in country and traditional music, had appeared in New York City before, there was no need to introduce Patsy Cline, as she was near the top of the charts and played constantly on WABC-AM, New York's highest rated top 40 radio station. The *New York Times* also explained that the Carnegie Hall benefit show had been set up to create more funds for the Musicians Aid Society, a group formed in New York City in April 1960, to help aged musicians through the establishment of a home for their final years—five years before Medicare was established as a national health insurance program for the elderly.[25]

On November 15, Patsy wrote her cousin's family: "Dear Aunt Nellie, I have been on the go so much I haven't had time to do anything hardly except work. I [want to] be with the children what little time I have at home. I think I've had nine days at home in a month. But while these records are hot I've got to get the hay 'in' while the sun shines." She told her aunt, uncle, and cousins that Hilda and Sylvia had come to Nashville for the CMA convention and were stunned by the Carnegie Hall announcement. Patsy expressed her good luck, writing:

"Sure was glad something <u>good</u> happened for a change. Maybe now, I'll be able to pay all my bills at last." Patsy reported on her grueling schedule: "This coming Thurs. I'll leave for Moline, Ill., Des Moines Iowa and Alabama. Then home and three days later in to Missouri." Patsy fully appreciated what Carnegie Hall symbolized. She wrote her aunt and uncle: "[On] the 29th [of November] I'll work Carnegie Hall in New York. . . . I'll bet Daddy would turn over if he could see [my new fame]. He said once that I'd never be or make anything of myself. I wish sometime he could have been a good father." [26]

On November 27, two days before Carnegie Hall, Decca released Patsy's second LP album, *Patsy Cline Showcase,* featuring "I Fall to Pieces," "Crazy," and second versions of "Walkin' After Midnight," and "A Poor Man's Roses." The market for recordings was changing, so Decca also released a reel-to-reel version with the same cover—meant for high-tech buffs. The LP sold well, and has been in continuous print since its release.[27]

On Tuesday, November 28, came national publicity: The Associated Press (AP) issued a photo of Patsy Cline, Minnie Pearl, Jim Reeves, Faron Young, Bill Monroe, and Grandpa Jones, arriving on an airplane at New York City's LaGuargia airport. As the AP was the largest news service in the United States, this image was printed in dozens of newspapers across the country. The accompanying AP story heralded Patsy as a star worthy of appearing at Carnegie Hall. That afternoon, Patsy and her fellow stars gathered at New York's City Hall to receive a gold key to the city from Robert W. Watt, Director of Commerce for New York City, standing in for Mayor Robert Wagner. Patsy, her mother, her sister, and her cousin Bobbi Patterson stayed at the posh Barbizon Plaza Hotel, on Central Park South.

The Carnegie Hall show—officially called "WSM Presents the 'Grand Ole Opry'"— started at 8:30 p.m., with Patsy Cline singing just before intermission. Patsy's position before the intermission meant that she came on early enough to make the deadlines for the morning newspapers. Patricia Brannon remembered that her sister, Bobbi went and told me, "You wouldn't believe [the] diamonds and furs.' She said [the show] was sold out. Not ordinary folks like us.." Bobbi told her sister Patricia Ginny was called back on stage twice.[28]

Indeed, The *New York Times* headlined its review, published the next day: "An unusual sort of opera was staged last night at Carnegie Hall. Its musical score was very much in the American idiom; its libretto was casual and folksy." Patsy wore a black cocktail dress, pinned with a white orchid (no cowgirl here). The *Times* reviewer, who only stayed through the intermission, called Patsy Cline a pop singer who had a convincing way with the "heart song," the country cousin of the torch song.[29]

A clue as to why Carnegie Hall booked the Opry can be found at the bottom of the official program, inside the last page: "For Rental Information of all halls, call the Booking Manager, Suite 100, Carnegie Hall at Circle 7-1350." In the early 1960s, Carnegie Hall needed bookings. On June 16, 1960, it ownership passed to a government foundation, as the fabled hall had not been able to sustain itself. Occupying the east stretch of Seventh Avenue between West

56th Street and West 57th Street, it had been built by philanthropist Andrew Carnegie in 1890, as one of the most significant venues for classical music in the United States—known for fine acoustics but not large audiences. It was in the process of being saved in 1961, just as Lincoln Center was about to open. Patsy Cline almost did not get to perform at Carnegie Hall because it had been scheduled to be torn down in 1960. But it was saved by such great musicians as Leonard Bernstein and Isaac Stern.[30]

Patsy's appearance stemmed from a last-minute cancellation. For November 29, 1961, Carnegie Hall had originally booked classical pianist John Browning (1933–2003). Despite the competition from Van Cliburn and other virtuoso American pianists of the same generation, Browning had developed a busy career, giving some hundred concerts a season. But in late October, Browning cancelled, and Carnegie Hall bookers and officials of the Musicians Aid Society called WSM, and scrambled at the Nashville Convention to craft a program. Thus, Patsy Cline had her chance to sing at one of the most important venues for music in the United States.[31]

Since this date had booked at the last minute, the Opry stars immediately went back on the road. After the show and a dinner, the stars returned to their hotels, and at 2:00 a.m., they boarded a bus for the trip to LaGuardia Airport. At 3:30 a.m., all flew back to Nashville to resume touring. Two days later, for example, Patsy Cline appeared for the Forsyth, North Carolina, Rescue Squad in a package show called Stars of the Grand Ole Opry at the Winston-Salem (North Carolina) Memorial Coliseum. The Forsyth Rescue Squad had been created on February 28, 1959, by the North Carolina Civil Defense office. This represented a typical example of Patsy Cline's means of earning money. While doing better, she still needed to tour relatively out-of-the-way venues to make a living.[32]

"Advertisement for Forsyth gig"

On December 2, 1961, the following Saturday, Patsy appeared on Atlanta's *Dixie Jubilee,* a weekly TV program, and some engineer made an audio recording of the TV show—hot off her appearance at Carnegie Hall in New York City. "Hot doggies, she told her audience, "you talk about a hen out of a coop. I really felt like one up there. But you know what? They were setting up there stompin' their feet and yellin', just like a bunch of hillbillies, just like we do. And I was real surprised. Carnegie Hall was real fabulous, but you know it ain't as big as the Grand Ole Opry." Patsy then paused and choked up—and for once in her life, she was speechless.

Back in Winchester, Hilda Hensley and her family awaited a notice in the *Winchester Evening Star* of Patsy's appearance at Carnegie Hall. It took almost a week, but finally, on December 5, the *Winchester Evening Star* noted in an article buried inside, on page 7: "Patsy Cline Featured at Carnegie Hall," telling readers that "Miss Cline sang five numbers including her latest hits, 'Walking [sic] After Midnight,' 'Crazy,' and 'I Fall to Pieces.'" Had she appeared singing classical music, she would have been headlined on the front page. The elite were having a hard time reconciling why, of all people, that girl from South Kent Street was singing at Carnegie Hall.

Finally Patsy had gotten a large royalty check from Decca. With this windfall, bass player Bob Moore sold Charles and Patsy his old house; Moore had grown wealthy doing so many sessions and he and his family were moving to a larger place. Bob Moore later remembered, "Charlie and Patsy were in the studio and Patsy said she couldn't come to the baseball game that evening because Charlie was coming into [Nashville] and they were going to look for a home to buy." They purchased Moore's nice little brick home, at 5024 Hillhurst Drive, off Dickerson Road, in northeast Nashville. The success of "I Fall to Pieces" had made a significant difference to their socioeconomic status.[33]

Patsy was back—after years of financial struggle since her 1957 marriage and the end of the busy schedule of bookings in the wake of "Walkin' After Midnight." (Patsy Cline received less than $1,000 in total royalties from 4-Star for this hit song!) With "I Fall to Pieces," she went on to national fame. For example, on Wednesday, November 8, 1961, three weeks before her Carnegie Hall appearance, Patsy performed on ABC's *American Bandstand*. (Sadly, copies of the show have not survived.) On August 5, 1957, *American Bandstand* had gone national on the ABC-TV network—from its Philadelphia, Pennsylvania, base. But Dick Clark and ABC still ran the show on the cheap and booked no live bands, so singers appeared in person to lip-sync their latest hit singles—in Patsy Cline's case, "I Fall to Pieces." To promote her hit to a teen audience of record buyers, Patsy gladly joined host Dick Clark.[34]

On December 18, 1961, *Billboard* summarized the past year in pop music. Patsy suddenly was in the pop music hierarchy—listed alongside Connie Francis, Roy Orbison, Dion, the Shirelles, Ricky Nelson, and Bobby Darin. It had been a year of important transition, as retail stores had finally begun to sell a significant number of pop and C&W LPs in stereo.

On December 30, according to the *Winnipeg Free Press,* Patsy began a tour across Canada, traveling with a package show. It was like being back in Washington, DC in 1956, with Jimmy Dean atop the bill, Patsy Cline second, followed by George Hamilton IV and Billy Grammar. They played the largest venues in Canadian cities, such as the Winnipeg Auditorium which held 4,000 persons. Next, New Year's Day of 1962, the group stopped in Billings, Montana—a long, twelve-hundred-mile journey. Here local impresario Marlin Payne topped the lineup with Patsy Cline and added Kitty Wells and Leroy Van Dyke.[35]

On January 4, the *Long Beach* (California) *Independent* reported that Patsy Cline's popularity seemed centered on Baby Boomers. Gilbert Youth Research Company's president, Eugene Gilbert, reported his latest research that there was an age separation in musical tastes between parents and their offspring. Gilbert wrote, "Few adults—parents in particular—have ever heard of Patsy Cline or Bobby Vee. Who are these two? Well at the moment they happen to be the leading recording artists in the country." Nearly 100 percent of teens could identify Patsy

Cline. This was a nationally fed wire service article, published in scores of newspapers across the United States. The next day, in the *San Antonio* (Texas) *Light* newspaper, a back page ad for the local Joske Department Store's eighty-ninth birthday announced a sale of 45s—marked down from ninety-eight cents to seventy-five—including salient examples as "Run to Him," by Bobby Vee; "The Twist," by Chubby Checker; and "Crazy," by Patsy Cline. Joskes ranked as downtown San Antonio's top department store at the time.[36]

On January 10, Decca released "She's Got You," which, during 1962, would go to number 1 C&W, number 14 Pop, and number 3 Easy Listening on *Billboard* charts. "She's Got You" stood at the core of *Sentimentally Yours,* Patsy's third and final LP released during her lifetime. Hank Cochran had pitched "She's Got You" to Owen Bradley as a follow up to "I Fall to Pieces." By late March, "She's Got You" was all over the *Billboard* charts. At about the same time, the *Showcase* LP was released. Patsy Cline pioneered—with "Crazy" and "She's Got You"—an appearance on *Billboard*'s new Easy Listening (purchases by adults, not teens) chart. Patsy Cline was popular all across the board.[37]

On January 22, Patsy wrote Louise Seger of her busy schedule, already touring the Midwest with Johnny Cash—from small cities in South Dakota to Chicago, from small venues in Indiana to the largest hall in Kansas City. She was scheduled to finish this tour in seven days, then return home to Nashville for a couple of days, then two days in Toronto, then return home for four days, and then start another tour. Her life was busy, but the money was finally flowing in. Patsy Cline wrote, "Got [on the tour] a twelve-year-old girl who plays steel guitar out of this world. My ole ears have never heard anything like it. She also plays a sax and sings. Looks like a blonde doll. Her name is Barbara Mandrell."[38]

Mandrell later wrote in her autobiography that, in early 1962, she had joined a package tour put together by Johnny Cash's management, with Don Gibson, Patsy Cline, and June Carter. "My job, as a specialist act, was to open with a couple of songs, one on the steel guitar, one on the saxophone, trying out my voice on a couple of choruses." From Patsy Cline, Mandrell "got the feeling that a woman could be a star, just like a man." Mandrell remembered Cline as a true professional. And she added that Patsy wore no western outfits, but in her tasteful dresses, provided a model of a country singer who could cross over to pop.[39]

Touring provided quick money but required long journeys over two-lane roads in large sedans, with several performers packed into each vehicle, pulling trailers loaded with instruments. (Patsy never had a tour bus.) Life on the road proved an ordeal. As Patsy's popularity rose, her manager, Randy Hughes, contemplated purchasing a private airplane to help his busy client fly instead of drive.[40]

"Advertisement for the Randy Hughes Agency"

On January 27, on stationary from the Hill Hotel, in Omaha, Nebraska, and mailed from Joplin, Missouri, Patsy again wrote Louise Seger, complaining about her busy schedule: "Go, go, go." On February 22, Patsy escaped touring for her second appearance on Dick Clark's *American Bandstand,* lip-synching "She's Got You" on a Thursday afternoon show. Still images exist of this appearance, but no film or video copies do.[41]

The February 1962 issue of *Song Hits* magazine ran an unusual headline: "What is this thing now called country music?" What the editors concluded: "It is as basic to popular music today as is R&B. Rock is an outgrowth of these two forms." It offered Patsy Cline as an example of the "new" country music. *Song Hits* underscored that "I Fall to Pieces" and "Crazy" provided successful examples of crossover hits.[42]

By late March, tired of the long auto rides and having to work around the schedules of commercial airlines, Randy Hughes purchased a green and white Piper Comanche. Thereafter, Patsy Cline could and would ride in style. So on March 25, according to the *San Antonio* (Texas) *Express and News,* she flew to and played the nine-thousand-seat San Antonio Municipal Auditorium—with Jerry Lee Lewis. Then, on April 8, the *Cedar Rapids* (Iowa) *Gazette* advertised Opry stars at its Memorial Coliseum—the largest venue in town. Suddenly the day-long drives to San Antonio and trips to Cedar Rapids could be completed in a few hours in Randy Hughes's plane. In April 1962, in Peoria, Illinois, she told an interviewer for a school newspaper, the *Limelight,* "I am very nervous due to my automobile accident last year." A private airplane solved that issue. Nevertheless, she also observed that her success meant dozens of tour dates and that she never had "any time to spend with my family." Nothing could be done about that; she had been cash strapped for so long that she was going to tour and make money as fast as she could. By April 22, the *Kingsport* (Tennessee) *Times-News* reported that Patsy sang on Sunday night, after the Bristol Volunteer 500 race at Bristol International Speedway—before more than one hundred thousand fans.[43]

By spring of 1962, Patsy Cline was making money so fast that she even began to contemplate building a dream home. She and Charles looked at many places and found one off Dickerson Pike, a section of Highway 41, north of Nashville—at 815 Nella Drive. This classic suburban split-level, red brick home, stood half-built in a then newly developed area, surrounded by beautiful trees. Patsy saw a huge house under construction and it fit her image of suburban success: dotted with white shutters, and with a small portico of wrought iron. The price tag was $30,000 (about $150,000 in 2011 dollars), but Patsy wanted it and was willing to work more dates to pay for this dream house. The house sat back off the street and with a backyard for leisure, not gardening.

"Patsy at her new home on Nella Drive"

The first floor of Nella Drive had a huge living room and dining room, a master bedroom, a bath, and a state-of-the-art kitchen—with a serving counter, plus informal dining room. The children's rooms and the guest bedroom were on the second floor. The basement, which opened onto a stone patio, had a spacious den with a wet bar, which Patsy dubbed her music room. An intercom system was installed throughout. Patsy ordered custom-made furniture, drapes, and carpeting, in what might be called an American Heritage look. Her fancy dining room table could expand to seat ten, and next to the table she placed a solid mahogany credenza. For the master bathroom, Patsy Cline bought gold-speckled wallpaper that she claimed she had seen in Hollywood movies years before.[44]

So that Patsy could afford the new home, Randy Hughes booked her in top venues. On June 15, she appeared at the Hollywood Bowl, where she co-headlined with Johnny Cash. She sang "Crazy," "I Fall to Pieces," "Won't You Come Home Bill Bailey," and "Lovesick Blues." The lineup that night included Roger Miller, Mother Maybelle Carter and the Carter family, Leroy Van Dyke, and Tompall and the Glaser Brothers. And as an added touch for Hollywood, the booker also included long-time singing cowboy, Gene Autry, as well as TV star Lorne Greene, and actor Walter Brennan—each of whom had a recitation on the pop charts. This was the kickoff of the Shower of Stars tour of the southwestern United States.[45]

"Poster for Johnny Cash 'Shower of Stars"at the Hollywood Bowl"

If Carnegie Hall was known as a classical music venue, pop music constituted the usual entertainment at the Hollywood Bowl. In 1943, teen-idol Frank Sinatra had made his Hollywood debut, not on film but at the Hollywood Bowl. Through the 1950s, the Hollywood Bowl booked the likes of Nat "King" Cole, Bobby Darin, Ray Charles, Johnnie Ray, Mahalia Jackson, Sammy Davis, Jr., and Little Richard. The stage measured ninety feet across, a vast space. "When you play the Hollywood Bowl," singer-songwriter James Taylor would later say, "You have a feeling—like at Carnegie Hall or the Royal Albert Hall in London—that you are playing in a major place, a place that has a lot of weight and is an important part of musical history. You have a feeling of having arrived." We can imagine that Patsy Cline had the same reaction as Taylor.[46]

The Hollywood Bowl had opened on July 11, 1922, and it sat in one of the largest natural amphitheaters in the world, seating almost twenty thousand attendees. Legendary figures had graced its vast stage: FDR speaking, Jascha Heifetz playing his violin, Fred Astaire dancing, and Billie Holiday, Al Jolson, and Judy Garland singing. Johnny Cash's bass player, Marshall Grant, remembered that "a lot of important people from the entertainment industry attended that show, and it was very well received." Hollywood movie fan Virginia Hensley must have thought she was in a dream. She could look out into the audience and see her favorite movie stars applauding.[47]

In July 1962, when her husband's brother, Melvin Dick, visited Nashville, he remembered being at the center of a whirlwind. During his week-long visit, Melvin Dick, who was a teenager at the time, came to fully appreciate Patsy. He tagged along on a short stop Cline made to her record company, Decca. As soon as she entered Decca's offices, Dick remembered all employees "buzzed" around his casually clad sister-in-law, "asking for her opinion on a host of matters." He contrasted this to the indifference back in Winchester, where upper class teens he knew at Handley High School seemed to go out of their way to avoid Cline's music. While people would request Cline's songs on WINC radio's afternoon *Platter Party*, Melvin Dick did not experience the star status of his brother's spouse until he walked into Decca records in Nashville with her.[48]

Teenager Brenda Lee was equally impressed. She remembered her fellow Decca star's closets were filled with sweaters, slacks, dresses, boots, spike heels, and slippers, among them gold lame slippers. In the closet of honor, Lee remembered Patsy's silver fox stole, and several formal gowns. The music room had a beautiful parquet floor, with a bar padded in red Naugahyde (an artificial leather made by the United States Rubber Company and popular in suburban homes)—with the words *Patsy and Charlie* in studs on the faux-leather covering. In the music room, Patsy had placed her collection of salt and pepper shakers and—in a suburban tradition—a couch that turned into a bed, an overstuffed recliner, and a hi-fi on a rollout table—with records scattered everywhere.[49]

On August 12, the *Anderson* (Indiana) *Herald* reported Patsy Cline's appearance at Plantation Park in shows at two p.m., five p.m., and eight p.m. the night before. On August 15, the *Syracuse Post-Standard* reported that Patsy Cline had appeared at the Franklin County Fair the night before. Then, on August 22 and 23, according to the *Abilene* (Texas) *Reporter-News*, she played the West Texas Fair. And then, on September 16, the *Dallas Morning News* printed a photo of Patsy in her blond wig for a gig sponsored by the *Big D Jamboree* before three thousand fans.[50]

The very next day, Patsy and Randy flew to Rapid City, South Dakota, for an appearance, and the day after that, she appeared in Cheyenne, Wyoming, for the city's annual Frontier Days. They then flew to Minneapolis and next Des Moines. All these transcontinental bookings were now possible because of Randy Hughes's private plane. Patsy wrote her new friend, Anne Armstrong, "Just got in from Minnesota and I worked a show in the down pouring rain. And the damn fool people sat in it and yelled for more. Over 5,000 of them."[51]

On November 7, the eleventh annual WSM Country Music Festival convention began in Nashville. Disc Jockeys from across the United States and Canada sought Patsy out for interviews. From ceremonies held at the Maxwell House Hotel, Patsy took home 10 honors, including *Billboard*'s Favorite Female Country Artist, *Cash Box*'s Most Programmed LP of the Year of 1962 *(Showcase)*, *Cash Box*'s Most Programmed Country and Western Female Vocalist, the *Music Reporter*'s Female Vocalist of the Year. Patsy accepted all these awards—dressed in a gold brocade evening suit, wearing spike high heels and draped in her silver fox stole. Newspapers across the United States correctly reported that Patsy would be going to Las Vegas, beginning November 23. She arranged for her mother to come to Nashville to look after the children, as her husband would go along to Las Vegas to handle the business affairs. The music trade press heralded the Las Vegas booking because it was a five week gig in the live pop music entertainment capital of the United States.[52]

If Carnegie Hall and the Hollywood Bowl glowed with historic prestige, Las Vegas symbolized the future of popular entertainment.

On November 23, Patsy opened at the Mint Casino in downtown Las Vegas, accompanied by the Glaser Brothers band—Chuck, Jim, and Tompall. Patsy was booked for thirty-five days, and Charles Dick has stated that Patsy grossed $6,300 a week—out of which she paid the band, an intermission band, and manager Randy Hughes's commission. Decades later, Charles Dick estimated they netted about $2,000 a week—thus making three times in a week what an average U.S. family did in a year. Finally Patsy was making a substantial income.[53]

The length of the gig proved Randy Hughes's skill as a manager—as he had negotiated a six-week booking versus the usual week-long engagement. In 1962, downtown Las Vegas still competed with the Strip; the Mint and the Golden Nugget ranked as the equals of the Sands and Last Frontier, out on the still barren Las Vegas Strip. While Carnegie Hall and the Hollywood Bowl held thousands who paid top dollar for tickets, the hundred patrons who sat in the Merri-Mint lounge only paid for drinks and were entertained for free. Patsy's job was to help gamblers relax—and then send them back to the tables. Las Vegas proved the biggest payday of her career.[54]

"Patsy in costume standing in front of the Mint
Casino"

By that time, noted developer Del Webb owned the Mint
casino. Webb was far more famous for his building Sun City retirement
villages in Arizona, but he helped—with shell companies—to build
much of Las Vegas. Publicly, he was "a builder," not a gambler. He
stayed one step away from gaming investigations by "renting" the Mint
to Sam Boyd for $2.5 million per year—just as he did with the new
shopping malls he constructed and then rented to others, like Sears
or Montgomery Ward. Webb was so skilled at his "one-step-removed"
legal strategy that Major League baseball permitted him to own the
New York Yankees.[55]

While by the twenty-first century, neon defined the Strip; in 1962 the Mint's neon excess defined Las Vegas, with the largest sign in town: M-I-N-T. Taking the entire facade of the casino as its domain, the MINT sign glowed as a three-dimensional sculpture, and was always in motion. It swooped in red neon across an entire city block—between First and Second on Freemont Street. Eighteen feet wide at its widest, its trajectory shot up eighty-two feet in the air, capped by a sixteen-foot-wide burst of white neon—that capped every 30 seconds. Noted writer Tom Wolfe called it "Mint Elliptical."[56]

Once a person stepped from Fremont Street into the Mint, he or she faced scores of slot machines and gaming tables. The entertainment required patrons to journey to the rear, passing all forms of gaming temptation. Downtown customers in 1962 dressed informally, a "come as you are" casual dress code, while the Strip hotels demanded suits and dresses simply to be admitted. The main performance venues of the Strip hotels required reservations for a show. Downtown hotels offered continuous entertainment. Walk in, sit down, order a drink, and stay for the whole forty-minute show. The Strip hotels served meals; the Mint did not.[57]

For five city blocks, on both sides of Fremont Street, it was all gambling, all the time. With so many alternatives—the bait became talent who could pull in the potential gamblers. That was Patsy's job. Del Webb liked that she was an easy-listening (read, adult) draw. Only in April of 1962 had Webb and Boyd switched from big band pop stars to adult contemporary stars, and after her Hollywood Bowl success, Patsy Cline was an obvious choice [58]

Patsy Cline and the Glaser Brothers did a total of forty minutes, rotating with a local trio of musicians for their break. That way the show never stopped. The Glaser Brothers—Chuck, Jim and Tompall—were also a Decca act, and while Tompall became during the 1970s the most famous of the brothers, as a member of the Outlaw movement with Willie Nelson, it was Jim Glaser (b. 1937) who handled the trio's business. Jim Glaser remembered, "My brothers and I traveled with the Johnny Cash show in 1962, and met Patsy. Working Vegas with her in 1962 was a really big deal at the time, and Patsy was very excited." The Glaser Brothers did sets starting in the afternoon, while Patsy entertained from early evening to past midnight. Jim Glaser remembered that Patsy Cline caught "Vegas throat," caused by excessive dryness, for the first couple of days, and had to lip-synch to her records.[59]

Once a week, Charles Dick and Jim Glaser would go to Sam Boyd to collect their money. Then Dick and Glaser would journey to the offices of the Musician's Union and pay the work dues for that week and for the relief band. Their next stop would be the motel where everyone stayed, as the Mint at the time did not have a hotel attached. Patsy chose her own music, and according to Jim Glaser, she wowed the people in that tiny lounge with her powerful pop voice. But she was on only for about twenty minutes each hour, to send lounge patrons back to the tables and slots, ready to gamble.[60]

The local American Federation of Musicians Union demanded that its members work, too. For her opening night, November 23, Embert Mishner was there. Why? He was the head of the "relief trio." If a show ran seven days a week, the Musicians Union required a relief band. Embert (and his wife Betty Mishler) described the experience with Patsy Cline vividly. They played for about one hundred folks, who were sitting at the bar or at tables around the lounge. The dressing rooms were in the back, behind the small stage. Embert Mishler and two union musicians did old standards—as requested by the audience. (Patsy Cline also took requests.) Embert Mishler made sure he never did a number that Patsy was doing. The trio consisted of Embert singing and playing guitar, an acoustical bass player, and a drummer. As for

Patsy, she simply walked out, took the mike, and sang—accompanied by the Glasers.

"Patsy performing at the Mint"

Embert's wife, Betty, was there, and she recalled, "[Patsy and I] ran together because Charlie was always drinking and Patsy did not drink as she was working. Patsy liked to go to other casinos and listen to other singers. [We] would drive to the strip to the Dunes, Sahara, the Sands and others." To combat the dryness, Patsy always took a glass of water onto the stage with her, and sipped during her twenty-minute performances. Patsy Cline proved an ideal lounge act, as she captured the attention of the patrons, and sent the gamblers went back to the tables.[61]

Patsy wore a black gown (as in the picture of her standing in front of the Mint) or a white gown (shown the image on the cover of this book. .) She chose her wardrobe carefully. Her shoes, for example, were the shoes for a woman who had to stand for hours and could not afford to get tired. What were Patsy's criteria for selection? Height and slimness had to be perfectly balanced. The heels could not be so high that she could not stand for long periods of time without getting tired. The heels were tapered, but not so spikey that she could not walk on any surface. Patsy also balanced the toe with the heel. Pointedness meant elegance, but bluntness meant comfort. If the toe was too long, she would need higher heels, thus making them uncomfortable. But if heels were too low, she would walk less elegantly. Patsy demanded that the toes not be cut too low (which would make her feet look too wide when performing) or too high (which would make her legs look too short). In fact, Patsy picked her shoes with the same meticulous care that she brought to bear on the subtle details of her singing.[62]

On November 22, the *Las Vegas Review Journal* contained an ad for the new Mint act, and listed the awards that Patsy had won earlier that month at the CMA Convention in Nashville. The newspaper listed "Tompall & Glaser Bros." as "an added attraction." The Mint promised "plenty of free parking—5 giant lots." On the same page the reader found out who was on the Strip: Harry James at the Flamingo, Nat King Cole at the Sands; Rosemary Clooney at the Desert Inn, Betty Grable at the Dunes, Debbie Reynolds at the Riviera, and Roberta Sherwood at the Stardust. Patsy Cline had admired pop singers (and learned from them) while listening at W&L, watching them in movies, and hearing them on radio. Charles Dick remembered the act that most impressed Patsy in Las Vegas was Roberta Sherwood, a bespectacled suburban housewife who in 1956 rose from obscurity to become a headline pop torch singer. Dick reports that Patsy stared in awe as Sherwood performed at the Stardust. Sherwood, like Jo Stafford, was a pure pop singer.[63]

The *Las Vegas Sun*'s reviewer wrote, "Much decorated Patsy Cline shows the stuff that got her there in her Vegas debut in the Merri-Mint Theatre. Pretty and poised, Patsy just stands there and sings with that big, go-get-'em voice, few gestures, no razzle-dazzle gimmicks, and she holds every eye and ear." (This agrees with the multitude of reports of how Patsy Cline sang on stage.) The unnamed reviewer—who was used to top-drawer talent, as he reviewed every act that came through Las Vegas at the time—told his readers that, while Patsy Cline was primarily renowned as a country star, she "does equal justice to a pop tune. It may be her first time in Vegas, but man, it won't be her last!" Indeed, before she left, in late December, Randy Hughes was already talking about a March 1963 return.

As 1962 ended, Patsy had proved herself, but the six-week, seven-days-a-week schedule proved a grind that she was not used to. So as her gig ended, Patsy Cline was not celebrating, but she was looking forward to returning to Nashville and reuniting with her children. As Christmas approached, Patsy called home twice a day, just to hear Julie and Randy's voices. As new friend Betty Mishler reminisced, Patsy repeatedly remarked, "I am never going to spend a Christmas away from kids ever again."

———————

Patsy returned to Nashville on January 1, 1963. One magazine summed up her career to that point: "Patsy Cline had it rough during her early professional career, but . . . [with] 'Crazy,' 'She's Got You,' and her current hit 'Leavin' on Your Mind,' she had risen to become a major star." That very month, "Leavin' on Your Mind" peaked at number 8 on *Billboard*'s country chart and also charted Pop and Easy Listening. *Billboard* noted Patsy's broad appeal.[64]

Beginning on February 4, Owen Bradley scheduled four recording sessions in four days. Bradley brought in Brenton Banks's biggest team so far—five violins, two violas, and two cellos. Bradley scheduled album fillers for the beginning of the week—covers of "Faded Love," (Bob Wills), "Someday (You'll Want Me to Want You)" (Mills Brothers), and "Love Letters in the Sand" (a 1931 pop song remade as a pop teen hit in 1957 by Pat Boone). On the next night, they covered Bill Monroe's "Blue Moon of Kentucky," Don Gibson's "Sweet Dreams (of You)," and Irving Berlin's "Always." Bradley was still experimenting with covers, ranging from bluegrass to prior country hits to Tin Pan Alley standards.

We can best hear Bradley's vision for Patsy Cline's future in "Sweet Dreams (of You)." Now associated solely with Cline, Banks's strings, the A Team, and the Jordanaires helped fashion a female ballad from a hit written and recorded in 1956 by Don Gibson, then covered by Faron Young, whose version took "Sweet Dreams" all the way to number 2 on *Billboard*'s country charts. In 1962, "Sweet Dreams" was considered a man's song; Patsy made it dreamy ballad aimed at female record buyers.

On the night of Wednesday, February 6, the ensemble covered two pop standards: "Does Your Heart Beat for Me" (Russ Morgan, 1936), and "Bill Bailey, Won't You Please Come Home" (written by Hughie Cannon in 1902). Finally, on Thursday, February 7, in Patsy Cline's twenty-ninth (and final) session, Owen Bradley tried two new songs: Harlan Howard's "He Called Me Baby" and "You Took Him Off My Hands," plus a Ray Price classic, "Crazy Arms (1956), and a cover of Moon Mullican's "I'll Sail My Ship Alone" (1950). The four February 1963 evening sessions accounted for one-eighth of Patsy Cline's total recorded work.

Patsy then went on the road to promote her current hit, "Leavin' On Your Mind." On Friday February 22, she was in Lima, Ohio, and then, on Saturday, February 23, she was in Toledo, Ohio, to sing with a full orchestra. She flew up and back, nine hundred miles, in Randy

Hughes's private plane. Patsy was back in Nashville by February 28, when she paid a surprise visit to Loretta Lynn and helped her put up the drapes in her home. Later that night Loretta and her husband went to visit Patsy and Charles and, in the music room, listened to playbacks of Patsy's early February sessions.[65]

As she took to the road, Patsy Cline faced a bright future. She loved her new home, and faced a guaranteed future of getting regular royalties and well-paying gigs like Las Vegas. She had an oeuvre of 102 recordings, five of which were second versions of songs she had already recorded. If this were a standard biography, it would end with her death on March 5, 1963, in an airplane crash. While this sad ending, at the age of thirty, has become closure of the Patsy Cline legend; instead this book ends with her musical recoding career. .

Then logically I explain why her recordings offer complex and appealing music that would be embraced by later generations. Her death simply started a new relationship of these recordings. Between 1963 and 1980 Patsy Cline was rediscovered and then in 1980, Hollywood jump-started her rise to iconic status.

But that could have not happened if the music Patsy Cline left had not been complex enough to engage new fans and appealing enough to provoke the new fans to purchase her records. Thus, the following chapter takes up and provides a musical analysis of the recordings that Patsy Cline left to the world.

NOTES

Chapter 6

1 Midwest Today, June1998: 22.

2 Paul Kingsbury Liner Notes for "Live at Cimarron."

3 countrydiscography.

4 Billboard, June 28, 1997:33.

5 Charles Wolfe, Classic Country (New York: Routledge, 2001): 175-177; The Weakley County Press (Martin, Tennessee), May 11, 2004: B1; www.jordanaires.net – accessed 10 January 2009.

6 Michael Kosser's How Nashville Became Music City U.S.A.: 50 Years of Music Row (Milwaukee, WI: Hal Leonard, 2006).

7 www.charliemccoy.com – accessed April 12, 2009.

8 www.rayedenton.com – accessed 8 January 2009.

9 ORAL HISTORY – at CMA – Ray Edenton by Bill Lloyd – 6 October 2006.

10 John Rumble, "Let's Cut a Hit: The A-Team Talks,"The Journal of Country Music, 20/2: (1998): 4-15.

11 ORAL HISTORY - Brenton Banks by Michael Streissguth, 13 November 1995.

12 Susan Alton, The Encyclopedia of African-American Heritage (New York: Facts on File, 1997): 22.

13 Paul Hemphill, The Nashville Sound (New York: Pocket Books, 1970)

14 The Independent (UK), 14 February 14, 1998: Arts1; WPost, November 15, 1991: A17.

15 Peter Fornatale, and Joshua E. Mills, Radio in the Television Age (Woodstock, NY: Overlook Press, 1980); David R. McFarland, The Development of the Top 40 Radio Format (New York: Arno Press, 1979).

16 Michael Kosser's How Nashville Became Music City U.S.A.: 50 Years of Music Row (Milwaukee, WI: Hal Leonard, 2006): 44-55.

17 The [Nashville] Tennessean, January 22, 2005: B1.

18 Rich Kienzle, "Owen Bradley," The Journal of the American Academy of Old-Time Country Music, 24 (December 1994): 13-15.

19 Alanna Nash, Behind Closed Doors: Talking with Legends of Country Music (New York: Knopf, 1988): 46, 48; Paul Kingsbury (editor), The Encyclopedia of Country Music (New York: Oxford University Press, 1998), Chapter 13.

20 Michael Kosser's How Nashville Became Music City U.S.A.: 50 Years of Music Row (Milwaukee, WI: Hal Leonard, 2006): 46.

21 Country Music, October 1979: 64-66; Goldmine, December 4, 1987: 22-26.

22 Ralph Emery, The View From Nashville (New York: William Morrow, 1998).

23 Pro Sound News, February 1998: 15-19.

24 Variety, November 8, 1961: 55.

25 NYT, November 8, 1961: 42.

26 The Patricia Brannon Collection.

27 TRIAL.

28 ORAL HISTORY – 12 June 2007.

29 NYT, November 30, 1961: 41.

30 Theodore O. Cron and Burt Goldblatt, Portrait of Carnegie Hall (New York: The Macmillan Company, 1966); NYT, July 7, 1984: 33.

31 The New Yorker, November 16, 1963: 44-52; author's hand written notes from booking files at the Carnegie Hall Archives.

32 Author's copy of souvenir booklet promoting the show.

[33] May 18, 2008 e-mail from Bob Moore to author; November 20, 2008 e-mail from Moore to the author.

[34] American Bandstand at the Internet Movie Database – accessed August 8, 2005.

[35] The Winnipeg Free Press, December 30, 1961: 15.

[36] The Long Beach (CA) Independent, January 4,1962: 44.

[37] countrydiscography.

[38] CMA, Louise Seger Collection, January 22, 1962.

[39] Barbara Mandrell, Get to the Heart: My Story (New York: Bantam, 1990): 74-80.

[40] Midwest Today, June1998: 33.

[41] Michael Shore with Dick Clark, The History of American Bandstand (New York: Ballantine Books, 1985): 130.

[42] TRIAL.

[43] The Kingsport [TN] Times-News, April 22, 1962: 22; TRIAL.

[44] TRIAL.

[45] E-mails to the author from Carol Merrill-Mirsky Curator Hollywood Bowl Museum – February 2007.

[46] Michael Brickland and John Henken (editors), The Hollywood Bowl: Tales of a Summer Night (Los Angeles: Los Angeles Philharmonic Association, 1996): 101-108.

[47] Marshall Grant, I Was There When It Happened: My life with Johnny Cash (Nashville, TN: Cumberland House, 2006): 112; Kenneth Marcus, "The Hollywood Bowl and the Democratization of Music," The Cal Pomona Journal of Interdisciplinary Studies, Fall, 1999: 32.

[48] WS, May 3, 2001: A1.

[49] Brenda Lee, Little Miss Dynamite (New York: Hyperion Books, 2002): 101.

[50] The Dallas Morning News, February 22, 2003: D1; countrydisography.

[51] "Remembering Patsy Cline" DVD (1994).

[52] TRIAL.

[53] ORAL HISTORY – Charles Dick, November 12, 2006.

[54] The Las Vegas Review Journal, May 17, 1964: 43; Fred E. Baston, and Charles Phoenix, Fabulous Las Vegas in the 1950s (Santa Monica: Angel City Press, 1999); Albin J. Dahl, Nevada's Economic Resources," Bureau of Business and Economic Research, State of Nevada, Carson City, 1964.

[55] Margaret Finnerty, Del Webb: The Man, A Company (Flagstaff, AZ: Heritage Publications, 1991): 128-130; Tom Alexander, Del Webb," Fortune, May 1965: 33-36; Robert Venturi, Denise Scott Brown, and Steven Izenour, Learning from Las Vegas (Cambridge, Mass., MIT Press, 1977).

[56] Tom Wolfe, The Kandy-Kolored Tangerine-Flake Streamline Baby (New York: (New York: Farrar Straus & Giroux, 1965); Horace Sutton, "Cowboys and Croupiers," Saturday Review, 43 (5 March 1960): 32-33.

[57] Ed Reid, Las Vegas: City without Clocks (Englewood Cliffs, NJ: Prentice Hall, 1961).

[58] Ed Reid and Ovid Demaris, The Green Felt Jungle (New York: Trident Press, 1963): 233-240; Tax Records for Sahara-Nevada Corporation, located at Clark County Government Center; The Las Vegas Review Journal, July 12, 1961: 7-8.

[59] www.jimglaser.com – accessed February 3, 2007.

[60] jim.glaser@comcast.net – email to author October 14, 2007

[61] ORAL HISTORY – Embert and Betty Mishler – Oct 11, 2007

[62] jim.glaser@comcast.net – e-mail October 14, 2007.

[63] The Las Vegas Review Journal, November 22, 1962: 12; "Show Guide" The Las Vegas Review Journal, November 30, 1962:18; The Las Vegas Review-Journal, November 24, 1962: 4.

[64] Cowboy Songs, January 1963: 8.

[65] Loretta Lynn, Coal Miner's Daughter (New York: Warners Books, 1976): 134-139.

Chapter 7

Patsy Cline's Musical Heritage

The recordings of Patsy Cline combine both musical complexity and popular appeal. In his groundbreaking *Foundations of Rock* (New York: Oxford University Press, 2009), Walter Everett, a trained musicologist, analyzes popular music recorded from 1955 to 1969, finding Patsy Cline recordings among the most complex. Everett based his musicological analysis on listening to all the singles that appeared in the top 20 on *Billboard*'s pop charts, including "Walkin' After Midnight," "I Fall to Pieces," "Crazy," and "She's Got You."

The architect of the complex Patsy Cline recorded sound was arranger-producer Owen Bradley. For musicologist Walter Everett, Bradley ranked as one of the top producers of the late 1950s and through the 1960s. In fact, Bradley proves a quintessential example of *The Producer as Composer,* as characterized by Virgil Moorehead's book of the same name (Cambridge: MIT Press, 2005). Like Phil Spector with his "Wall of Sound" in "girl group" rock music, Bradley widened the producer's role from primarily technical matters to conceptual and artistic ones. Also like Spector, he assumed the central role in hiring musicians and making the musical arrangements from the demo recordings. Artistically, he created an Owen Bradley sound.

Bradley often was the only person in the studio who could read music. So he taught head players the songs he arranged. Then, like jazz producers, Bradley worked with his group of singers and musicians to improvise real-time interpretations. He proved a skilled session leader as he embraced suggestions from players and singers he knew well. He would try various takes until he approved the musical mix. Then the group recorded a take, and then another—until Bradley selected a final version for release.

Over the space of Patsy Cline's final fifteen sessions for Decca (August 1961 through February 1963), Owen Bradley showed Nashville how to make recordings that sounded better than live concerts, with the singer surrounded by the world's best musicians—all arranged by Bradley in the recording space he had designed. As the mediator between the two worlds of inspiration and know-how, Owen Bradley became the central figure in a Patsy Cline recording. He called himself a referee, but a better sports analogy would be a coach. He formed a game plan, called the plays, and chose the players. This required consummate producing skills.

Bradley was the first in Nashville to embrace multi-track recording. He took full advantage of the rise of high fidelity by producing Patsy Cline's recording sessions as "cleanly" as possible. Decca New York cared only about sales and loved that Bradley made Decca the top label in Nashville. But Bradley went further.

Patsy Cline had taught herself to be a great singer through constant practice. Bradley's greatest contribution lay in his selection of musicians. As Walter Everett emphasizes in *The Aesthetics of Rock,* rare was the pop record that sold well between 1955 and 1969 that was not defined by its beat. Bradley never recorded Patsy Cline without a drummer. Teens danced to the beat, slow or fast—and purchased Patsy's recordings.

Second, to Walter Everett, making popular music from 1955 to 1969 meant electric guitars but no brass or woodwinds. In the middle 1950s, this meant Scotty Moore's guitar behind Elvis, Chuck Berry's adapting piano chords to his electric guitar playing, and Carl Perkins' playing the electric guitar in his country fashion. Starting with Patsy Cline's first 1955 recording session and continuing through her twenty-ninth and last, on February 7, 1963, a constant in Owen Bradley's session work was Grady Martin, playing lead electric guitar.

Martin established the complex treblelike sounds and the mellow tones that made Patsy Cline music sound seem unique. Grady Martin proved as versatile a lead guitarist as there was in Nashville—or anywhere in pop music. For example, Martin shaped countless rock classics, including Elvis Presley's "(You're the) Devil in Disguise," Brenda Lee's "I'm Sorry" and "Rockin' Around the Christmas Tree" (both produced by Owen Bradley), Ray Price's "For the Good Times," and Patsy Cline's "Crazy" and "She's Got You."

Everett's third necessity for popular music was the piano. This was Owen Bradley's own instrument of choice; Patsy also embraced piano sounds. Owen Bradley, working with Floyd Cramer, changed the status of the piano in Nashville. Everett ranks Cramer as a session master among all the popular recordings he studied. With the piano, Bradley added greater complexity to the music coming from Nashville. He could teach sessions, from his arrangements of taped demos, from the piano, and expand the possibilities of the sonic structure. Cramer and fellow pianist Harold "Pig" Robbins added to all forms of musical timbre (color of the sound) that had been lacking in most earlier Nashville recordings because earlier producers did not use piano players.

Once he had signed Patsy Cline exclusively to Decca, in 1961, and finding songs like "I Fall to Pieces," Bradley began to expand his sound even further. However, fans and scholars alike have misunderstood one addition: the steel guitar. Prior to Bradley producers hired steel guitar players as up-front players, along side guitarists.. What Bradley did was push his steel players into the rhythm section to fashion a more complex beat. In fact, he used the steel guitar to create a stronger beat than rock bands.

With the July 1961 ascendency of "I Fall to Pieces" on the country, pop, and easy listening *Billboard* charts, Decca New York called for a second LP, and Bradley had Cline record pop standards, literally starting with Cole Porter's "True Love." Bradley sweetened this session with six strings playing in unison: four violins, one viola, and one cello. This made the sound more accessible to adult record buyers who had grown up with "sweet" Big Bands. Thereafter rock stars—from Bobby Vee to Aretha Franklin—used strings in the same way, to create a sweet sound.

Strings worked so well that, from Patsy's twenty-second to twenty-ninth (and final) sessions, Bradley used different combinations of strings. He also hired Ray Edenton, a talented electric guitar player, to create an even fuller guitar sound. From sessions 23 to 29, it was Grady Martin on electric guitar lead, Ray Edenton on electric rhythm guitar, the unheard Randy Hughes on acoustic guitar, Harold Bradley on six-string eclectic bass, Bob Moore on acoustic bass, Buddy Harman on drums, Floyd Cramer on piano, a selection of strings, and the Jordanaires. These were the sweet Patsy Cline instrumentals heard in "Faded Love," "Sweet Dreams," and "Bill Bailey, Won't You Please Come on Home," all now Patsy Cline classics.

It is interesting to note that, in Walter Everett's initial five chapters, describing sources of pop music of the 1960s, the shortest chapter is the one on vocals. Everett admits that "each singer has a distinctive tonal quality, range, and method of articulation." This is what the fan paid for in the end. Everett praises Patsy Cline as an alto role model. While she sang lower than a classic soprano, she had a very wide range—from E below middle C to the C an octave above middle C. Like Elvis, Owen Bradley encouraged Patsy to use all her physicality to invest emotion into what she sang. But what separated her from all others of her generation was her skill with vocal ornamentation. Everett uses, as an example, the "bent note" at Patsy Cline's ending of "Faded Love." She sings it "Lo—ve," bending the note as she sings the final word. But he also found she often added swoops (in technical language, glissandi or portamenti) to create what Everett describes as her vocal complexity. For Everett, Patsy Cline's vocal ornaments differentiated her and made her popular. In a stunning contrast, Everett compares her with soul singer James Brown. He lists her uses of vocal ornamentation: She sings notes in rapid alternation with the notes above or below (labeled a "mordant," from the Latin *mordere,* meaning "to bite," in which a singer vocalizes notes above or below the major chord in rapid alternation). Using other such complex techniques, found in Walter Everett's massive catalog of vocal ornamentation, Patsy Cline stands out with her now familiar "Crazy," which includes broken syllables, a strong dynamic range in her voice, and a continuous use of vocal ornaments.

Vocal ornaments are what make Patsy Cline melodies sound so complex when first heard. She was vastly more complex than any other singer of her generation.

Richard Leppert's "Gender Sonics: The Voice of Patsy Cline," in *Musicological Identities* (edited by Steven Bauer, Raymond Knapp, and Jacqueline Warwick, Burlington, VT: Ashgate Publishing, 2008), takes for granted the complexity that Everett examines and expands on its complexity for scholarly musicologists. For example, according to Leppert, Patsy Cline's singing betrays no break between her use of both a chest voice and a head voice. The chest voice is often associated with deep, warm, rich, thick sounds. In contrast, the head voice, with female singers, is most associated with light, bright singing tones that are higher in pitch and resonate within the upper sinus cavities. Patsy's low and middle range is richly colorful, and her high range crystalline, argues Leppert. Indeed, he directly praises the complexity of her slow-moving "torch songs," as she expresses key words and phrases, drawing them out with a kind of reverence that gives these performances their notable power.

Leppert argues that Patsy Cline proved best at singing "torch songs," typically slow- to moderate-tempo ballads about failed relationships, and love lost. For Leppert, Patsy Cline's recording of "I Fall to Pieces," spanning over an octave and a major third, dramatically exploits an extraordinary octave leap, of which she was a master. "The expressive effects are principally accomplished through extremely skilled phrasing . . . all of it without deviating from what seems to be an effortless floating quality, achieved in part by extremely subtle variation in dynamics on single words and notes—slight crescendos, slight decrescendos."

For Leppert, the first phrase of "I Fall to Pieces" offers up an abstract of the Patsy Cline style: "the slight hesitancy in finding the note on 'fall,' a delicate [vocal slide between two pitches] on 'pieces,' the note then extended over the beat on the final syllable," sung with an almost imperceptible gruffness as she scoops up to notes, then drifts downward, and hesitates finding the final note. Thereafter, as she repeats the title phrase, she sings "I Fall to Pieces" slightly differently, not with full force of the complete improvisation that a jazz singer might embellish, but with careful attention to tiny variations. Patsy sings so subtly and with such skill that repeated close analysis rewards the listener with a more complete understanding and appreciation.

Owen Bradley had Patsy experiment from the beginning. For example, for her first hit, "Walkin' After Midnight," the first thing we hear is a steel guitar coming in with a three-note windup to the downbeat, and then drums and the acoustic bass with a heavy swing beat. The steel guitar signals that this is a country song, but drums indicate that this is a different kind of country song. Significantly, on that same downbeat, Grady Martin's guitar lands on a relatively unstable pitch, and then slides down to the root of the chord of the melody, prefiguring the song's most important motif: the two-note descent heard on *walkin'*, and later with *midnight, moonlight, miles,* and so forth. Here fans hear the complexity of Grady Martin's guiitar playing contrast while the steel guitar, after building a little momentum with a rhythmic fill, quickly comes to rest firmly on the tonic pitch (the *do* of *do-re-mi*). This instability explains and underscores Patsy Cline's obsession. "I go out walkin', after midnight, out in the moonlight, just like we used to do. . . ." The restless obsession begins in the first line.

By 1961, when Owen Bradley rerecorded "Walkin' After Midnight," he added the Jordanaires, a six-string electric bass, and an organ—and eliminated the fiddle and steel guitar. This version opens, not with a steel guitar but with the almost marchlike *om-pah, om-pah, om-pah*s of the Jordanaires, and the three guitars (electric, electric bass, and acoustic bass). Then Patsy begins to sing, bending certain notes, or hits them a little flat, to add what is called a blue note. (Blue notes are lowered by a third, seventh, or sometimes a fifth degree.) Any of the capitalized syllables can be sung as a blue note by hitting it a little flat. "I go out WALKin' after MIDnight out in the MOONlight" This second version contains the same words as the first but is altogether musically different.

"Crazy" ranks as the most praised of Patsy Cline's songs. Indeed, in 2004, a set of experts advised the Librarian of Congress to place "Crazy" on a national list of the most important recorded sounds ever made. "Crazy" divides into an A section, then an A' section, then a B section, and finally an A" section—sung twice—with a modulation for the repeat singing of A"—a half step higher. This is a typical thirty-two-bar pop song. "Crazy" lasts two minutes and forty-four seconds in the key of B flat and then B major for a dramatic and emotional closing.

"The sheet music for 'Crazy'"

"Crazy" opens with a four-bar piano introduction (four beats per measure, in a slow, almost plodding tempo). Then the beat slows for a moment, then speeds up again, in what musicologists call a rubato. Such a slowing-then-speeding-up is used for expressive purposes, and usually conveys strong sentiment. Here is one source of Patsy Cline's emotional expression. Floyd Cramer's nightclub piano and drummer Buddy Harman's sultry brushwork begin; then come the Jordanaires' *do-do-doos*; Harold Bradley's six-string electric bass doubling Bob Moore's stand-up for a clicking tic-tac effect that turns each bass note into a tiny explosion; and finally Patsy herself expressing the misery and confusion in Willie Nelson's lyric by making her voice break and sob. Every element of "Crazy" integrates with the whole, yet each offers an endlessly compelling hook in its own right. These multitudes of musical elements create a whole effect where no listener feels manipulated: Here's just a woman in pain, and somehow, suddenly, wherever we are, we hear her voice again and are swept up with the pain she's feeling at the time of the recording

Most popular music uses a major scale. Minor scales are rare in popular music, but "Crazy" moves immediately to an unstable C minor on *lonely*, so that Patsy can obtain a bluesy quality through frequent use of notes outside the major scale. This iteration establishes the Patsy Cline recording as something different. The second phrase of A, "crazy for feelin' so blue," moves subtly across tones, and almost as an afterthought, moves smoothly back to set up the A' section, which follows the same harmonic pattern as the first: tonic, supertonic, dominant, then tonic (B-flat). This modulation of tonics is repeated in section A", to be a variant of the first and second sections. The main difference can be heard in increased rhythmic and harmonic motion that add a great deal more complexity. Patsy Cline's verbal outburst of "I'm crazy for tryin' and crazy for cryin'" is set to a stepwise, descending set of harmonies, and the resolution is postponed to the end of the phrase, which closes with a three-measure tag in the new key.

"Crazy" is characteristic of the late Patsy Cline style, with a wide range of vocal intonation and numerous melodic leaps, notably the downward one on the first word ("Crazy") and the upward one on "for feelin." When arranging from the demo, Bradley masterfully combined the main rhythmic motif with two contrasting melodic motifs. "Crazy, crazy, I knew, someday" features descending intervals, while "lonely" and "wanted" ascend. Patsy sings broken chords, conveying tension and frustration. The rhythmic material of "Crazy" is remarkably economical, through repetition and variation, combined with melodic contrast, as Bradley arranged for the listener a sense of familiarity without monotony.

The "crazy motif" also has variants. It can be preceded by an eighth-note upbeat, by a grace note (a small ornamentation on another note; it usually is very, very short, about a thirty-second note, and is played slightly before another note.) Floyd Cramer's piano further abridges the crazy motif to merely a grace note and then a downbeat. Patsy often parallels the piano's grace notes with an upward slide into the first pitch, either on the beat, or after the beat. Her use of grace notes offers a distinctive vocal ornament, further defining the complexity of the Patsy Cline singing style.

It takes great skill and practice to sing grace notes that occur of short duration before singing the relatively longer lasting note that immediately follows. How did Patsy Cline learn this rare skill? She listened to Big Band and Jazz singers on the radio, and then sought to imitate them. She practiced and practiced even more. She then gauged audience reaction at Moose Hall gigs and on television. That is, she taught herself.

Owen Bradley knew Patsy's vocal skills instinctively, and patterned the instrumental makeup and arrangement to fit her vocal skills. In short, Bradley rearranged Willie Nelson's demo tape for Patsy Cline's vocal "comfort zone." Bradley made sure Patsy Cline would be using the strongest and most beautiful part of her voice most of the time. Thus, Patsy Cline's "Crazy" is personalized for her with subtle but pervasive alterations to the pitches and rhythms found on Willie Nelson's demo.

Bradley had Patsy sing off the steadiness of the session players with an elastic sense of rhythm, delaying entrances, stretching and shortening note lengths, and thus resynchronizing with the other musicians just often enough that it seems like a collaboration. Her first line demonstrates this well. "I'm" and "feel" line up with the instrumentals, but little else does. She delays the second "crazy" until after the Jordanaires hit their specified chord, then rushes to get to "feelin'" on time. She delays the next words, "so lonely," for emphasis, so that both words fall after the downbeat. Because she interrupts the last syllable ("ly") with a break, her sustained vocal offers a postponement of 1½ beats, or roughly, a full second. This hanging back conveys emotional fragility, as if the singer struggles a moment for composure.

Patsy's musical accompaniment drops back to underscore this feeling: "so lonely" has only drums, bass, and shimmering steel guitar for most of the measure. (The accompaniment creates a similar effect at the same point in the A" section, when she sings "could hold you.") Patsy Cline's rhythmic liberties nuance what would otherwise be a clear-cut distinction between the triplet motif and its variants, and occasionally between the two motifs themselves. Her rubato and her musical ornaments Patsy Cline's vocal style contained at least four common vocal ornaments: mordants, trills, glissandi, and swoops.

A *mordant* is a musical ornament in which a principal tone is rapidly alternated with the tone a half or full step away.

A *trill* is a rapid alternation between a melodic indicated note and the one above.

A *glissando* (plural *glissandi)* is the rapid scale achieved by sliding the nail of the thumb or third finger over the white keys of the piano. This is what Floyd Cramer called a slip-note.

A *swoop* is a rapid sliding up or down the musical scale. Like a glissando, the swoop creates extra rhythmic spaces by pushing ahead and hanging back.

In the last five beats of the B section of "Crazy," Cline hits the listener with ornaments, one after the other: A mordant precedes the held G of "do," which soon gives way to the song's only glissando, which ends in a growl on an inserted neighbor tone (1:28 to 1:36 on the recording). Patsy Cline also trills and swoops in "Crazy," as the other musicians, including the Jordanaires, keep strict time. Only pianist Cramer accompanies her with matching ornaments.

In "Crazy," the most important session player is Floyd Cramer. He offers a sort of duet with Patsy Cline; prefigures her ornamentation, has much more variety in rhythmic and melodic figures than other band members, and lends a bluesy feel especially with grace notes. Cramer has the lead melody in the introduction, during solo breaks between eight-bar sections, and in the coda. Cramer plays tinkles in the highest register, adding intensity and a breadth of range.

In short, Patsy Cline's recording of "Crazy" is complex music making. It was part of Bradley's skill set that he could hear in his brain a new version beyond what Willie Nelson's demo contained. Bradley figured out what he could do with Patsy Cline's singing, his team of musicians, and the Jordanaires. He tossed out Willie Nelson's phrasing and rearranged "Crazy" for Patsy and his selected session players.

Harold Bradley recalled for the August 2003 issue of *Mix* magazine the configuration of the musicians and singers that his brother used to record "Crazy." Owen Bradley had set up his control room beside the back door to the Quonset hut. Patsy stood one-third of the way into the sonic space, away from that door, near Harold Bradley on electric bass. Floyd Cramer played a piano placed about two feet in front of Harold Bradley but behind Patsy Cline. Bob Moore on acoustic bass stood five feet to Harold Bradley's left, and drummer Buddy Harman was five feet from Harold Bradley's other side. All were enclosed in "shed" houses, to prevent bleeding into Patsy Cline's singing. These sheds were four feet high and consisted of boards on rollers. At the other end of the space stood the Jordanaires.

Owen Bradley sought to create a record to meet the goal of Decca management, which told him that "I Fall to Pieces" was a little too country, so could he could make the next one a little more acceptable to cosmopolitan radio stations. What he did with the complexity of "Crazy" by Walter Everett's detailed musical analysis was so rare and so special that Everett cites Patsy's singing as *the* example of the use of ornamentation in pop music from 1955 to 1969. Patsy Cline had learned her lessons from the radio well—and Owen Bradley ingeniously tapped into her considerable skills.

As an aspiring pop singer, Virginia Hensley taught herself to sing for a mass audience in the United States. To sing like Jo Stafford, she had to jettison any level of Southern accent she had developed. She did that with her self-training, and after 1951, when she turned to country music singing, she had never developed a southern-twang singing style. As Patsy Cline, she sang country music sounding like a pop singer. Owen Bradley encouraged this. Decca New York bosses loved Patsy's skill to appeal to C&W audiences, as well as rock and pop music fans.

Her vocal English offended some C&W purists, but not Decca or Bradley. In fact, they admired her ability to sing non-hillbilly English. This took practice. In 1939 when a British movie star, Vivien Leigh, was preparing for her role as Scarlett O'Hara in *Gone with the Wind,* she worked hard to develop an accent that would evoke the languid plantation life of the antebellum South. A southern drawl makes one-syllable words sound like two syllables. Pronunciation of words such as *bait* becomes *bay-uht, bid* becomes *bee-uhd, and bed* turns into *bay-uhd.* One need not be a trained linguist to think that Hank Williams was a southerner. His southern nasal twang labeled him a country singer; when Tony Bennett covered Hank Williams, Bennett sounded like a pop singer singing a great song.

Vowel pronunciation became the major component of the southern accent. To appeal to national audiences, Patsy sang the number *nine* in the non-southern way. For mass-marketing, professional pop singers in the United States tended to downplay their southern accents if they wanted to work regularly on a national basis. Patsy Cline had long studied pop singing star Jo Stafford, always praised for her clearly articulated non-Southern singing.

With Patsy's recordings, fans across the United States—and later, around the world—had no trouble listening to and loving Patsy's singing. Indeed, Linda Echols Perry, of suburban Washington, DC, taught English as a second language by playing Patsy Cline recordings. Perry told students in her instruction manual, "Patsy Cline's music endures today because of her warm, expressive voice." In 2002, Perry claimed she was having great success, as nonnative students embraced Patsy Cline's singing and learned to evoke her accentless English.

When Patsy was performing in the South, she could evoke a southern accent, as country fans expected, when speaking to her audience. Southern fans expected her to speak as they did. And she did. For example, consider her speaking on an Atlanta, Georgia, local TV C&W show, recorded a week after her performance at Carnegie Hall: "Oh I tell ya. Your cuttin' up tonight." She knew fans in Georgia used *your cuttin' up* to stand for *you're having a good time,* and *ya* was southern speak for *you.*

And then she sang – as she recorded -- in her accentless voice. After the song ended, Patsy Cline's act returned to Southern-speak: "Ah, granny, this ain't like New York but it's uptown. . . . They sittin' up there stompin' their feet and yellin' just like a bunch hillbillies, just like we do. . . . We were auffally proud of havin' the opportunity to go up there in high cotton." This is Patsy Cline seeking an identity with the Georgia audience, with *high cotton* translating as "citified."

To make extra money, Patsy created recruiting radio shows for all major branches of the U.S. military: the Army, Air Force, Navy, and Marine Corps. These were sent to radio stations across the United States. For example, in November 1956, a male announcer began, after theme music, "It's the Country Hoedown, brought to you by your local Navy recruiter." Later when asked to read an advertisement for the U.S. Navy to recruit women, Patsy read, in accentless English, "Have you ever noticed the attractive WAVE officers' uniform? It's really a beauty. An outfit that any young lady would wear with pride. Today the new Navy needs more smart women to serve in the Navy WAVES." She read the text as written, with no *y'alls,* as a southern audience might expect. Her accentless English was necessary because this recruitment show was to be broadcast by stations in the North, South, East, and West.

Patsy Cline's rarest recording of her speaking came when she spoke to Arthur Godfrey on national television. In early 1958, per Godfrey's request, she read from an award she had won: "The Billboard Award for outstanding achievement in recorded music presented to Patsy Cline voted by America's disc jockeys as the most promising country and western female artist of 1957." Then Godfrey asked his announcer, Tony Marvin, to read the next award. Marvin, a New York City– based speaker, did what his boss requested, and there again was no accent. Then Godfrey asked, "Any more?" "Well I received a couple more, also. From the *Country and Western* magazine for the new number one female singer of 1957 and also the juke box vendors magazine for the 1957's new most played on records girl singer." Arthur Godfrey offered his congratulations, and Patsy, on cue, responded: "I would like to say that this wouldn't have happened if I hadn't come before the folks to get across the whole United States on your program." Her speech would seem "normal" all across the United States.

Thus, Patsy Cline not only trained herself as a pop singer but trained herself to sing country music without an accent. This certainly proved a source of her universal appeal. Critic after critic, as praise, remarked that Patsy Cline was a country singer who did not sound like a country singer. Indeed. Bradley made complex pop music that sought to appeal to all listeners of pop music. Fans who bought her recordings after the success of the movie *Coal Miner's Daughter* loved her as another skilled pop singer.

Four decades after her death, on an international Web site, a fan wrote from Brazil, "I just had to write since I've been a fan of Patsy Cline's for a long, long time. One thing I bet the rest of you didn't ever think about, native English speakers like I also am, is that Patsy Cline is one of the few American singers that can be understood easily by non-native English speakers. My husband, a Brazilian, fell in love with Patsy Cline not only because her music and her voice were so beautiful but because it was so easy to understand her!" So the accentless singing also pushed her sales internationally, an economic trait Decca management loved.

What, specifically, about the music made it so appealing? In the final chapter of Daniel J. Levitin's *This Is Your Brain on Music: The Science of a Human Obsession* (New York: Penguin, 2006), the author teaches the reader that the music instinct serves as evolution's number one hit. Why, many have asked, does the human species even need music? Levitin ends his book with three key sentences: "As a tool for activation of specific thoughts, music is not as good as language. As a tool for arousing feelings and emotions, music is better than language. The combination of singing and music making is best understood as found in the love song—and its use in courtship rituals."

For cognitive psychologists, courtship leads to reproduction of the species, which provides an essential basis for the theory of evolution. Certain human skills and traits—notably, like singing—have evolved because of the singular advantages they offer in wooing a mate. Creating new music involves a display of human flexibility to new circumstances and an ability to solve problems, for example, Patsy Cline's use of musical ornaments. Singing and making music, as cognitive skills, developed into meaningful patterns to engage the attention of other humans, to find compatible mates. Because they needed courtship appeals, humans evolved built-in incentives to learn to articulate forms of singing. This can be best appreciated by the music of Elivis to the Beatles which would kick off a wave of nostalgia a generation later, as now settled Baby Boomers remembered the singing that was affiliated with their courtship.

Patsy and Owen Bradley tried to create new pop music. By understanding the norms of singing and making music, humans use their intelligence to praise the skill, daring, and emotional power of music makers. Pop singing never started from scratch; rather, it recombined elements already developed by live singers on the vaudeville circuits. Such a tradition reached a mass audience by recordings and radio. To attract attention, singing and music making through the twentieth century—the age of recording— have exploited constant variation. Patsy simply started from a different base than the one expected from country music singers. She grew up, not with the Grand Ole Opry stylings but with Big Band jazz music made for middle-class white audiences across the United States. She never abandoned this style, even as she was publicized as a C&W singer. Owen Bradley placed the Patsy Po stylings on record to differentiate the nard country coming from his Nashville studio. For southerners, Bradley already had Kitty Wells and Loretta Lynn. Bradley wanted to make Patsy Cline something different.

New musical variations activate the same parts of the brain that create a neurochemical "cocktail" with other pleasurable activities, like laughing at comedic wit or eating chocolate. Cognitive psychologists assert that most people in Western society use music to regulate moods, and Patsy's "torch songs" calmed those frustrated when faced with the social contradictions of courtship. Thus, she appealed to an audience beyond typical country music fans.

What is the secret of music's strange power? Evolution suggests that human minds have been trained to love music. More than forty thousand years ago, early humans were playing sophisticated bone flutes and percussive instruments. In the fall of 2008, in a cave in southwestern Germany, archeologists found early homo sapiens' sophisticated bone pipes with five finger holes. This discovery suggests that this early civilization was musically oriented. And the singing of myths helped pass down ancient tales over time. Even the Bible needed music to make verses accessible for mass religion.

Patsy Cline taught herself to sing. Cognitive psychologists now have evidence from a number of biographically based research studies that singing offers no exception to the general rule that "practice makes perfect." Patsy Cline had been singing day after day since the early 1940s. Her exceptional skill is something that developed gradually through practice—a minimum of 10,000 hours. It is not very easy for a young person to accumulate ten thousand hours of practice. To get some idea of the workload that figure implies, consider that accumulating ten thousand hours would require two hours every day of the year for fourteen years.

Patsy practiced at four times that rate. A person committed to practice, often for economic reasons, sees performing and practice as an essential part of life—in Patsy's case, a way out of poverty.

This contrasts with the talent myth, which posits humans are born with "natural talent." In contrast, cognitive psychologists have concluded that music-making ability is a general characteristic of the human species, rather than a rare talent. Virtually every member of any society is capable of listening to and understanding music, even if he or she cannot read notes, which are written for experts. Collective music experience has historically served to promote feelings of group togetherness. But expert singing requires an extraordinary commitment to practice.

For Patsy playing the piano and singing, and constantly listening to the radio and singing the words and melodies she heard, proved key. The innovation of radio was crucial, as Virginia Hensley practiced by singing along with the Jo Straffords who populated the radio air waves through the 1940s and into the 1950s.

Cognitive psychologists have also found that parents of complex singers were less accomplished musically than the parents of average children. These same studies found that complex singers were motivated to practice, practice, practice. The rich qualitative data suggest a socioeconomic motivation for persons wanting to practice. Frank Sinatra did it in a city, Johnny Cash on a farm, and Virginia Hensley in town and country. She stepped up her practice as she sought to earn money for her fatherless family by singing. And these new studies by cognitive psychologists stress self-teaching—particularly by persons of color and females who were not expected to perform music for a living.

As Daniel J. Levitin writes in *A World in Six Songs* (New York: Penguin 2008), we can best understand music as coming in six basic forms. One is the love song, which binds humans together as they express love desired, love found, and love lost. The last of these was the Patsy Cline specialty: ballads of heartache, as encouraged by Owen Bradley. For fans of Patsy Cline, she walked after midnight thinking of lost love, she fell to pieces because of a lost love, she was driven crazy, and she laments that "she's got you" —all in hit songs. Patsy Cline's recordings proved to be so skillfully performed so that listeners could feel with her, and that emotional tug of lost love is universal, argue cognitive psychologists who have studied music making. A basic idea of cognitive psychological analysis of music posits that sad people are made to feel better by sad songs.

The skill in singing about love lies in sounding honest. And as cognitive psychologists have demonstrated, humans believe that a message of love found or love lost comes through more honestly with singing than with speaking. A great singer can make us feel a truth of love lost even if she does not necessarily feel sad. For reasons even cognitive psychologists admit they do not fully understand, humans seem exquisitely sensitive to the emotional state of singers.   Levitin posits that love songs reflect four stages of human to human love: I want you, I got you, I miss you, and it is over and I am heart broken. Patsy Cline sang about themes between love missed and love lost. Owen Bradley succeeded with Patsy when he matched her with such songs whether written by Tin Pan Alley's Irving Berlin and Cole Porter, or Nashville's Hank Cochran and Willie Nelson. Patsy complexly walks the themes in her recordings of emotional fragility, of missing her lost love, and of dealing with the fact that her relationship is over.

Her singing style convinces the listener that she deeply cares and that caring affects her mental state and emotional state as she sings. Patsy Cline possessed the skill to make listeners feel her caring about love missed and lost, and taught herself to sing this in a complex fashion. She benefitted from the changes in recording techniques; since the listener hears this with both ears (stereo) from one track Patsy's vocals flood their brains. She makes listeners feel human by lamenting what seem to be her own tragedies, and she sings so skillfully that fans honestly believe she is simply emoting, not expressing well-worn clichés.

Music's origins functioned as part of public events and promoted social solidarity. And Patsy Cline had practiced at dances at fraternal organizations. But with radio, the solitary listener depended on new electronics and was therefore historically a newcomer. Music's function changed in the late twentieth century, as millions listened alone to Patsy Cline "singing to them."

With the advent of modern recording studios—which Owen Bradley pioneered— we can listen to a well-crafted, "ideal" performance, not available at any live venue. And this advanced modern recording enables new fans to emerge for singers no longer alive. Critics of recorded music are right to point out that repeatedly hearing a particular performance may cause the listener to think that the interpretation that she or he has become accustomed to is the only possible one. Bradley's use of Patsy's complex singing has made her an auteur, even though she never wrote any of her songs.

This modern technology has also enabled listeners to come to terms with complex music through repeated listening. The Owen Bradley combination of Patsy's singing, surrounded by skilled instrumentalists and matched vocal backups, offers a familiar but complex sound. Metaphorically we might call Patsy's singing smoky, silky, and sultry, using a voice that pulls the listeners in and makes them "live" the lyrics emotionally. But her singing was carefully crafted to do just this. As Owen Bradley has reminded us, he was making records that would sell at the time and decades later.

Bradley took a pop genre, the "torch" song, with lyrics of heartache involved in the ritual of courting in the United States, and made it appeal to a wide spectrum of fans. Patsy and Owen Bradley were big part of the constant historical evolution of popular music in the United States. They sought to make and sell something new and different. Elvis led the way into this pop/rock split and as Walter Everett correctly argues, he changed forever the aesthetic of popular music. Genre divides were torn down, and with Patsy's voice, Owen Bradley led Patsy into another musical world.

Yet, a tradition of change has never been absent from country music. For example, in 1949, Ernest Tubb created a quartet with a pop trio, the Andrews Sisters, for "I'm Bitin' My Fingernails and Thinking of You." George Jones recorded with R&B great Ray Charles, with rockers Elvis Costello and Keith Richards. Willie Nelson has sung with, among others, Duane Eddy, Diana Krall, Aerosmith's Steve Tyler,

Wyclef Jean, ZZ Top, and Julio Iglesias. And Johnny Cash, on his TV show, sang with many varied artists -- including duets with jazz great Louis Armstrong, teen rockers Derek and the Dominos, R&B legend Stevie Wonder, and pop icon Neil Diamond. Popular music embraced and transformed country music, and Owen Bradley and Patsy led the way.

Cognitive psychologists in the twenty-first century place what Patsy and Owen Bradley did at the core of musical engagement distributed throughout the brain. The singing of Patsy Cline, with its complexity within popular norms, taps into a long-evolved wiring of the human brain.

New musical variations retune the brain, so that more cells respond best to complex sounds, in whatever musical genres. The human brain stores the learned importance of varying musical stimuli by devoting more brain cells to the processing of those stimuli. The long-term memory effects of brain retuning explain why anyone familiar with Patsy Cline can immediately recognize her Owen Bradley recordings even in a room filled with hundreds of humans conversing.

The choice of music thus has important social consequences. Particularly when humans are young, and in search of an identity and a mate, they form groups that they believe they have something in common with. As a way of externalizing the bonds, they dress alike, share activities, and listen to the same music. This ties all of us into the evolutionary idea of music as a vehicle for social bonding and societal cohesion. Music and musical preferences become a mark of personal and group identity, and of distinction. To some degree, we might say that personality characteristics are associated with, or predictive of, the kind of music that people like. While the average woman was settling down and raising a family, as gender roles demanded in the 1950s, Patsy Cline was singing to please young men and women who were courting.

To a certain extent, all humans surrender psychologically to music when they listen to it. Even when music doesn't transport humans to a transcendent emotional place, music usually changes human moods. This is why filmmakers use it to establish mood within sequences, even if there is no source for the music in the story line. Music fans are understandably reluctant to let down their guard and embrace just any singer. But as more and more people heard "Patsy Cline," they have embraced her recordings and thus have kept purchasing them. This added of course has added to her iconic status.

Accessible recordings lead to fandom for certain popular musicians, whether the Grateful Dead, the Beatles, or Patsy Cline. Listeners learn "Patsy Cline," and then turn to her to lift their spirits during a blue mood, to comfort them in times of stress, and to inspire them. They let her into their ears, directly, through earbuds and headphones, when they're not communicating with anybody else in the world. And then, in the twenty-first century, they shared these feelings—one step removed from face-to-face reality—by sharing their thoughts on the Internet.

When a musical piece sounds too simple, new listeners tend not to like it, finding it trivial. When it is too complex, listeners tend not to like it, either, finding it unpredictable, not grounded in anything familiar. Popular music has to strike the right balance between simplicity and complexity in order for fans to embrace it. Simplicity and complexity relate to familiarity, and familiarity is just another word for a schema, which is how cognitive psychologists distinguish their theory of brain activity. We listen through our ears; we hear with our brains.

Singers and musicians who practice many hours a day for years exhibit a certain hyperdevelopment of certain areas in their brains that nonpracticed singers and players do not have. So for example, when musicians who worked with Owen Bradley listened to his instructive piano playing, about 25 percent more of left-hemisphere auditory regions responded than would have in nonmusicians. This effect is specific to musical tones and does not occur with similar but nonmusical sounds. Creating music requires significant brain work. Patsy Cline was not an educated woman by traditional standards, but her brain was a well-trained one, self-trained to fashion sounds few of us can even imagine making.

Once Owen Bradley discovered Patsy's skills, he taught her to do new stylings. He took advantage of neuroplasticity, or the ability of the brain to reorganize itself. She was remarkably quick to learn. And just as some people can heal faster than others, so, too, can some people forge new brain connections more easily than others. This was Patsy Cline's "talent."

Each musical genre has its own set of rules and its own forms. The more fans listen, the more those rules and forms become instilled in their brains' memory. Unfamiliarity with the structure can lead to frustration; usually new songs fit a category. But there can be new variations that are "fuzzy" members of an older category. Patsy Cline was sold as country because of her contract with Decca, but was not really country. She was as "fuzzy" as one could be and still work as a country singer.

One of the reasons that people are willing to make themselves vulnerable to a musician like Patsy Cline is that she herself often seems vulnerable to them. Owen Bradley tapped this vulnerability when he constructed his sessions with Patsy. She had learned to convey vulnerability through her singing in Bradley sessions. The power and appeal of her singing is that it can connect humans to larger truths about what it means to be alive and what it means to be human. Listening to Patsy sing about "Faded Love," all who have engaged in courtship can remember lost relationships. She sings about losing love, and this theme resonates with them. We hear her vulnerability, and it brings us all closer to Patsy Cline. Thus, new fans come into being.

In sum, cognitive psychologists argue music's function in sexual selection is key to a most meaningful stage in life. Music's evolutionary origin is present across all humans (meeting the biologists' criterion of being widespread in a species). The courtship ritual involves specialized brain structures, including dedicated memory systems that can remain functional when other memory systems fail. When, in the twenty-first century, Web sites began to promise to help people find mates, there was one called Rocknrolldating.com, which included Patsy Cline recordings. The Web site recognized the relevance of music compatibility in relationships, stating, "Ever gone out with someone only to find that their tastes in music are so far off the mark, that you couldn't imagine being in a long-term relationship with them?" This site helped singles who liked certain singers or groups find relationship matches on the Internet. Music plays an important part in all lives of all humans.

─────────────

Music therapy reaches the inner brain. So, for example, when the hospice nurse first suggested to Bill Blake that music therapy might be helpful for his wife, Delores, his first thought was, "It'll be a waste of time." Delores was only in her fifties, but she had advanced Alzheimer's and hadn't spoken in a long time. That changed the day the music therapist came over with her guitar and a microphone. When they were younger, Bill and Delores had loved to sing karaoke, and the therapist was trying to recreate that time. The therapist started singing "Crazy," a song that Delores had loved, and then put the microphone in Delores's hand. Suddenly, Delores was no longer silent and unresponsive. Her face lit up and she sang every word of the song. "It was unbelievable, a miracle." This offers but one example documented by Levitin and other cognitive scientists.

This connection hinged on the vocal color of Patsy Cline's voice. Her unique timbre, Daniel J. Levitin believes, lies at the center of the power of music during the late twentieth century as millions of fans learned it from the recordings they could easily access. Patsy Cline's vocal timbre has long been associated with the slow tempo of sadness at failed courtship. Tribute singers have continually proved that Patsy Cline's vocal timbre was unique. But on timbre, cognitive psychologists have little to say, other than that it stands as the next frontier of brain research.

Timbre (pronounced tamber) is the quality of a musical sound that distinguishes one instrument from another, or in this case, Patsy Cline from Billie Holiday. The physical characteristics of sound that mediate the perception of timbre include its color, pitch, and volume. When recorded by Owen Bradley and surrounded by a vocal group and instrumentation, the Patsy Cline vocal timbre becomes the center of the recording.

Patsy Cline's session recordings established a standard version of many songs. Once these sessions were played and replayed, then even the composer Willie Nelson lost control of a song he composed; he was reduced to simply being the composer of *the* prototypical version of "Crazy." Millions have heard the official session version by

Patsy Cline, and encoded this as the "correct" version. Listeners store the correct version of "Crazy" in their brains, and recognize how close a tribute artist might be to the "real" Patsy Cline song. They encode the ornaments of her voice, the timbre of her voice, and the sonic tone of the Bradley studio. This is what makes her fans experts. They cannot create a Patsy Cline session, but have stored what she did and note that no one can replicate her recording. These recordings—as we have learned and stored them—have become the basis of her growing popularity after her death.

No wonder Patsy Cline's singing has appealed to ensuing generations. It was sonically recorded so well that it still sounds "clean" and digital, as if made today. It was complex popular music, which required the listener to feel it, but not so complex as to overwhelm the listener. Patsy Cline's (as recorded by Owen Bradley) is popular music at its best, and its appeal is universal.

Chapter 8

Keeping Patsy Cline in Circulation After Her Death

The death of Patsy Cline, on Tuesday, March 5, 1963, in an airplane crash ended her recording and performing career. She was a popular singer but was hardly a major star – nothing like her iconic status of the late twentieth century. So in early March 1963, the crash was just a short-lived radio and newspaper story. Patsy died before network TV even offered thirty minutes of nightly news. Most fans heard about the crash on the radio or read about it almost a day after it happened.

Hilda Hensley remembered, "[My daughter] called me that day (March 5, 1963) and said, 'I'm still out here—we're fog-bound. The fog should be lifting soon. Mama, I'll get back to you.'" The next morning, when the phone rang at 605 South Kent Street, in Winchester, Virginia, Hilda thought it was Patsy calling back. Instead it was a radio DJ calling Hilda for her reaction to Patsy's death in the plane crash. Hilda Hensley went into a state of shock; Patsy was only thirty years old. Hilda, her son and daughter, and other family members then drove for 12 hours to get to Nashville (no one wanted to fly), where a memorial service was held on Friday. March 8. Then Patsy Cline's body was flown back to Winchester, and the funeral was held the following Sunday afternoon.[1]

Since the crash site was not discovered until after dawn on March 6, most people heard the news on the radio later that morning. Newspapers did not report it until that afternoon, and morning papers, like the *New York Times* and the *Washington Post*, were not able to print the story until the following day.

George Hamilton IV recalled, "I was at home in Nashville [on the morning after the crash] and a [radio] DJ from my home town of Winston-Salem [North Carolina] telephoned me to ask for my reaction to 'the news.' I asked rather tersely what 'news' he was talking about and the DJ went on to tell me. . . ." Like everyone who had worked with Patsy Cline, Hamilton was stunned; he knew all four in the plane: forty-nine-year-old "Cowboy" Copas, forty-two-year-old Hawkshaw Hawkins, thirty-four- year-old Randy Hughes 34, and of course Patsy, age thirty, who was the youngest and best known. Hamilton remembered, "When I went to bed the night before, none of [my family] had even heard that Patsy's plane was in trouble or missing."[2]

Kathy Copas Hughes, wife of Randy Hughes and daughter of Cowboy Copas, found out the same way Hilda Hensley did—from a call from a radio DJ. Starting at 6:20 a.m., a search party found the small plane. Its contents and passengers were crushed into small parts as the plane had plunged to earth in such a tight vertical spiral that it destroyed only a single tree, leaving a crater about six feet deep, filled with water from the rain.

After landing in Dyersburg, Tennessee, Hughes, the pilot, had been advised to expect limited visibility and isolated thunderstorms, and was advised to drive the 170 miles to Nashville. But his passengers urged him to take a risk. He took off, flew about 100 miles, lost control, and crashed. To hide the gruesome scene from the public, Raymer Stockdale, of Stockdale and Milan Funeral Home, located in Camden,

Tennessee, quickly cleared the scene of the remains. He later stated, in the formal investigation, that he had made identification of the men by their billfolds but that "Patsy was not very well identified." The cause: Hughes,

a non-instrument pilot attempting visual flight in adverse weather conditions, resulting in a loss of control.[3]

Music's Broken Wings: Fifty Years of Aviation Accidents in the Music Industry, self-published in 2003 by William P. (Phil) Heitman, an experienced flight instructor and an avid popular music fan, concludes that the crash was identical to the February 3, 1959, private plane accident that killed Buddy Holly, Richie Valens, and the Big Bopper. In both cases, an inexperienced pilot had experienced disorientation that led to swift death. Hughes quickly lost total "situational awareness." Within three minutes, Randy Hughes went from flying his plane to being little more than a helpless passenger as gravity took over.

Heitman cites a research study conducted by the University of Illinois that the average time for a pilot to become spatially disoriented is less than three minutes. A publication called *FAA* [Federal Aeronautics Administration] *Aviation News* paints a chilling but short scenario: "178 Seconds to Live." Hughes piloted his airplane into clouds, expecting to come out into sunshine after a few seconds. Instead Hughes remained inside the clouds with no land markers— or even the horizon—to guide him. Not knowing what to do, he accelerated straight ahead. Or so he thought.

Instead of flying parallel to the earth, he was headed directly toward the ground. He had no idea that he had about one hundred seconds to do something; so instinctively he sped up his airplane—and seconds later, crashed. Hughes unknowingly had entered "a graveyard spiral." On May 20, 1964, the Federal Aeronautics Administration issued a report concluding that "poor judgment" explained the crash.[4]

Why the rush? On March 3, the quartet had stayed in Kansas City, Kansas, after the late Sunday night benefit show. They tried to leave on Monday March 4, 1963 from Kansas City but were not permitted to fly out because the airport was closed—fogged in. The flight was postponed until Tuesday morning and then delayed until Tuesday afternoon. At about 1:30 p.m., Hughes started off and flew at full speed, about 120 miles per hour, so that he could stay ahead of the edge of the front as he flew across Missouri and then south, following the Mississippi River. Hughes stopped after 3 ½ hours in Dyersburg, Tennessee, to refuel.[5]

Why were the four in Kansas City, Kansas? To do two Sunday benefit shows at the three-thousand-seat Soldiers & Sailors Memorial Building, which was filled to near capacity with fans who had paid $1.50 admission to hear Patsy and the other acts and to raise money for the family of DJ Cactus Jack Call, who had died in a car accident on January 25 of that year. Promoter Harry A. "Hap" Peebles, the most powerful booker in the Midwest, organized and emceed the show. Mildred Keith knew Peebles and was able to go backstage to meet Patsy Cline, after which Mildred recalled, "When we got to the steps, she was getting ready to go on-stage, and it dawned on me, I said 'Patsy, could I get one picture?' And she said 'Sure.' And she just stopped and I just took the one picture. She then went on and she did that show and I'm telling you, she just brought the house down."

This event was just another gig on the road. The *Kansas City Star* didn't even cover Patsy Cline's appearances. The *Star* printed only ads for the Sunday show. Through radio publicity, the two shows raised three thousand dollars for Jack Call's widow and family.[6]

It had been a busy weekend, as Patsy had played gigs in New Orleans, Birmingham, Alabama, and finally Kansas City. On Saturday, March 2, just after breakfast, Patsy Cline, Randy Hughes, and Charles Dick left New Orleans after the Friday gig, bound for Birmingham, Alabama, to do two sold-out shows Saturday evening. Hughes had negotiated three thousand dollars for these two shows. Roy Orbison opened for Patsy. As one fan said, "Boutwell Auditorium was the place to be for big shows, especially the WVOK Parade of Stars." This hall held six thousand fans and so provided one of the single best pay-dates in Patsy Cline's career.[7]

On Sunday, March 3, again after breakfast, Hughes flew Patsy and Charles Dick to Nashville so that Charles could get off and be with Randy, his and Patsy's twenty-five-month-old son, who was sick, and return to work on Monday. A copy of the March 3 Kansas City program lists an all-star group: Patsy Cline, George Jones, Cowboy Copas, Hawkshaw Hawkins, and Dottie West. While the unpaid benefit show that featured country stars has been used to define her career, more typical was the Roy Obison date in Birmingham was far more typical of her gigs in 1963.[8]

A reporter for the March 7 (Nashville) *Tennessean* noted, "I have deliberately decided to refrain from discussion of too much detail of the remains of the crashed airplane and the people involved out of respect for the families." But all this absence of detail did was to open the doors for mythologizing the crash. Millions of words have been created to explain a simple act of incompetence.[9]

On March 6, the *Washington Evening Star* put the AP story on page 1, with only five hundred words of reporting. Other newspapers reprinted this story, with little additional detail. By March 7, the news was considered so old that even the *Frederick* (Maryland) *Post,* based where Patsy Cline had once lived, placed it on page 18, well inside the newspaper. [10]

On March 6, the *Winchester Star* printed on its obituary page that the burial would take place at Shenandoah Memorial Park, south of Winchester. In 1957, Bob Casey had purchased a farm and made it a new cemetery, affordable for working-class folk. Casey's thirty-two-acre cemetery had identical plaques flush with the ground and inexpensive to maintain. Doris Casey, Bob's wife, later recalled Patsy's service as the largest in the history of the cemetery: "Cars were lined up on both sides of Front Royal Pike back to [downtown] Winchester." As the twenty-first century started, Cline's grave was still the most-visited site in the cemetery. [11]

The service, scheduled for Sunday, March 10, at 3:30 p.m., was planned by late Friday night, when in a closed casket, the "body" of Patsy Cline came back to Winchester on a Tennessee National Guard airplane. Her old mentor, Jack Fretwell, was honest enough to say, "Very little of her came back to Winchester; so they had a closed casket." [12]

Jones Funeral Home handled the arrangements. For Laurens and Nancy Jones it was just another job. Later matriarch Nancy Jones stated bluntly, "The most memorable funeral held at [the downtown facility] was that of Patsy Cline, in March 1963." The Jones were not Patsy Cline fans and so did not anticipate that 1,500 people would try to pack into the small chapel the Jones Funeral Hall maintained for nondenominational services. Indeed, the Joneses had scheduled two funerals to be held before Cline's that Sunday. Nancy Jones recalled, "We had people come to the 11 a.m. funeral and stay for the 1 p.m. funeral. Then even more of those people stayed, because they wanted to have a seat for Patsy's funeral at 3 p.m." [13]

On its front page, on Monday, March 11, the *Winchester Evening Star* described a "mob scene." After the service, the Star reported, hundreds of fans stole floral arrangements so they could to get their own Patsy Cline souvenir. The *Star* headlined the story, "They Were Her People," and concluded: "They acted as if it was a 'dollar day' at the department store. It's unlikely that Patsy—killed Tuesday in the crash of a light airplane— would have minded."

Out-of-town newspapers proved less class conscious in describing the events. On Monday, March 11, the *Washington Evening Star*, as conservative as the *Winchester Evening Star* but caring little about the Winchester small-town elite, headlined, "5,000 Attend Winchester Rites for Patsy Cline," and then it simply printed an AP account of a dignified but crowded set of funeral. The Washington paper made no mention of a mob scene; only the Winchester paper reported that. Even the *Northern Virginia Daily*, which was published in Strasburg, just sixteen miles up the Shenandoah Valley from Winchester, handled the account quite differently. Its story began "The Lord is my shepherd; I shall not want. The comforting words of the old Psalm were intoned by Rev. Nathan Williamson as 500 people jammed the chapel of the Jones Funeral Home." The article referred to the service at the cemetery, where "a stately choir sang 'Shall We Gather at the River,'" concluding that the proceedings were very dignified , and that Patsy Cline received a proper burial as the most famous citizen of Winchester.[14]

––––––––––––––

Since Virginia Hensley Dick died with no legal will, the probate process took some time. Under Tennessee law, her husband inherited everything, although on May 14, 1964, Charles Dick revealed that on April 22, 1961, Virginia Hensley Dick had handwritten a will (but never named an executor). Charles asked to be named the executor under Tennessee law. He was. But Charles left Julie and Randy in

Hilda Hensley's care. In July 1965 Charles Dick remarried (and later divorced) an aspiring singer, Jamey Ryan, with whom he had a son, Charles Allen Dick, Jr. After the marriage, he journeyed to Winchester to take his children for a vacation and then never returned them. The sole items Hilda Hensley inherited were a vast number of Patsy Cline outfits and dresses, some of which Hilda herself had made.[15]

In the 2001 interview, Charles Dick said he considered moving back to Virginia after Patsy's death, but country stars Dottie West and Loretta Lynn, as well as their respective husbands, Bill and Mooney, convinced him to stay in Nashville by. A friend named Timothy Hill told Charles about a record-promotion job with Starday records, but Charles said he was unsure about his qualifications. Hill assured Charles that he had already been doing the work for Patsy. Charles applied, got the position, and stayed for eight years. He formally abandoned his work as a Linotype operator.[16]

Hilda Hensley got no part of Patsy's insurance monies, either. In May 1966, the Stuyvesant Insurance Company of Pennsylvania filed for a "declaratory judgment," claiming that it did not have to pay for full damage or personal liability of the insured aircraft while piloted by Randy Hughes, as the federal government reported that the crash was not an accident but simple pilot error. Kathy Hughes, Randy Hughes's widow, along with the executors of the other three estates, filed a $2.5 million suit, asking for $750,000. In the May of 1966, in an out-of-court settlement, Stuyvesant paid each beneficiary $33,333 and another $15,500 to Kathy Hughes.[17]

Thus Hilda Hensley, with no access to money from Patsy, had to find work. She went back to being a seamstress, but legal records and Patsy's relatives also tell of Hilda's attempts to become a restaurant owner. It appears that Hilda opened one restaurant in downtown Winchester, across from City Hall, another on Route 522 South, past the cemetery where her daughter was buried, and possibly one more. Hilda was a good cook, but she lacked business acumen. On July 15, 1971, Hilda Hensley gave up and sold what was left of her venture, called the Third Base. This was a joint venture with Hilda Hensley, her friend Wendell Whitlock, and Arthur Wadsworth, who owned the Terminal café in the bus terminal. Whitlock and Wadsworth bought her out for $2,500, including her equipment.[18]

At age fifty-four, Hilda returned to her work as a seamstress and married. The records at the Winchester City Clerk's office show that Hilda Patterson Hensley and Andrew Marshall Lake married on January 12, 1971, in Hagerstown, Maryland, where eloping Virginia residents went to evade the more restrictive marriage laws of the Commonwealth. Hilda and Andy, as the family called him, then lived together at 605 South Kent while Lake ran the Little Tavern restaurant-bar, about three miles south. By March 3, 1971, they decided that the marriage was a mistake, and Hilda filed for divorce. But on March 12, Hilda withdrew her divorce application. It was not until February 3, 1975, that Lake filed for divorce. By then he was living in Stephens City, Virginia, nine miles from Hilda. Then, four days later, Hilda counter-filed for divorce, and in a deposition on March 7, Hilda admitted that she was still legally Mrs. Lake but called herself Mrs. Hensley. This 1975 divorce proved easy, as no party contested it, and on March 13, Judge Robert Woltz approved the divorce. Patsy's cousin put this in perspective: "Aunt Hilda got married on whim; even her son did not know." So from 1975 to her death in 1998, Hilda Hensley remained mired at the bottom of the socioeconomic ladder, on South Kent Street.[19]

On the corporate level, Decca executives also had been caught off guard, and small labels scrambled to take advantage of the death of Patsy Cline. Within a week, Patsy Cline tribute records began to appear in advertisements. For example, the March 13, 1963, *Auburn* (New York) *Citizen Advertiser* ran an ad for the Family Bargain Center "Patsy Cline" sale. For Decca executives, "Leavin'on Your Mind" was already climbing the charts, and the publicity from the crash sent it to number 8 on the *Billboard* country charts. On April 15, Decca executives chose "Sweet Dreams" to release as the first new post crash single. It climbed the *Billboard* country chart to number 5, on the easy listening chart to number15, and on *Billboard's* pop chart to number 44.[20]

Then, on June 16, Decca released *The Patsy Cline Story,* a two-disc album Decca sought to take advantage of the popularity of "Sweet Dreams" as a single. This twenty-four-cut LP offered nearly sixty-one minutes of singing, and was the first to contain all the now iconic hits: "Walkin' After Midnight" (the 1961 remake), "I Fall to Pieces," "Crazy," and "She's Got You." *The Patsy Cline Story* made it all the way to number 9 on *Billboard's* country albums chart.[21]

This two-disc LP also offered two pages of liner notes, which filled the inside of the two connected record sleeves. The notes were written by Trudy Stamper, of WSM's PR Department, and they became the basis of the Patsy Cline biography. Stampler started with a supposed quotation: "Oh Lord, I sing just like I hurt inside," as the way Patsy Cline supposedly liked to describe her singing, the unabashed emotion that she put into each song. Stampler described her as a country singer who put emotion into all her singing.

In Stampler's characterization, Patsy thought that "hurting" and "loving" were almost synonymous. But Stampler offered few details on Patsy's personal life of struggle. Instead, she quoted Charles Dick as saying that "every day was Christmas!" to portray their marriage.

Stampler stated that Patsy Cline's weakness was "loving all who loved her back." Stampler provided only modest details of Patsy Cline's life before she arrived in Nashville. She cited "a band from Martinsburg, Va."—meaning Bill Peer—and Patsy's frustrations while she auditioned for the *Arthur Godfrey Talent Scouts* show. Stampler did not have time to check that Bill Peer worked in Martinsburg, West Virginia. Nashville became Patsy's Promised Land.

Stampler claimed, "Hers was not a happy childhood, and at sixteen it became necessary for her to leave school and go to work to help support the family." This left out all the details of Patsy's learning Big Band music. Stampler had Patsy Cline singing "everywhere, any place she could, on street corners, in church, in honkytonks, with or without bands, for nickels and quarters, occasionally for dollars . . . but too often, for nothing," ignoring the vital amateur contest experiences and her work with Jack Fretwell and Jumbo Rinker. Then Stampler boldly proclaimed that "At heart, she was a country/western singer."

In the end, Stampler concluded that "for the first time in [Patsy's] life," just before she died, money was not an issue. And aiming proper mythology, the PR writer stated that Patsy was putting her life in financial order, as if she knew she was going to die. Stampler asserted that Patsy Cline left "annuities for both Mom and Charlie." Then Stampler got personal: "I like to think of Patsy as I saw her last. She came by the office only a few days after the June 1961 accident [not possible as Patsy Cline was in Madison Hospital] to tell me about her new album." Stampler exposed her agenda as a public relations expert, writing liner notes to help make the two-disc album sell more copies, with little attention to the actual facts.

On August 5, 1963 Decca followed up the release of *The Patsy Cline Story* two-disc album with the released of "Faded Love" as a single. By Labor Day, Decca had had three top 50 Patsy Cline singles since her death: "Sweet Dreams," "Leavin' on Your Mind" and "Faded Love," which climbed to number 7 on the country charts and made a small dent in the pop charts. Thus, as expected, when on November 1, the twelfth annual Country Music Festival commenced, surveyed DJs voted her *Billboard's* Favorite Female Country Artist and *Cash Box* named her the Most Programmed Country Female Vocalist of 1963. The Juke Box Association of America named her one of the ten most-played artists of 1963, and so Decca executives concluded that the label should continue to regularly release Patsy Cline songs and occasional LPs.[22]

Starting on January 11, 1964, Decca issued "When You Need a Laugh" as a single. "When You Need a Laugh" was written by Hank Cochran, who had co-created "I Fall to Pieces," and "She's Got You," both of her number 1 hits during her lifetime. Decca executives figured that this single had a chance of being another major hit. Instead, the single stopped at number 47 on the *Billboard* country charts. On July 26, 1964, Decca released a new LP: *A Portrait of Patsy Cline,* topped by "Faded Love" and containing eleven tracks of the pop covers that Patsy Cline had recorded with Owen Bradley in February 1963. Decca sold her pop covers as country recordings, as Decca executives—by then taking firm orders from MCA, Decca's new owner—tried to extract money from Patsy Cline fans. Since Owen Bradley produced all these recordings in stereo, they particularly appealed to teenagers around the world, who were then buying cheap stereo record players in increasing numbers.[23]

To keep feeding radio stations with singles, on September 14, Decca released "He Called Me Baby," backed by "Bill Bailey, Won't

You Please Come Home," both from her last two recording sessions. An increasing number of country-formatted radio stations played this single as if it were new, and it climbed to number 23 on *Billboard*'s country singles chart. So again, Decca timed it to capitalize on the publicity coming from the now extensively media-covered CMA meetings, to be held in November 1964. In addition, on November 2, Decca released an LP called *That's How a Heartache Begins,* containing "He Called Me Baby," "Bill Bailey, Won't You Please Come Home," "That's How a Heartache Begins," "Love Letters in the Sand," "Shoes," "Lovesick Blues," and "Lovin' in Vain." This was Decca's Patsy Cline Christmas album, which benefitted from the wave of publicity that the Nashville Sound received from a lengthy article in the November 27 issue of *Time* magazine. *Time* praised Owen Bradley as the top producer in Nashville, and noted, in a single line, that "Patsy Cline records continued to sell long after her death."[24]

Decca kept to its singles strategy but stopped making new LPs. Starting on March 15, 1965, Decca released three "new" singles, starting with "Your Cheatin' Heart." Then, in 1966, Decca issued an additional three singles, then three in 1967 and three in 1968. None charted, but the releases did keep Patsy's sound in circulation. In November 1968, Decca ended its release of Patsy Cline singles, as the vault was empty.[25]

On March 13, 1967, Decca released another LP, *Patsy Cline's Greatest Hits,* and at the time, it peaked at number 17 on *Billboard*'s country albums chart. This release defined the classic Patsy Cline body of work -- including "Walkin' After Midnight"(2nd version), "Sweet Dreams," "Crazy," "I Fall to Pieces," "So Wrong," "Strange," "Back in Baby's Arms," "She's Got You," "Faded Love," "Why Can't He Be You?" "You're Stronger Than Me," and "Leavin' On Your Mind."[26]

The lead article on the front page of the June 8, 1968, issue of *Billboard* reported that *Patsy Cline's Greatest Hits* had sold better than expected, and so Decca issued greatest-hits LPs of Loretta Lynn, Kitty Wells, Red Foley, Ernest Tubb, Bill Monroe, and Jimmie Davis. One can see the firm hand of Lew Wasserman, head of MCA, who was always looking for a way to milk the most revenues from any product that MCA owned. This was Wasserman's initial promotion of *Patsy Cline's Greatest Hits* once he had discovered her popularity from internal sales data. Yet not even Wasserman expected that, when MCA's Decca division reissued the album on CD three decades later, SoundScan would place it at the acme of top-selling "greatest hits" albums of the 1990s.[27]

But Decca controlled only half of Patsy Cline's cuts; the 4-Star company owned the rest. Even before the airplane accident, the new ownership of 4-Star had started licensing its tracks. In May 1960, Bill McCall, who had signed Patsy Cline in September 1954, sold his 4-Star company to former-movie-cowboy-turned-millionaire Gene Autry. The new management, under Autry, gambled they could exploit Patsy Cline. Autry's first deal came with independent record label Everest in 1962, which released a single of "Walkin' After Midnight" (first version) backed with "That Wonderful Someone." It bubbled under the *Billboard* Hot-100 chart for three weeks, peaking at number 108 before Patsy's death.

But this was not the return Autry had expected, and so in April 1963, he sold 4-Star to Joe Johnson. In turn, Johnson started to rent Patsy Cline 4-Star cuts to all who would pay. A new discount LP market was opening up as independent labels compiled "Patsy

Cline" in some manner, created new artwork, and aimed sales at Baby Boomers who were acquiring new stereo systems. Johnson negotiated with Everest management, which late in 1963, released an LP called *In Memoriam*, containing "Walkin' After Midnight" (first version), "Never No More," "I Cried All the Way to the Altar," "Honky Tonk Merry Go Round," "If I Could Only Stay Asleep," "Hidin' Out," "Cry Not for Me," "Walking Dream," "Come On In (and Make Yourself at Home)," "Pick Me Up on Your Way Down," "Let the Teardrops Fall," and "Turn the Cards Slowly." Everest even gained a review in the *Los Angeles Times*.[28]

But the Hilltop and Pickwick discount labels led sales. In 1964 Hilltop released its Patsy 4-Star compilation LP *Today, Tomorrow, and Forever,* which did well enough that, in 1965, Hilltop issued a second Patsy Cline LP, *I Can't Forget You;* in 1966 a third, *Stop the World and Let Me Off;* in 1968 a fourth, *Miss Country Music;* and in 1969 a fifth, *In Care of the Blues.* With these five LPs, fans could acquire and listen to the totality of the 4-Star material for less than ten dollars.[29]

"An example of a Pickwick LP reissue"

While Hilltop issued five LP compilations, in terms of total sales, Pickwick Records did far better, as its technicians refashioned the mono cuts from 4-Star into a crude form of stereo. Indeed, Pickwick specialized in stereo-converted discount LPs. Owner Cy Leslie made considerable profit from discounting and recrafting mono recordings, and in 1977, he was able to cash out for a profit of one million dollars.[30]

New suburban discount stores throughout the United States sold these discount LPs. For example, on September 18, 1963, the *Holland* (Michigan) *Evening Standard* contained an advertisement for Thrifty Acres, a discount store that sold Hilltop Patsy Cline LPs for sixty-nine cents. On October 2 of that year, the *Oxnard* (California) *Press-Courier* printed an ad for Disco Fair, another discount store, which sold Patsy Cline on Pickwick for forty-nine cents. And on November 25, 1964, the *Gettysburg* (Pennsylvania) *Times* ran a full-page ad for the Bargain Town United States store, with Patsy Cline Hilltop and Pickwick LPs for fifty-eight cents. These prices were lower than those that department stores charged for new singles.

What gave rise to this wave of discount stores? All were open on Sundays, when downtown record and department stores were closed. In 1961, in a test case that went all the way to the U.S. Supreme Court, the justices ruled that discount stores had the right to open on Sundays. In *Two Guys from Harrison-Allentown, Inc. v. McGinley* 366 US 568 (1961), the U.S. Supreme Court ruled that discounter Two Guys from Harrison-Allentown was well within its rights to open on Sundays, despite Pennsylvania's blue laws. As the only discount store serving a city of 100,000 people, Two Guys was always mobbed on Sundays. In other states, others successfully challenged other existing blue laws, based on the Two Guys precedent. All sold Patsy Cline discount LPs as one of their drawing cards—loss leaders to get people into the stores and walking their length to the rear, to find the discount LP section.[31]

As Baby Boomers heard Patsy Cline Decca singles on local radio, they drove to discounters for well-advertised specials. For example, on March 10, 1964, the *Corpus Christi* (Texas) *Times* announced the opening of a local Woolco and its "record riot" with "top artist's 45s including Patsy Cline, Kay Starr, and Dinah Washington for 77 cents." On September 8 of that year, the *Bridgeport* (Connecticut) *Telegram* ran a half-page ad for E. J. Korvette's "One Day Sale" with all LPs for fifty-nine cents, including Patsy Cline's. Woolco and E. J. Korvette were the largest chains of discount stores in the eastern part of the United States.[32]

"A 45 rpm re-issue"

Patsy was sold as a pop and C&W singer. On February 18, 1965, the *Albuquerque* (New Mexico) *Tribune* advertised "Furr's Family Center's Quality Merchandise at Discount Prices!" featuring "Famous Artists LPs—both mono and stereo at 67 cents," from Patsy Cline to Nat King Cole to Tony Bennett. On May 6, 1965, the *Appleton* (Wisconsin) *Post Crescent* printed an ad for "Prange's Budget Store—The Store of Lower Prices," featuring a sale of "2,000 popular LP albums at one low price" and prominently displaying an image of Patsy Cline.[33]

On September 24, 1965, the *Cumberland* (Maryland) *Evening Times* profiled the Tri-State Discount Center, which regularly sold all Pickwick and Hilltop LP offerings for ninety-nine cents. Long before Wal-Mart, Tri-State was the place to shop in Cumberland. Trucks constantly arrived with regular shipments of Quaker State oil, bags of peat moss, fertilizer, and boxes of 33 1/3 rpm (revolutions per minute), or LP, discount records. Long lines were a constant, reported one tired worker in 1965. Every month the store featured "circular sales," which had appeared in local newspapers for three days—and which always featured discounted Patsy Cline LPs for ninety-nine cents. Those special sales brought customers to the checkout counters nonstop for hours at a time. One former worker recalled working eight hours straight during one of the "circular sales" before finally getting a break.[34]

By 1967, discounting had even become a retail strategy for chain drug stores. For example, on September 20 of that year, the *Lumberton* (North Carolina) *Robesonian* newspaper a special inset for the opening of a new shopping center, featuring the "Grand Opening Sale" for Eckert's Drug Store , which in turn featured a Pickwick Patsy Cline LP for ninety-nine cents.

Sam Walton began his regional discount store chain in the late 1960s, and on April 16, 1975, the *Blytheville* (Arkansas) *Courier News* carried an ad for "Wal-Mart Discount City," which sold everything, including Pickwick LPs by Patsy Cline for ninety-nine cents. By 1997, Wal-Mart had become the largest retailer in the United States, as Walton's strategy of establishing stores only in small- and medium-size towns allowed him to monopolize local business and avoid the price wars that plagued discounters who built stores across from each other. The 4-Star material created "headlines" with their advertisements. Sales proved brisk—until the advent of the cheap audio cassette during the late 1970s.

During the late 1960s, a technological change made it possible buy eight-track tapes. Listeners could play these paperback-book-size cartridges in their cars, instead of hoping that a radio station would play their favorites. So for example, on July 5, 1969, the *Anderson* (Indiana) *Herald* advertised that the local Arlan's discount store was having a "Dollar-Rama Special" for "new" eight-track stereo cartridges by Patsy Cline; Pickwick had flooded suburban discount stores with low-priced eight-track tapes. By February 24, 1974, the *Lowell* (Massachusetts) *Sun* was advertising that the local Zayre discount store was selling eight-track tapes by Patsy Cline for $1.59 each.

Technologists had always sought some way to play music in autos. Vinyl records and reel-to-reel tapes proved impossible to use because of the size of equipment and problems from the vibration of the automobile. In the late 1960s came what was then heralded as revolutionary—the eight-track cartridge, designed play in the automobile. The car culture of the United States spawned the notion of these tapes as an automotive alternative to playing LPs at home.

Appearing in 1969, and lasting for about a decade, eight-track cartridges dominated in-car listening, and Decca and the low priced labels produced and sold them through discount auto centers. The eight-track technology was developed as a joint venture by the Ampex Magnetic Tape Company, the Lear Jet Company, and RCA Records. On September 15, 1965, Ford Motor Company offered eight-track players as an option for their complete line of 1966 model cars. At first, these tape players were simply an expensive luxury car accessory, but then the discount store auto centers began to offer them at lower prices. Such appendages to discount stores used low-priced eight-track tapes to tempt car owners into adding the players to their autos. This marketing proved so successful that, by 1970, all the major auto manufacturers offered eight-track the apparatus in new cars. Millions of fans discovered Patsy Cline throughout the 1970s.

The eight-track cartridge player was constructed with the three-minute song in mind. Want to listen to Bob Dylan go on for ten minutes? Fine—but do that at home with an LP disc. Want to hear Patsy Cline sing her three-minute hits? Purchase an eight-track player and some Patsy Cline eight-track tapes, and press a few buttons. By 1970, Decca-MCA had put out *Patsy Cline's Greatest Hits* and *The Patsy Cline Story* on eight-track. MCA, which owned the Decca Patsy Cline catalog, made deals with the largest discount chains so that "The Greatest Hits of Patsy Cline" could be used to tempt buyers to purchase the eight-track players and have them installed. MCA executives, led by Lew Wasserman, reasoned that the more installations of eight-track players in cars, the greater the potential for this new market.[35]

The demand for eight-track tapes and their apparatus lasted until the late 1970s. During the 1970s the sales of 8-track tape players in cars constituted a new market for record company executives to sell low-cost compilations by noted singers. But as the eight-track was proving car owners were also record buyers, scientists were at work on a far smaller—and cheaper—format, the audio cassette. During the 1980s, audio cassettes spawned another technological revolution for playing Patsy Cline at home, as well in the car.

How did even more fans come to hear Patsy Cline's voice? From television, of course. Starting on January 16, 1966, television became a vehicle for selling Patsy Cline discounted LPs. One TV advertising campaign used Jack Benny's former announcer, Don Wilson, to sell

"25 Country Music Greats, including Patsy Cline's 'Walkin' After Midnight.'" Wilson told audiences, "You get 25 of the most beautiful country hits ever created by 25 of the greatest stars who ever lived! All on one LP! Just send $1.50 to Great Stars, 420 Lexington Avenue, New York 17, New York." The key to that commercial was that audiences heard the voices of these "country greats" over and over again during the TV ads, particularly Patsy Cline singing the

4-Star version of "Walkin' After Midnight."

By the 1970s, K-Tel Records had become synonymous with late-night television. During the 1970s, K-Tel TV commercials provided a constant reminder of Patsy Cline, including ten-bar reprises of all her 4-Star hits. K-Tel was founded in 1962 by a salesman named Philip Kives, who began using TV to sell household gadgets. In 1956, Kives branched out into LP sales by first releasing the best-selling "25 Polka Classics." More than a million copies of the LP were sold via TV advertising. Millions upon millions of K-Tel records were sold over the course of the next decade, thanks largely to TV. Patsy Cline's 4-Star masters stood at the heart of the company's ads. Joe Johnson, who was still running 4-Star Music, had gained another sales outlet.[36]

But Patsy Cline also had a moment in the spotlight on prime-time TV when, on October 15, 1973, the annual CMA Awards show was broadcast nationally on the CBS television network. Viewers saw Patsy Cline enshrined in the Country Music Hall of Fame. On national TV, Johnny Cash inducted Cline, televised live from the Ryman Auditorium, in Nashville. This induction signified that Nashville thought Patsy Cline belonged in a special, select group, and soon thereafter, fans could tour the CMA Museum, in Nashville, and see a handful of her stage outfits and personal effects recovered from the crash site. Her election to the Country Music Hall of Fame boosted her record sales, just as people were looking for something to buy as an inexpensive Christmas present.

Discount record labels issued at least two "new" LPs and eight-tracks with "Country Music Hall of Fame" in the title.[37]

Hilda Hensley remembered the 1973 awards show: "They called me to Nashville and told me she was one of five nominated and I thought that was wonderful." At the ceremony, Patsy Cline's mother heard Johnny Cash's booming voice say, "she" and knew her daughter had been selected, as Patsy was the only woman nominated. But the family was still split; Charles Dick and Hilda Hensley could not agree on who should accept the award. So no one did.[38]

On the same 1973 telecast, the Vocal Duo of the Year went to Conway Twitty and Loretta Lynn, who had a hit with "Louisiana Woman, Mississippi Man," and the Female Vocalist of the Year went to Lynn. On stage Lynn openly thanked Patsy. In October 1973, nearly every newspaper in United States reported that Lynn thought the selection of Patsy Cline was overdue. The CMA show drew millions of viewers, and those viewers watched the assorted clips and listened to the four-minute tribute to Patsy Cline.[39]

As Nashville voters considered Patsy's nomination, the June 17 *Kingsport* (Tennessee) *Times-News* and 500 other newspapers printed a wire service story about the CMA museum in Nashville that led with, "[The tourist] was a big man with a camera slung around his neck. The blonde wig of Patsy Cline fascinated him. 'Didn't even know she wore a wig,' he whispered." He then spotted Patsy Cline's lighter, which the museum indicated still played "Dixie."

Prior to the CMA broadcast, the *New York Times* published a basic discography of Country Music, and *Patsy Cline's Greatest Hits* made the list. Later, the front page of the March 16, 1974, *Galveston* (Texas) *Daily News* ran a wire service article on the closing of the Ryman Theater. The story ended with a Minnie Pearl quote: "I hate to have to leave. It's killing me. . . . Patsy Cline, Hank Williams. I just feel like they're little ghosts down here." Soon after that, Loretta Lynn came out with her autobiography, *Coal Miner's Daughter,* featuring a chapter on her relationship with Patsy.[40]

Through the 1970s, Patsy Cline was acknowledged as helping break down barriers for women in country music. For example, on November 13, 1971, an analysis of *Billboard's* top country singles showed that more than a quarter were by women. This report, "What You Don't Know About Country Music Is Probably Costing You Money," cited the crossover appeal started by Patsy Cline that had moved country music into the American suburbs.[41]

Many noted female singers started covering songs associated with Patsy Cline. In 1968, for example, Tammy Wynette covered "Sweet Dreams." Thereafter, many female singers wanted to do their variations of "Patsy Cline" songs, particularly after Patsy was elected to the CMA Hall of Fame.[42]

By December 1975, Emmylou Harris's cover of "Sweet Dreams" graced her album *Elite Hotel.* Harris walked the same fine line as a pop-sounding singer who was labeled country. But reviewers' attitudes had changed. And they praised *Elite Hotel* for its impeccable arrangements and Emmylou's tough and tender vibrating soprano voice. They argued that Emmylou's passionate delivery transcended all musical genres, and critics praised her choice of material—especially her cover of Patsy Cline. Like Patsy Cline, whom she openly praised, Emmylou seemed better suited to slow country ballads – in particular Patsy Cline's "Sweet Dreams." After *Elite Hotel* won a Grammy in 1976 for Best Country Vocal Performance, Female, Harris' fans then looked for LPs containing the Patsy Cline original.[43]

Harris hailed her influences in interviews: "Patsy Cline, but also Edith Piaf and Billie Holliday. There's a spark of individuality in all of them." Harris' new style was fashioned as pop-country-folk, cross-genre vocals that evoked Patsy Cline, only an octave higher. While *Elite Hotel* ranked number1 as a country album, it also landed on *Billboard's* pop charts. Harris, like Cline, appealed to listeners who were not fans of hard-core country music, and reaffirmed that Emmylou Harris and Patsy Cline were "something different." By 1981, as country and pop music meshed, Harris was regularly charting on *Billboard's* Hot 100 pop chart.[44]

In 1972, Linda Ronstadt had also begun covering Patsy Cline in concert. By November 1976, Ronstadt was arguably the most popular female vocalist in the United States, atop the pop charts as a solo artist. By 1976, she had won her second Grammy Award for Best Pop Vocal Performance, Female, for her third consecutive platinum album, *Hasten Down the Wind,* which included "Crazy." Her interpretation of "Crazy" became a *Billboard* top 10 pop hit in early 1977.[45]

In 1976 the *New York Times* called Ronstadt's cover of "Crazy" "a vampish jazzy love song." Ronstadt was the first female "arena class" star, setting records as one of the top-grossing concert artists. By 1979, she was recognized as the most successful female pop singer of the decade as voted by *Cash_Box* magazine. She was so popular that her image appeared six times on the cover of *Rolling Stone* magazine, and once on the cover of *Newsweek* and *Time* magazines. By 1979, the *Chicago Sun Times* described her as the best "of the 1970s school of female singers." Like Patsy Cline, Linda Ronstadt defied music stereotypes. Of Ronstadt, *Country Western Stars* magazine wrote in 1979, "Rock people thought she was too gentle, folk people thought she was too pop, and pop people didn't quite understand where she was at, but country people really love Linda." And this hot pop singer was regularly singing Patsy Cline covers.[46]

In her popular best selling autobiography, Loretta Lynn openly professed that her main influence was Patsy Cline. But her link to Patsy was not with her singing; rather, Lynn celebrated "Patsy's independent streak." From Loretta Lynn's very first record, "Honky Tonk Girl," she carved out a persona more independent and feisty than traditional Kitty Wells's. Many of Lynn's numbers were answer songs, not to individual hits but to whole genres of country music: "Don't Come Home A' Drinkin'" was a barroom ballad, and "You Ain't Woman Enough" a cheatin' song. While many had covered Patsy Cline's songs, Lynn used her clout at MCA in 1977 to create a whole album of Patsy Cline covers, an LP entitled *I Remember Patsy*. Lynn's cover "She's Got You" ranked among the top country singles in February 1977.

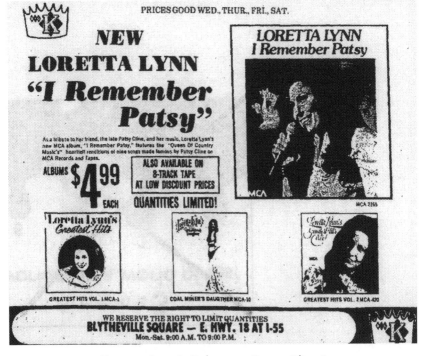

"Loretta Lynn's Tribute to Patsy Cline"

Thereafter, writers constantly linked Loretta Lynn and Patsy Cline, "as a bond seems to have forged between two of country music's strongest-willed and most down-to-earth women." These writers told how, after the plane crash, Loretta had named her daughter Patsy, in honor of her mentor. In her book, *Coal Miner's Daughter,* Loretta wrote, "She taught me a lot of things about show business, like how to get onto a stage, how to get off stage, and how to dress. She even bought me lots of clothes, and if she bought herself an outfit, she'd git me one like it." Lynn revitalized and legitimized Patsy Cline as a true "legend of country music" because of her difficult youth, her emotional singing, and her pathbreaking efforts on behalf of solo female country music singers.[47]

In 1979, Reba McEntire first tasted the top 20 with her "Sweet Dreams" cover. As a tribute to Patsy Cline, Reba always used "Sweet Dreams" to conclude her concerts at this early stage in her career. Indeed, *Out of a Dream,* Reba McEntire's second studio album, contained her cover of "Sweet Dreams." Reba embraced Patsy Cline in interview after interview: "I love [her song] 'I Fall to Pieces;' I had very good teachers— including Patsy Cline." McEntire praised Patsy Cline for "Crazy:" "You can almost hear her cry from her guts, you know. That's the kind of stuff I wanted to do. Patsy Cline was my real influence."[48]

For her first appearance on the Grand Ole Opry, on September 17, 1977, Reba McEntire admitted, "I was really scared when I walked out on the stage at the Grand Ole Opry. Patsy Cline was always a favorite singer to me. I remember sitting out in the car with the tape player, singing along with her tapes. That's why I performed 'Sweet Dreams' in my Opry debut, dedicating it to Patsy's memory before I sang." This was high praise, not from a sentimental old-timer, but from a contemporary hit-maker.[49]

So with these accolades from the likes of crossover star Emmylou Harris, pop sensation Linda Ronstadt, country icon Loretta Lynn, and new country star Reba McEntire, by 1979 Patsy Cline stood at the cusp of rediscovery by a whole new generation. Fans of pop and country music around the world became familiar with "Patsy Cline" songs.

PATSY CLINE

LET THE TEARDROPS FALL

"Patsy Cline with her image converted to Asian appeal."

In October 1979, Susan Nadler Gantry published "A Portrait of Patsy Cline" in *Country Music* magazine. Owen Bradley told Gantry that Patsy Cline was "way ahead of her times as she was the first female country singer with a smooth, polished voice." Gantry interviewed Chic Dougherty, head of record sales at MCA, who revealed that Patsy Cline LPs were steady sellers—some sixteen years after her death. MCA kept a dozen in print. Dougherty singled out *Patsy Cline's Greatest Hits* as MCA's best selling greatest-hits LP. And Dougherty and MCA were readying a "new" release of *Patsy Cline's Greatest Hits,* on audio cassette. Patsy Cline was ready to be discovered by Hollywood— as she would be, with the *Coal Miner's Daughter* movie, as I have described chapter 1. This would be the beginning of her path to iconic status.

NOTES

Chapter 8

1. WS, 6 March 1993: B1.

2. Paul Davis, <u>George Hamilton IV: Ambassador of Country Music,</u> <u>The Authorized Biography</u> (New York: Harper Collins, 2000); 55.

3. FAA-Report Docket file 2-1324, on file at Southeast Branch, National Archives, Atlanta, Georgia.

4. NYT, 7 March 1963: 5.

5. As posted on <u>www.patsified.com</u> -- accessed March 5, 2004.

6. WS, September 5, 1995: A1

7. <u>The Birmingham [AL] Daily Mountain Eagle</u>, March 6,1999: B1

8. <u>The Kansas City Star</u>, March 2, 1993: B1.

9. As posted on www.patsified.com – accessed March 5, 2004.

10. Based on articles in newspapers provided by NewspaperArchive. com

11. WS, May 13, 1998: F1.

12. ORAL HISTORY – Jack Fretwell – by Fern Adams – September 9,1993.

13. WS, September 18, 1997: F1; WS, March 29,,1997: B1.

14. <u>The Northern Virginia Daily</u> [hereafter NVD], March 1, 1963: 1.

15. Filed May 14, 1965.

16. WS, May 5, 2001: B1.

17. National Archives, , Southeast Region, Civil Case #3547 from the U.S. District Court Stuyvesant Insurance Company v. Kathy Loma Copas, Jean S. Hawkins, Gary Copas, Lucille Copas and Charles A. Dick, June 1966.

[18] ORAL HISTORY, JULY 31, 2007; TRIAL; WS, September 1, 2001: F1; Winchester City Clerk's Office, Deed Book, 121/ 238.

[19] ORAL HISTORY – JULY 31, 2007.

[20] countrydiscography

[21] Goldmine, August 2, 1996: 20-32.

[22] The [Nashville] Tennessean, November 11, 1963: 33.

[23] LA Times, July 26, 1964: D1.

[24] Time, November 27, 1964: 44-45.

[25] Joel Whitburn, Country Annual, First Edition 1944-1997 (New York: Billboard, 1998): 44-45.

[26] Tad Richards and Melvin B. Shestack, The New Country Music Encyclopedia (New York: Simon & Schuster, 1993): 59.

[27] Billboard, February 10, 1973: 44.

[28] Billboard, April 28, 1963: 1; Variety April 28, 1963: 44; The Estate of William A. McCall v. Four Star Music Company, et al, the court of appeal of the State of California, Second Appellate District (1996).

[29] LATimes, January 5,1964: A15; countrydiscography.

[30] Frank Hoffmann, & Howard Ferstler (editors), Technical Encyclopedia of Recorded Sound (New York: Routledge, 2005)

[31] The author grew up in Allentown and lived there when Two Guys from Harrison opened, and shopped there often.

[32] Discount Merchandiser, July 1988: 33-35; Robert Sobel, When Giants Stumble (Englewood Cliffs, NJ: Prentice Hall, 1999): 77-92.

[33] Discount Store News, May23, 1988: 22.

[34] The Cumberland [MD] Times-News, July 27, 2007, B1.

[35] David Morton, "A History of The Eight Track Tape" 8-Track Mind magazine, August 1995: 22-23.

[36] www.ktel.com – accessed August 9, 2008.

37 LA Times, October 17, 1973: D15.

38 Unknown radio show, March 1975 – track 13 – CPC Collection.

39 Wpost, October 16, 1973:C1.

40 NYT, September 23, 1973: 33.

41 Linnell Gentry, A History and Encyclopedia of Country, Western, and Gospel Music, (Nashville: Clairmont Press, Second Edition, 1969).

42 Bill Malone, "Classic Country Music: A Smithsonian Collection" (booklet included with Classic Country Music: A Smithsonian Collection 4-disc set, 1990: 51.

43 www.emmylouharris.com – accessed December 12, 2007.

44 www.grammy.com – accessed March 21, 2008; Jim Brown, Emmylou Harris: Angel in Disguise (New York: Fox Music Books, 2004).

45 LA Times, November 11,1976: D3.

46 Goldmine, August 2, 1996: 54-66.

47 Country Music, October 1979, 65-66.

48 Alanna Nash, Behind Closed Doors: Talking with Legends of Country Music (New York: Knopf, 1988): 318-319.

49 Don Cusic, Reba McEntire (New York: St. Martin's, 1994): 71, 127-128.

Chapter 9

Riding the Wave of the Pasty Cline Iconography

One condition of iconic status is ubiquity. That came for Patsy Cline after March 1980, with the popularity of the movie *Coal Miner's Daughter.* Hollywood's publicity caused new fans to discover Patsy Cline's vocals on audio cassettes and later on CDs. In 1991, SoundScan confirmed this phenomenon; by November 24, 1996, the *New York Times Magazine* celebrated the new iconic status of Patsy Cline.

The success of *Coal Miner's Daughter* produced externalities, as the hit movie sparked renewed Patsy Cline record sales. Of course, a soundtrack was planned by Universal studios but parent company MCA also started by reissuing Patsy Cline recordings to take advantage of the wave of positive publicity. For example, two months after *Coal Miner's Daughter*'s March 1980 premiere, the *Nashville Banner* straight forwardly told readers, "Patsy Cline's music is still living today. Her popularity is greater now than when she was on earth." The *Banner* correctly pointed out that Patsy Cline had had a substantial number of fans before the film. It reported that MCA Nashville had stated that sales of her old albums were "good 'n' plenty." So good, in fact, that MCA lured Owen Bradley was lured out of retirement to take his recordings and remix them.[1]

MCA issued a press release announcing that it was ready to rerelease six LPs of Patsy Cline and her *Greatest Hits*. The press release detailed how Bradley was going to "lift her vocals from the three-track masters and place them on a new musical bed." While Owen Bradley was the producer, David Briggs handled the actual sessions, and replaced the all-male Jordanaires with an all-female backup group. MCA wanted to focus on the pop music market and so wrapped its "new" releases around the rerelease of Patsy Cline singing Irving Berlin's "Always." Berlin, the most fabled composer in Tin Pan Alley history, had written "Always" for his bride, and then in 1942, Sam Goldwyn used this as theme music for the popular film *The Pride of the Yankees,* a biopic about baseball player Lou Gehrig, who, at age thirty-seven, had his career cut short when he was stricken with amyotrophic lateral sclerosis (ALS, which would later be known as "Lou Gehrig's Disease"). Commentators made a link to the death of Patsy Cline—also "too young." "Always" reintroduced Patsy Cline to a new audience, who thereafter knew she sounded "pop," even though MCA still labeled her a country star.

Briggs and Bradley were going to reproduce not only "Always" but new versions of "Foolin' Round" (eliminating the original 1961 "Latin" rhythm) and a full LP filled with overdubs of "Love Letters in the Sand," "Bill Bailey, Won't You Please Come Home," "Have You Ever Been Lonely (Have You Ever Been Blue)," "You Made Me Love You (I Didn't Want to Do It)," "I Can See an Angel," "That's My Desire," "That's How a Heartache Begins," "I Love You So Much, It Hurts," and "You Belong to Me." These selections emphasized the pop, lost-love side of Patsy Cline. Only long-time fans complained that these overdub sessions did not use the A Team, or strings, or the Jordanaires.[2]

In the fall of 1980, MCA released "Always" as a single and as an LP. The single went on to become a country hit, peaking at number 18 on the *Billboard* charts; the LP reached number 27 on the *Billboard* country albums chart. Even Irving Berlin helped with the publicity, declaring that the Patsy Cline version of "Always" was his favorite.

In 1981, Mary Reeves Davis, widow of country crooner Jim Reeves, who had died in 1964, at the age of thirty-nine, approached Owen Bradley with the idea of putting Cline and Reeves together technologically to create a "duet" album. MCA management embraced the idea of creating two Cline and Reeves electronic duets. Reeves' label RCA was by then a desperate label, and Lew Wasserman negotiated a favorable deal for MCA, to milk more money from the popular MCA-Universal movie *Coal Miner's Daughter*. Wasserman's agreement with RCA called for two albums, one from each label. Owen Bradley stood at the core of the deal, as his son Jerry was then head of RCA in Nashville.

The Bradleys, father and son, knew that "Have You Ever Been Lonely," and "I Fall to Pieces" were had been recorded in the same key. Owen Bradley later recalled: "We found that it was probably going to be easier to fit Jim to Patsy's track rather than to fit her to his track," so while they sounded like duets, it was Cline's voice that dominated. The Bradleys took the voice tracks off their stereo master tapes, and created new background music. In a pre-digital age, the project kept Owen Bradley and his son in the studio five days a week for almost five months.[3]

The November 14, 1981, *Los Angeles Times* reviewed their efforts: "Where there's a (possible) hit, there's a way and so one of the fastest-rising singles in country music is Jim Reeves and Patsy Cline's duet on 'Have You Ever Been Lonely (Have You Ever Been Blue).'" If that pairing sounded strange, there was a good reason, the reviewer told his readers. Both were dead—both killed in airplane accidents. Reeves and Cline had never stepped into a recording studio together. But hot off Patsy's role in *Coal Miner's Daughter,* the demand was high for something new. For Christmas 1981, MCA released *Remembering: Patsy Cline & Jim Reeves,* containing the electronic duet "I Fall to Pieces," as part of its Special Products series. The rest of the album was filled with past hits by the individual artists: "So Wrong"(Cline), "Misty Moonlight" (Reeves), " Back in Baby's Arms" (Cline), "Missing You" (Reeves), "Walkin' After Midnight" (second version, Cline), "The Blizzard" (Reeves), "Why Can't He Be You" (Cline), "Distant Drums" (Reeves), and "Leavin' On Your Mind" (Cline). For this MCA album, Lew Wasserman negotiated that the new song be one of Cline's hits. The electronic duet of "I Fall to Pieces" went to *Billboard* number 61, while the album went gold, according to the Recording Industry Association of American (hereafter RIAA).

Next RCA issued the *Jim Reeves & Patsy Cline—Greatest Hits* album, featuring "Have You Ever Been Lonely (Have You Ever Been Blue)" as a duet. RCA also included songs of each performer, including Patsy Cline's "Crazy," "Sweet Dreams," "I Fall to Pieces," and "She's Got You." Despite MCA's plans, it was the RCA duet of "Have You Ever Been Lonely" that became the single that soared to number 15 on *Billboard*'s country singles chart, although the LP failed to chart.[4]

———————————

Both MCA and RCA also released the duet albums in the then new form of audio cassette. Although audio cassettes were originally intended as a medium for dictation, improvements in fidelity had led to audio cassettes' supplanting eight-tracks in autos, innovating portable Sony Walkman, and finally also replacing phonograph records

records. Audio cassettes consist of two miniature spools, between which a magnetic tape passes. These spools and their attendant parts are held inside a protective plastic shell. When combined with Dolby type B noise reduction and chromium dioxide tape, audio cassettes result in quality sound for anything less than complex orchestral pieces.[5]

The audio cassette came to dominate music listening in the 1980s. By 1986, RIAA estimated sales of a third of a billion prerecorded audio cassettes. Patsy Cline was rediscovered by the public, which could buy a cassette for just a few dollars and listen on the way to work or school. Fans could often find a used audio cassette Patsy Cline on sale for ninety-nine cents. Or they could copy a friend's for the price of a blank tape. As the portable CD player defined the 1990s, the audio cassette defined listening during the 1980s.[6]

Throughout the 1980s, MCA reissued Patsy Cline recordings on multiple audio cassettes, as did smaller companies with her 4-Star material. New fans purchased so many Patsy Cline audio cassettes each year that MCA commenced an effort to locate heretofore unissued audio material. But first, in 1987, MCA released a new, remastered audio cassette version of *Patsy Cline's Greatest Hits,* retitled *Patsy Cline: 12 Greatest Hits.* This album hit the *Billboard* charts in August 1987 and would stay on the country album charts until May 1991, when SoundScan bumped it into a new category, "catalog country," where it was number 1 on the new SoundScan chart. Thereafter, MCA issued eighteen audio cassettes filled with Patsy Cline.

In July 1988, MCA released *Live at the Opry,* an audio cassette comprising recordings of the Grand Ole Opry from 1956 to 1962, and it climbed to number 60 on the country album charts. At the time, the trendsetting *Rolling Stone* magazine praised the live cassette "because Cline's wonderful legacy deserves every bit of trendy revivalism it can get. In the way that Aretha Franklin is Lady Soul, Cline is surely Lady

Country." *Rolling Stone* crowned Patsy Cline—twenty-five years after her death—an undisputed rock standard-bearer. According to *Rolling Stone,* Cline's voice "rippled the heartstrings." But the magazine felt it necessary to explain Patsy Cline to younger fans: "Though you might be better acquainted with Linda Ronstadt's version of 'Crazy' or Elvis Costello's performance of 'She's Got You,' you haven't really heard those songs until you've heard Cline's unmatched blend of silky and earthy blues." *Rolling Stone* praised MCA for releasing all her past LPs on audio cassette, and then going the extra step to make widely available, first-ever live recordings, culled from radio broadcasts.[7]

In 1989 MCA issued *Patsy Cline Live, Volume Two,* and drew even more praise because it had sought out her vocals from the military recruiting shows she had done. Released at the time her *12 Greatest Hits* went double-platinum, this audio cassette consisted of recordings that had been sitting in the public domain since she created them thirty years earlier. The cost of recovering the masters, cleaning them up, and preparing audio cassettes was undertaken by MCA. Its sales pitch: The cassettes contained five songs Patsy Cline had never recorded commercially, covers of Sonny James's "For Rent," Webb Pierce's "Yes, I Know Why," Little Jimmie Dickens' "When Your House Is Not a Home," Connie Francis' "Stupid Cupid," and the pop standard "Side By Side." The other six cuts were new versions of "Strange," "Turn the Cards Slowly," "Come on In," "The Wayward Wind," "Stop, Look and Listen," and "Just a Closer Walk with Thee." *Volume Two* was like an archeological discovery for all her new fans—and it charted.[8]

In 1989, a Los Angeles-based, specialized reissue label, Rhino Records, put out a complete set of her 4-Star material, in order of original release, on three audio cassettes. Rhino's *Patsy's First Recordings Volumes 1, 2 & 3* offered a new experience for fans, as listeners could hear how Owen Bradley experimented with Patsy's voice. Rhino Records started as a reissue label in the late 1970s because audio cassettes were inexpensive, and as Baby Boomers aged, they wanted to hear the songs of their youth. Dozens of cassettes containing 4-Star material were available, but no series contained all her 4-Star recordings in order, and with Rhino's superior sound quality (with remastering of the original tapes under the direction of Bill Inglot) and creative packaging, the three-cassette series garnered rave reviews.[9]

New fans discovered a Patsy Cline whose range spanned blues to rock. Review after review of this Rhino compilation stressed her sassy voice. Reviewers discovered gems, including "Yes I Understand," in which Cline's voice is double-tracked; "Life's Railway to Heaven," a haunting gospel number; and "Gotta Lot of Rhythm in My Soul," a growl-filled rockabilly masterwork. Critics noted guitarist Grady Martin did all her early sessions and also played on Roy Orbison's "Pretty Woman." They praised Martin's riff on "Let the Teardrops Fall," where Cline also "rocked." Taking Patsy seriously began with this Rhino three-cassette reissue.[10]

*

But it took a Canadian to make Patsy hip. k.d. lang (born Kathryn Dawn Lang, but known professionally with all lower case letters) had been one of those fans who was inspired by getting a discount LP for Christmas in 1982. She was so moved by Patsy Cline's vocals that, soon thereafter, she formed a band called the Reclines and toured college campuses, honoring Patsy by singing "Three Cigarettes in an Ashtray." (She learned the 4-Star song from her discount LP.) When she attended Red Deer College, in Alberta, Canada (halfway between Calgary and Edmonton), lang stated, she wanted to become the new Patsy Cline—but with an edge. She reflected: "I listened to

[Patsy Cline] sing and how Patsy and Owen Bradley incorporated blues, swing and some rockabilly stuff. She had a type of soul that is hard to find in a singer." She claimed to interviewer after interviewer that she could hear Patsy Cline "cry from her guts singing in 'Crazy.'" But lang dressed in what could best be called "cowgirl punk," and appealed to hip alternative music fans.[11]

In 1983 the Reclines recorded their debut album, "Friday Dance Promenade," which got good reviews for an indie release. She continued to record on small labels and in 1985 earned a Juno Award for Most Promising Female Vocalist. In 1986, she signed a contract with Sire, a U.S. record producer in Nashville, and received critical acclaim for her 1987 album, "Angel with a Lariat." Her career then received a huge boost when Roy Orbison chose her to record a duet of his standard, "Crying," a collaboration that won them the Grammy Award for Best Country Collaboration with Vocals.[12]

Then lang persuaded the seventy-two-year-old Owen Bradley to come out of retirement to create *Shadowland,* an album of torch songs to honor Patsy Cline. That lang was a lesbian and was a transsexual did not offend Owen Bradley. Her voice appealed to him, and he imagined that, like Patsy Cline, lang could cross over and appeal to a vast audience.

Owen Bradley produced *Shadowland* at his new studio in Mt. Juliet, Tennessee, for Warner Communications owned the Sire label, which even drew in Kitty Wells, Loretta Lynn, and Brenda Lee on its most touted track, "Honky Tonk Angels' Medley." For session players, Bradley brought back his brother Harold on guitar, Hargus "Pig" Robbins on piano, and Buddy Harman on drums—all of whom played on original Patsy Cline sessions—as well as the Jordanaires. Bradley hired a dozen strings to create the sound that he had started to use with Patsy Cline at the end of her recording career. Bradley and lang covered country classics: "Sugar Moon" (written by Cindy Walker and Bob Wills), "Don't Let the Stars Get in Your Eyes" (Slim Willet), and "I'm Down to My Last Cigarette" (Harlan Howard, Billy Walker). Bradley and lang also recorded pop standards, including "I Wish I Didn't Love You So" (Frank Loesser), "Black Coffee" (Sonny Burke and Paul Francis Webster), and "Shadowland" (Dick Hyman and Charles Tobias). *Shadowland*, as an album, went to number 73 pop, and number 9 country.

On the front page of the July 1988 issue, *Country Music News* praised the recording: "Just watch k.d. lang perform and . . . for whatever else she might be, she's also unlike anyone else in country music. She has literally taken the Nashville music community by storm with her high-spirited, no-holds-barred live stage show, and her powerful, versatile vocal abilities." The reviewer went on to warn that any hard-core country fan might be put off by lang's androgynous appearance, close-cropped hair, and lack of makeup, but like Owen Bradley, they should listen to her voice. In 1988, lang and Bradley were showered by praise from all media reviewers. "She's as good as Patsy Cline," enthused Owen Bradley over and over again.[13]

But it was the New York City underground magazine *Details* that quoted lang to praise Patsy Cline in its October 1985 issue: "What self-respecting person can listen to Patsy Cline's 'I Fall to Pieces' without having a nervous breakdown?" To appeal to its lesbian and gay readership, *Details* compared Patsy Cline and k.d. lang to Judy Garland. *Details* applauded the way Patsy seemed to suffer with every word she sang. According to *Details*, Cline didn't just sing her songs, she cried them. "Hurt me now, get it over," she sang as if the sooner she was hurt, the quicker she could come out with the next torch song to relive her pain.[14]

Suddenly college students across the United States, who generally didn't like country music, embraced k.d. lang's extraordinary talent. They discovered complex harmonies in *Shadowland*. With Owen Bradley producing lang and declaring her the second coming of Patsy Cline, the sons and daughters of Baby Boomers learned what their parents already knew.

Consider the collective embrace at the University of Michigan, as described in the November 6 , 1989, *Michigan Daily*: "There aren't many stars today that can tinker with and mildly subvert the cultural mainstream. To be enormously popular and actually have something of substance to offer often seem incompatible, and it's only [a] very few of our most potent cultural icons that accomplish both."

On Friday, November 3, 1989, k.d. lang and the Reclines appeared at the Michigan Theater. The following Monday, the *Michigan Daily* raved, "It's patently clear that k.d. has charisma with a capital K, and an aura of star quality surrounding her. She and the Reclines did a varied set that showcased her more frisky country numbers as well as her wide repertoire of ballads." In her baggy, purple suit, k.d. lang seemed sexy like a retro Elvis, perfecting the Presley sneer in her rockabilly numbers. But the college newspaper noted, "It's when k.d. sings her slow songs that her voice is at her most moving." During her cover of Patsy Cline's "Three Cigarettes in an Ashtray," the crowd became still, the college audience silent—in awe.

k.d. lang made Patsy Cline a positive symbol for women, whatever their sexual preference. Suddenly her backstory of feminine struggle became part of the appeal. And lang bent country music into a more modern genre, and attributed her inspiration to Patsy Cline. By the early 1990s, as SoundScan proved millions were buying Patsy Cline audio cassettes at ever increasing rates, k.d. lang had turned Patsy

Cline into a symbol for progressive feminism—and complex modern singing.

All the fuss over *Coal Miner's Daughter* caused a resident of suburban Boston to approach Hilda Hensley about restarting the Patsy Cline Fan Club. Jimmie Bowen got Hilda's blessing, and fans journeyed to Winchester to meet Hilda, visit Patsy Cline's grave, and tour Winchester. This new fan club commenced modestly in September 1980, as Hilda agreed to become its honorary head.[15]

By April 1981, the *Winchester Star,* by then a morning newspaper, headlined in its local news section: "Scrambling Aboard the Patsy Cline Bandwagon." Ellis Nassour, a New York–based freelance writer, stopped in Winchester to promote his mass-market paperback biography of Cline. The *Winchester Star* correctly judged that Nassour was simply trying to "make a buck" on this new interest.

In 1982, Hilda Hensley and Sylvia Hensley Wilt, Patsy Cline's mother and sister, announced plans to organize a nonprofit "Patsy Cline Memorial Foundation" to raise monies to provide music scholarships to high school graduates. Hilda Hensley also mentioned she was planning a museum with her daughter, the first such public proclamation of such an idea.[16]

Bowen organized the fan club to lobby for honors for Patsy. So in its January 1984 issue, *Sunset* magazine, reported that the All-America Rose Selections committee had just approved a dozen new roses. One, a lavender hybrid tea rose with large flowers, was named the Patsy Cline. Jack E. Christensen, of California, had patented the Patsy Cline rose as Rose Plant #5556. During the 1980s and 1990s, Hilda Hensley planted them in the backyard of her home at 605 South Kent Street, to surround the vegetable garden she still grew each year.[17]

It was not until Labor Day weekend, 1985, that the Patsy Cline Fan Club meetings grew large enough to merit coverage by the local press. Winchester resident Teresa Bowers won the "Sweet Dreams Can Come True" Patsy Cline singing competition as part of a fan club celebration, as noted by both the *Winchester Star* and the *Northern Virginia Daily*. But if there seemed optimism surrounding the Labor Day events of 1985, the local reaction to the movie *Sweet Dreams* dampened any renewed spirit. The *Northern Virginia Daily* wrote, "[Patsy Cline] was never accepted by the Winchester establishment because of her brashness, her chosen profession, which at the time was considered somewhat seamy, and her upbringing. Cline lived on what is commonly referred to as "the wrong side of town." The *Winchester Star* simply found that this Hollywood biography was not worth seeing.[18]

In October 1985, the movie prompted follow up stories, most notably on the front page of the October 12 *Roanoke* (Virginia) *Times & World's* Style section. The headline read, "Will Patsy Cline Ever Get Enough Credit?" This major Virginia daily, published 175 miles southwest of Winchester, took Winchesterites to task for rejecting the location shooting of *Sweet Dreams,* and loathed that, with the exception of a memorial plaque on the cemetery gate, there was nothing to commemorate Patsy Cline in a city that openly honored short stays by General "Stonewall" Jackson, and George Washington. Local Winchester DJ Jim McCoy said for the record: "They just figured she was a local girl; we were nothing but a bunch of hillbillies. . . . That puts you on the wrong side of the tracks." Winchester Mayor Charles Zuckerman when asked about local apathy toward Patsy Cline: "I'll be getting in trouble, but, I guess I'd have to agree."

Embarrassed, in early 1986, local Winchester citizens started a petition drive to name Pleasant Valley Road to Patsy Cline Boulevard. This ad hoc committee presented a petition to the Winchester City Council. "I think it's a sin and a shame something like this has not been done earlier," said Winchester lawyer Eugene Gunter, who wrote the petition. While anyone could sign, Winchester Public Works Director Gary Lofton said the signatures of city residents who lived on Pleasant Valley Road would carry the most weight to convince the Winchester City Council to change the name of a street. Jack Fretwell appealed to his fellow citizens: "Can you think of anybody in this area who sang at Carnegie Hall?" No one could.[19]

During the petition drive, the April 16 *Winchester Star* printed a front-page article entitled "Patsy's Mom," by Ron Morris, then managing editor of the newspaper. Hilda commented on *Sweet Dreams:* "We were told they were going to make a beautiful love story. I saw it one time. That was enough." What about the street name? "I have kept quiet. I thought my absence in these things, would convey my feelings. It's a very nice gesture, but I think it's way too late. If they wanted to do something in her memory—let's face it, they can't do anything for Patsy now." Having just turned 70, Hilda Hensley had grown understandably bitter, living on Social Security, custom sewing for a few people, babysitting, and working on "my memories for a book." No one really thought she was at work on a book, but they should have taken Hilda's word.

On October 22, 1986, after dragging its heels for six months, the Winchester City Council voted *not* to change the name of Pleasant Valley Road. Knowing the outcome beforehand, Teresa Bowers switched venues and asked the Frederick County Board of Supervisors to have a portion of U.S. 522 renamed "Patsy Cline Memorial Highway." "I feel 522 is most appropriate because it goes right by where she's buried,"

Bowers told the Frederick County Board. The sections of Route 522 that Bowers referred to had no name in 1986, unlike U.S. 522 South, in nearby Clarke and Warren counties, which had long been "Stonewall Jackson Memorial Highway." County resident Jack Fretwell told the board, "This is where she was born. She's an international figure. This is a way of memorializing her that would cost very little to the county." A handful of country residents complained that they felt the road should have more of a historical name (such as for a general or president); they felt Patsy had not done anything worthy of such recognition.[20]

The front page of the November 7 *Winchester Star* reported, "Patsy Cline Gets Memorial Road" after the Frederick Country board unanimously decided to name Route 522 South "Patsy Cline Memorial Highway." No one appeared in person to speak in opposition. But winter delayed putting up the signs, so it was not until February 10, 1987, that the *Winchester Star*—again on its front page—could report that the Virginia Department of Transportation had begun to erect signs on 522 South, designating the eight miles of highway between Winchester and Double Tollgate "Patsy Cline Memorial Highway."

On January 3, 1987, Virginia's largest newspaper, the *Virginian-Pilot* (based in Norfolk) took Winchesterites to task for not doing more to honor Patsy Cline. "About the only thing Winchester ever gave Cline was a good funeral, according to "Bittersweet Dreams," a cover story in the "Tidewater Living" section of the newspaper. "When she was alive, she never got a Patsy Cline Day," the *Virginian-Pilot* reporter, Mike D'Orso, wrote. "The only thing the town ever gave her was a chance to ride in its Apple Blossom Parade. And when she did, they laughed." In the town that Patsy's mother had long called home, Hilda remained an outsider, the story concluded.

However, with the uncredited monetary help of Charles Dick, the August 22, 1987, *Winchester Star* could headline on its front page a description of cranes putting up a bell tower in the entryway of Shenandoah Memorial Park, where Patsy Cline was buried. The Bell Tower was dedicated on Sunday, September 6, 1987, as part of the fan club weekend. It cost $25,000, part of which was donated "in kind" by area residents: Crider & Shockey, Inc., created the concrete base, and Charles Zuckerman & Sons (the mayor's business) constructed the basic steel structure.

Charles Dick went to the dedication; Hilda Hensley did not. Buck Patterson, Hilda's brother was at the ceremony, however. The front page of the Tuesday, September 8, *Winchester Star* quoted Patterson as saying that his sister "can't take [the constant reminder of her elder daughter's death]. It heartbreaks her." In addition, Patterson said, it took too long for the community to erect a memorial to Cline, and there was criticism of the city government for not taking any official action to recognize her.

While Hilda Hensley privately wrote up stories of her life with Patsy Cline, and hoped to open a profit-making museum as a nest egg for her surviving son and daughter, newcomers Douglas and Fern L. Adams named a side road of one of the shopping mall developments "Patsy Cline Boulevard." The road was on private land, so the Adams did not need city or county permission. "It was my wife's idea," Douglas Adams said. "We're both fans." On December 10, 1987, the front page of the *Winchester Star* announced that the Adamses had formally opened "Patsy Cline Drive," a two-lane, 1,200-foot street that, ironically, connected to South Pleasant Valley Road. Douglas Adams told the press that the sale of twenty-six acres north of Patsy Cline Drive for a two-hundred-thousand-square-foot shopping center constituted the largest single real estate transaction ever recorded in Winchester. His wife, Fern Adams, said at the dedication, "I never knew anything about Patsy Cline until I saw "Sweet Dreams," but fell in love with the spirit of the woman."

In a letter to a fan dated May 1988, Sylvia Hensley Wilt stated the Hensley view on Winchester was bitter about the hesitancy of Winchester city officials to honor her sister. As for the Ellis Nassour biography, Sylvia said, "I hope you will not rely too heavily on the veracity of that item for accurate information." It was, Sylvia stated, full of inaccuracies. "We are learning that much of what is said about a celebrity is what makes print to sell, not necessarily tell the truth or create an accurate depiction." Hilda Hensley had rejected any help at this point from Fern Adams, or any rich persons from Winchester who sought to mount a competing museum effort. But to those Hilda Hensley liked, such as Jimmie Bowen, she was ever gracious.[21]

By the Labor Day weekend 1988, Bowen's fan club and Hilda Hensley's foundation had formally united. On September 4, they cosponsored a Sunday night banquet, before Labor Day Monday, to announce Hilda Hensley's Patsy Cline Memorial Foundation. Hilda chose not to give the story to the *Winchester Star,* but instead gave it to a newspaper based in Clifton Forge, Virginia, 150 miles southwest of Winchester. Hilda, her daughter, son-in-law, and other family members went there to raise money for their Patsy Cline Memorial Foundation with the hope of giving the first award in June of 1991. "We have had lots of people asking why her hometown hadn't done anything for Patsy," explained Sylvia Hensley Wilt. "We think [a foundation giving scholarships] is something Patsy would have approved of." Why Clifton Forge? Family friend Ed Loudermilk lived in Low Moor, Virginia, four miles away; Hilda Hensley did not want any help from the *Winchester Star.*[22]

Over the Labor Day weekends of 1989 and 1990, the fan club and the foundation acted as one. They began holding auctions to raise money for the Patsy Cline Memorial Foundation scholarships, usually from supporters bidding on items Hilda knitted. There were fan club meetings and dances on the Saturday before Labor Day, a graveside service on the following day, and a Sunday banquet for the foundation. This collaboration was a symbiotic relationship that worked smoothly. Patsy Cline's cousin remembered on July 31, 2007, remembered that Hilda Hensley had liked Bowen, who was a nice young man, "a Catholic boy who worked in a hospital."

On August 24, 1989, in order to publicize the Patsy Cline Memorial Foundation, Hilda Hensley broke her silence and granted her last interview to the *Winchester Star*. Ron Morris, still the managing editor of the *Star*, journeyed the six blocks down Kent Street to Hilda's home and talked to her in the living room of 605 South Kent Street. Morris portrayed the room as having a goldfish bowl, a TV set, several photographs of Patsy Cline, two gold Patsy Cline albums, and a platinum album from *Patsy Cline's Greatest Hits*. Hilda told him that the mail had tripled since the premiere of *Sweet Dreams*. Morris quoted Hilda as stating, "Last year, at the fan club meeting, I realized how much people really love my daughter. Some had ridden a bus from Canada to be here. I feel like I'd be letting my daughter's fans down if I didn't help, too."[23]

But that did not mean Hilda Hensley would cooperate with wealthy Winchesterites Fern and Douglas Adams. So on the weekend after the Labor Day weekend of 1989, the Adams family staged their own "Celebrating Patsy" downtown—without input or approval from Hilda Hensley. Fern and Douglas Adams aimed their event at the elite of Winchester, trying to convince them Patsy Cline was worth celebrating. Sonya Tolley, executive director of Winchester's Downtown Development Board, admitted that negative feelings still existed, and she met some resistance from a few long-time residents. Fern Adams stated at the time, "The next move is to create a museum." This placed the Adams in direct competition to Hilda Hensley's plans.[24]

Non-Winchester-based publications agreed that the community seemed to be doing nothing to honor Cline. Even slick magazines like the *Blue Ridge,* which in its September 1992 issue, took aim: "Patsy Cline: Why Her Home Town Still Turns Its Back; 30 Years After Her Death." *Blue Ridge* printed, "She would have turned 60 on 8 September 1992 and does anyone in Winchester care?" The magazine argued that the doctors, lawyers, and business executives of Winchester seemed more comfortable with museums for Stonewall Jackson and George Washington than even acknowledging the presence of Patsy Cline. By 1992, millions of fans knew Winchester as Patsy's hometown. "But you won't see a statue of her anywhere in town, no matter how hard you look," noted *Blue Ridge.*

On September 10, 1992, the *Washington Times,* a conservative newspaper hardly known for its exposes, also embarrassed Winchester. The *Times* argued that Winchester was bucking national trends. "Patsy's greatest hits CD reissue currently tops the country music compilation chart and United States Today recently reported that her signature tune 'Crazy' has replaced Elvis' 'Don't Be Cruel' as the most popular jukebox song of all time." To explain, the newspaper argued that, because Patsy Cline did not act like a proper Southern woman, and was considered by those in Winchester to be "poor white trash," Winchester seemed to be frozen in time, still filled with stories of Patsy shopping downtown with curlers in her hair. The Winchester elite dug in their collective heels

In 1992, Charles Dick formed Legacy, Inc., to deal with the national and international demand for all things Patsy Cline. So he decided to take over the fan club. On March 8, 1993, Jimmie Bowen sent the following letter to all members of his International Patsy Cline

Fan Club. "Dear Friends: After 13 years of running the Patsy Cline Fan Club, I have been ordered to cease the Fan Club by Charlie Dick's attorneys. He will now market Patsy Cline memorabilia through the new fan club run by his brother Melvin Dick." Thus, on the Labor Day weekend of 1993, Bowen was gone—and with him, any cooperation with Hilda's Patsy Cline Memorial Foundation. Ironically, over that Labor Day weekend, Hilda's foundation did give its first scholarship, but that weekend the new fan club went one way—and Hilda's foundation another.

Shortly before that weekend, on August 7, Hilda Hensley sent out the following letter to supporters of her foundation and to a list of members of Bowen's former fan club: "Dear Friend and Fan. Yes! There will be a memorial weekend for Patsy. The new fan club is having registration Fri. Evening Sept. 3 & Sat. several meetings-swap-business & a dance Sat. eve. at 9 pm. So we have cancelled our auction on Sat. eve. However, Sun, Sept. 5 as usual the grave side service memorial [will be held] in Shenandoah Mem. Park at 3p.m. and Sun. eve. at 5:30 social gathering in Banquet Hall Best Western Lee Jackson" [abbreviations in the original]. Hilda Hensley was sad to see Bowen go, but quietly she continued working on her book and planned museum.[25]

Fern Adams noticed the changeover and formally organized Celebrating Patsy Cline, Inc. (hereafter CPC), to promote a local museum. There seemed to be promise that something might finally happen because of the Adams' money. Then came a shock. On May 27, 1994, as reported on the front page of the *Winchester Star,* Fern Adams died at age sixty-six from lung cancer. The native Canadian, a Unitarian, an advocate for mental health, and the leader of CPC was gone. She was never able to mount a serious effort for a museum. The well-off of Winchester did business with her family, but never accepted her efforts on behalf of Patsy Cline. It was left to her son, Kevin Adams, to on carry the cause, in his mother's name.

Thereafter, the three organizations —the fan club, CPC, and the foundation—split the Labor Day weekend time slots. Events on Friday night were given to CPC; Saturdays were for the Fan Club; and on Sunday nights came Hilda Hensley's Foundation banquet. For fans who supported all three groups, it became awkward, at best.

Under oath, in a trial held in 2002 over the estate of Hilda Hensley, her son Sam, Jr., revealed what the plan was for the Patsy Cline costumes: "Question: Mr. Hensley, what did your mother tell you she intended to do with the stage outfits and items she had? Answer: She always wanted to have a museum to put them in, to display them. Question: And, why did she want to establish this museum? Answer: So she could display the Patsy Cline items. And, what she discussed with me was that at the time of her death if she had the museum, it would pass on to me and my sister for our benefit." In other words, Hilda Hensley had no reason, by the 1990s, to cooperate with any action by CPC, whose stated goal was to create a nonprofit museum.[26]

Hilda, who turned eighty in March 1996, openly gave up on Winchester as a site for her museum and started seeking other locations. Robby Meadows, a country performer based in Elkton, made contact with Hilda Hensley and her daughter about his hopes of starting a concert hall and museum honoring Patsy Cline in Elkton. In early May 1995, the Elkton Downtown Revitalization Corp. (EDRC) formally agreed to help Patsy Cline's family establish a museum in Elkton. But again the issue was money. EDRC never was willing to offer enough to entice Hilda Hensley. Sylvia Hensley Wilt was blunt: "What we are looking for is someone or some group that will help give us a building or charge a nominal lease." Sylvia added, "Earlier efforts by a number of different citizen groups from Winchester failed." So did the effort in Elkton.[27]

Charles Dick was not surprised that the Winchester elite ignored Patsy. "That's Virginia—a weird state. It's got its old ways." Dick told the Winchester Star reporter a story about a wealthy Winchester couple who approached Patsy and him in Las Vegas in 1962. "Of course, back in Winchester, they didn't know who we were." His younger brother Melvin Dick stated that, in Apple Blossom parades, Patsy was cheered in poor neighborhoods and snubbed "uptown on Washington Street," the wealthiest section of Winchester. Melvin Dick remembered an icy silence. "On certain streets they [the crowd] would holler and applaud, and then in the ritzy sections just absolutely ignore her as she went by." Eugene Gunter, a local attorney, who had spearheaded the petition drive to have a highway named for Patsy Cline, noted, "You've got to have been here two or three centuries to be considered a native. Hell, that girl put us on the map."[28]

In its July 30, 1996, issue, the leading country music fan magazine, Country Weekly, asked: Why nothing in Winchester? The answer was consistent with the ideas expressed in other publications. "The town did not accept her," Phil Whitney, long affiliated with WINC-AM, stated for the record. Whitney went on, "She was from the wrong side of the tracks." Judy Sue Huyett-Kempf, manager of the Chamber of Commerce's Visitor Center, stated that daily she witnessed visitors coming to the Visitor's Center, looking for anything relating to Patsy Cline. The current owner of the Shenandoah Memorial Park reported that people—some from outside the United States—came daily to find Patsy Cline's grave, and openly wept. Country Weekly found one tourist from England who said, "I'm here for Patsy. I'm going to touch what she touched, eat what she ate, walk where she walked and see what she saw." By the end of 1996, the singer had become an icon—but not in Winchester.

In 1996, a live tribute show, *Always . . . Patsy Cline* had just finished a two-year run at Nashville's Ryman Auditorium, where Patsy Cline once sang. Such tribute shows had long been a fixture since the Beatles broke up in the 1960s and Elvis died in 1977. The Patsy Cline tribute shows started simply enough. In 1988, a two-woman musical *Always . . . Patsy Cline* premiered at Stages Repertory Theatre in Houston, Texas. Ted Swindley, the theater's founding artistic director, wanted to fashion inexpensive plays to fill the smaller venues of the Houston complex. Swindley sought to develop ideas for a small summer musical that would have broad appeal for audiences that never made it to Broadway revivals. A young singer in his company spent her spare time singing the Patsy Cline repertoire, and Swindley penned a show on a very simple "local" idea: "Did Patsy ever perform in Houston?" After a little research, Swindley discovered a former Houston housewife, Louise Seger, who had corresponded with Patsy Cline. What intrigued Swindley most was that, at the end of each letter that Patsy wrote to Louise, was the closing "Always, Patsy Cline." He had his title.

The warmth and humanity of Patsy's letters surprised Swindley, who simply could not imagine Patsy Cline writing letters. Swindley used the letters as his organizational hook: Have a Louise Seger character tell of meeting her idol, Patsy Cline, and then talk to her idol at her kitchen table. Yet in 1988, Swindley was not so sure this idea would work; his initial production lasted only forty-five minutes. But the show became an instant audience pleaser, and Swindley doubled its length. In 1990, he repremiered this revised, longer version at the Spoleto festival, held annually in Charleston, South Carolina. Swindley had no idea that he was tapping directly into the wave of iconography of Patsy Cline.

While writer and director Ted Swindley gets the auteur credit, the national success of *Always . . . Patsy Cline* is due to producer Randy Johnson, who arranged to franchise bookings and dealt with Charles Dick for necessary rights. By 1992, Charles Dick, as executor of the Patsy Cline Estate, approved *Always . . . Patsy Cline* as the official Patsy Cline tribute play. Johnson scored national prominence and press coverage on June 9, 1994, when *Always . . . Patsy Cline* was chosen to reopen the Ryman Auditorium, after the former home of the Grand Ole Opry had sat empty in downtown Nashville for twenty-two years. The tribute show ran to critical acclaim and packed houses in Nashville for an amazing two years, and made a star of Mandy Barnett. From 1989 to 1997, Randy Johnson produced or co-produced more than five hundred productions of *Always . . . Patsy Cline,* including a remarkable five-year run at Denver's Arts and Culture Center. Johnson even persuaded MCA to release a "cast album" of the Ryman–Mandy Barnett show. Under Johnson's guidance, *Always . . . Patsy Cline* was, according to

American Theatre Magazine, one of the top ten most produced plays in the United States between 1992 and 1996. This tribute play continues to appear today, with a new production announced each week.[29]

The *Always . . . Patsy Cline* live soundtrack included Mandy Barnett singing eighteen Patsy Cline songs. Later versions of the live tribute expanded the number of songs to twenty-seven, as Randy Johnson negotiated with copyright holders. Johnson sold the show as "based on a true story" of Cline's friendship with a fan. This tale of female friendship provided the cues for the lead to sing the various Patsy Cline songs. The Seger character offered down-home humor and emotional support, and even encouraged audience participation.

By 1996, *Always . . . Patsy Cline* had become so popular that performing arts centers across the United States treated it as a reliable "cash cow." It was the Houston Stages Repertory Theatre's largest source of revenue. Houston Stages Repertory Theatre began to use revenues from *Always . . . Patsy Cline* to fund new plays and mount the classics. Ted Swindley had found exactly what he was looking for.[30]

But it was not clear that *Always . . . Patsy Cline* would become *the* tribute play. For example, on May 19, 1989, the Palms theater of St. Petersburg, Florida, created the show *For the Love of Patsy Cline*. This served as a nostalgic commentary, as an actor recited tales from his bland adolescence, alternating with a woman singing Patsy Cline. The story centered on the Baby Boomer male reflecting on how much Patsy Cline had meant to him when he was a boy. Like *Always . . . Patsy Cline,* the performance was judged on the basis of the Patsy Cline imitator's performance. By the time she slid into "Crazy," audience members demanded that "Patsy Cline" return for one last encore. The attraction of the songs worked, but the narrative failed. For *The Love of Patsy Cline* was not going to become an evergreen like the one fashioned in Houston. Fans seemed to prefer the tale of a fan meeting her idol.[31]

Fans also liked the loose narrative of two women bonding over coffee through a long night, and the back story of a fan, Louise Seger. The mass media loved the Seger story: how she never expected to hear from Cline again, how she received many letters and phone calls, how sad she became when learning of the death of her idol—and friend.

Only in Nevada did pure tribute one-woman Patsy Cline shows thrive, as Nevada had a unique state law that protected entertainers from having to pay fees to any estate. Sharon Haynes took her show to Las Vegas, and starred for years in a one-woman tribute, *Patsy Cline Memories: A Tribute to Patsy Cline* at the Gold Coast Hotel. Haynes's attorney advised her that doing a tribute show in Nevada was protected.

"I do a tribute," Haynes emphasized, indicating that she speaks in the third person, not first person, during the performance. Instead of saying, "I recorded this song in 1963," she said, "I say, 'It was 1963 when this song was recorded,'" to meet the Nevada statute.[32]

By May 1995, *Billboard* concluded that through these tribute plays, "Patsy Cline's Music Lives On." *Always . . . Patsy Cline* was setting box-office records at the newly reopened Ryman Auditorium, and the cast album, starring Mandy Barnett, was selling briskly. At record stores, MCA had the *Always . . . Patsy Cline* cast CD racked both in the Patsy Cline and the original cast recording bins. *Billboard* surveyed theater managers, who agreed that everywhere across the United States, *Always . . . Patsy Cline* drew excellent crowds and made extraordinary profits, since costs were so low: The production required only a two-woman cast, a five-piece band, inexpensive props, and two costume changes.[33]

By February 6, 1996, the fan magazine *Country Weekly* profiled Louise Seger as *Always . . . Patsy Cline* finished its two-year run at the Ryman. (At this point, Patsy Cline's *12 Greatest Hits* still stood atop the *Billboard* country catalog charts, after five years.)

Louise Seger recalled, "The first time I heard Patsy was back in 1957 on the Arthur Godfrey show and I thought, 'Good Lord, that's how I'd like to sing.'" But it took Seger four years before a Houston DJ informed her that Patsy Cline was scheduled to perform there. She arrived early with girlfriends, Seger remembered. "I saw a woman walk in and sit down at a table. I knew it was Patsy. I decided to get real brave and introduce myself. She turned to me with that open smile and we just clicked." Seger recalled: "We discussed loves lost, loves found, loves yet to be. We talked about her troubled marriage and the pain she endured being away from her children. It was just two people baring their souls." Early the next morning, Seger rushed Patsy to the airport, expecting never to hear from her again. But within two weeks, she received the first of what turned out to be many letters, and also phone calls, they would exchange before Cline's death. Seger saved these letters, and they became Ted Swindley's fortunate discovery.[34]

In September 1996, *Variety* explained how *Always . . . Patsy Cline* was changing the regional theatrical industry. It headlined, "Big Touring Productions Are Done." The trade magazine reported, "The live theater industry had come a long way from the big touring tuners [*Variety*-speak for Broadway musicals], but shows such as "Always ...Patsy Cline" were emerging as the growth sector of regional nonprofit arts centers: small, sit-down shows in cities where going to the theater is a rare occasion." *Always . . . Patsy Cline* was setting house records for runs from Cleveland to Denver. All provided a steady, reliable flow of cash that made them irresistible to regional theaters. For example, at the Denver Center for the Performing Arts, *Always . . . Patsy Cline* covered the center's entire overhead for the year. *Variety* even assigned this phenomenon its own term: "a sit-down classic."[35]

It was inevitable that someone would try to match *Always . . . Patsy Cline*. Canadian Dean Regan mounted *A Closer Walk with Patsy Cline* in Vancouver, British Columbia, and took his sold-out show on tour across Canada and then ran it for nine months at the Playhouse Theatre in Boston. Like Swindley, Regan personally directed the initial productions, and then began to license the concept to small venues that had had success with *Always . . . Patsy Cline*. Regan's *A Closer Walk with Patsy Cline* offered a looser biographical narrative, told by a Winchester radio station DJ. Regan, after securing permission from Charles Dick, provided regional theaters complete scripts and scores, press materials, and background slides. Regan even advised that (pending availability) he could book Charlie Dick to generate publicity. But *A Closer Walk with Patsy Cline* never had the success of *Always . . . Patsy Cline*.

The other character, who was there, like Seger, to offer cues for the Patsy Cline impersonator to sing, was a mythical DJ, Little Big Man, who narrated from his studio at WINC. Productions usually employed a set resembling an old-fashioned Wurlitzer jukebox to frame the bandstand, with the radio studio just off to the side. The script called for various locations at which Patsy performed, such as the Grand Ole Opry, which made the play more expensive than *Always . . . Patsy Cline* to create. And audiences still seemed to prefer the story of the fan to the pure biography.[36]

From the stages of Branson, Missouri, by then the new capital of live country music performance came Gail Bliss as Patsy Cline—also with Charles Dick's blessing. Bliss had toured extensively in the starring role of both *A Closer Walk with Patsy Cline* and *Always . . . Patsy Cline,* so in 1995, she created for Branson visitors *Patsy!* She spent 1995 packing two shows a day at the 3,800-seat Grand Palace. With eleven period costumes, four wigs, and the performance of twenty of Patsy's songs, Gail sought to highlight the tragedy and gift "from God" to give her audiences "a family tribute show." Bliss concentrated on looking back from the death of Patsy Cline as a blessing, as part of the larger Christian perspective of life.[37]

All these musical tributes reinforced the wave of iconization, as did the sales of Patsy Cline's *12 Greatest Hits* – now out on CD -- and constant praise and awards. Only icons commanded tribute shows. British producer Mervyn Conn created *Patsy Cline—the Musical,* a Patsy Cline musical tribute to tour the UK. Conn created a two-person musical, starring Irish singer Sandy Kelly and George Hamilton IV (who had worked with Patsy Cline on *Town and Country Jamboree* in 1956), with "Patsy Cline" and George Hamilton IV singing duets and telling stories. This musical tribute jumped from song to song, rather than using a narrator to cue the Patsy Cline imitator.

"Greatest Hits on CD"

"The playbill for Patsy Cline - The Musical"

Patsy Cline—The Musical proved so successful that, by 1994, it had landed in London's West End (the equivalent of Broadway). Remember in the show, Hamilton praised Kelly, "I've got a great respect for Sandy's talent. She's got the same spirit, strength, power and fire that made Patsy Cline so special. I've never seen anyone capture the 'essence' of Patsy on stage the way Sandy does."

Kelly's association with Cline's music went back to the late 1980s, when she covered "Crazy," and made it number 1 in her native Ireland. Kelly noted, "I told [Conn] from the start that there were substantial Cline impersonators—including a man who, according to [Owen and Harold Bradley], is the nearest thing to Patsy they've ever heard. . . ." She did not want to become Patsy Cline, but to honor her. The British press praised this tribute when it moved to London's West End. Following an acclaimed season at London's Whitehall Theater, *Patsy Cline—The Musical* again toured the United Kingdom, lasting six years in all.

This was conclusive proof of the international iconic status of Patsy Cline. Indeed fans abroad—particularly in the United Kingdom—seemed to bond with the recordings of Patsy Cline abroad.

NOTES

Chapter 9

[1] The Nashville Banner, May 1, 1980: 32.

[2] LA Times, March 30, 1982: L77.

[3] Joel Whitburn, Country Annual: First Edition 1944-1997 (New York: Billboard, 1998); Music City News, April 1982: 8; Michael Streissguth, Like a Moth to a Flame: The Jim Reeves Story (Nashville, TN: Rutledge Hill Press, 1998).

[4] See web site www.RIAA.com

[5] Eric. D. Daniel, Dennis Mee, and Marck H. Clark, Magnetic Recording: The First 100 Years (New York: The Institute of Electrical and Electronics Engineers, 1999); Robin James, Doing Cultural Studies: The Story of the Sony Walkman (Thousand Oaks, CA: Sage, 1997).

[6] NYT, September 2,1987: D1.

[7] Rolling Stone, July 14, 1988: 44.

[8] The Chicago Tribune, September 7, 1989: 17E.

[9] Billboard, August 29, 1992:10-11; Billboard, June 6, 1998: 71; Goldmine Annual 1994: 56-59; Forbes, January 30, 1995: 58.

[10] See, for example, The Boston Globe, February 26,1989: E2.

[11] Victoria Starr, k.d. lang: All You Get Is Me (New York: St Martin's Press, 1994); William Robertson, k.d. lang: Carrying the Torch (Toronto: ECW Press, 1994).

[12] Rolling Stone, July 1987:136, 139; Canadian Composer, November 1987: 44; Canadian Living, November, 1989: 38-39.

[13] Music City News, July 1988: 76; Billboard, March 10, 1990: 14; Variety, April 15, 1957: 210; Billboard, 18 August 1990:11.

[14] Details, October 1985: 33.

[15] WS, October 6, 1980: 33; WS, October 15, 1980: 31.

16 WS, April 29, 1981: B1.

17 WS, June 28, 1981: B1.

18 NVD, September 3, 1985: A1; NVD, October 11, 1985: A1; WS, October 11, 1985: A1.

19 WS, February 27, 1986: A1; WS, March 8, 1986: B1.

20 WS, October 23, 1986: A1; WS, October 24, 1986: A1.

21 Letter, dated May 15,1988, Sylvia (Hensley) Wilt to fan, in files of University of North Carolina Southern Folklife Collection, Chapel Hill, North Carolina.

22 The Allegheny Highlands (newspaper), November 3, 1990: B1.

23 WS, August 24, 1989: B1.

24 WS, September 11, 1989: B1.

25 TRIAL.

26 TRIAL.

27 The [Elkton, Virginia] Daily Banner, May 4, 1995: A1; Wpost, August 27, 1995: B3.

28 The Washington [D.C.] City Paper, April 7, 1995: 24-28.

29 web site www.randyjohnson1.com – accessed March 6, 2006.

30 web site   www.tedswidleyproductions.com -- accessed March 5, 2006.

31 The St. Petersburg [Florida] Times, May 20, 1989: 2D.

32 web site   www.broadwaytovegas.com – accessed September 21, 1998; Viewpoint magazine, February and June 1999.

33 Billboard, May 6, 1995: 22.

34 CW, February 6, 1996: 33-34.

35 Billboard, May 6, 1995: 22.

36 web site   www.walkwithpatsycline.com – accessed March 7, 2006.

37 web site www.gailbliss.com – accessed March 7, 2006.

Chapter 10

Iconography Contested: A Struggle in Winchester

During the events of the Labor Day weekend of August 29 through September 2, 1996, in Winchester, Virginia, the two stars of *Patsy Cline—The Musical* flew in from London to support the creation of a Patsy Cline Museum. Sandy Kelly and George Hamilton IV reprised their roles from their West End hit show to help CPC gain funds for the woman Kelly adored and Hamilton greatly praised. But the outcome proved disappointing. The silent auction where they entertained raised only $2,500, and their performance brought in another $2,500. This weekend simply proved that even Kelly and Hamilton, stars in a London hit, could not help Patsy Cline achieve iconic status in Winchester, Virginia, even though she held such status worldwide.

In 1996, the best hope Winchester had of gaining a Patsy Cline museum lay with the late Fern Adams' son, millionaire Kevin Adams. He was an energetic man about to turn forty, and in 1996, he took over his late mother's quest. Kevin Adams made no secret about the fact that he was willing to pay Hilda Hensley three times the appraised value of

608 South Kent Street. To Winchesterites, Adams symbolized the new Baby Boomers who had moved there to escape the suburban sprawl of Washington, DC. To Hilda Hensley, he came off as a person who sought to destroy her dream of a museum that she could pass on to her son and daughter. Hilda Hensley clung to her plan of eventually publishing her stories about Patsy Cline, garnering hundreds of thousands of dollars in royalties, opening her museum, and filling it with her costumes. It would be the sole place in the world for fans to see her collection of Patsy Cline's clothes and other memorabilia.

Yet in the decade from 1996 to 2005, no museum opened in Winchester. This period offers a fascinating case study of the struggle to have the town of Winchester to give Patsy the recognition the rest of the world thought she so richly deserved. As of 2005, there existed only one new attraction to celebrate Patsy Cline, a Commonwealth of Virginia historical marker standing in front of 608 South Kent Street.

As the *Winchester Star*'s resident local historian (his column "Valley Pike" ran every Wednesday in the *Star* throughout this period), Adrian O'Connor, summed up the way Winchester natives judged status: "In chatting with local folk, either they [are] natives or come-heres." He adroitly observed that he "had been told flat-out told or gently reminded that one can't consider yourself a true [Winchesterite] unless you've graduated from Handley High School." Patsy was still "an outsider" in the town where she had lived and was buried.[1]

Millionaire Kevin Adams, too, was an outsider when he decided to honor his mother's desire to fund a Patsy Cline museum. There was no question that Kevin Adams had the money, but he failed to enlist other members of Winchester's monied class to help him, and so decided to go it alone. At first he funded a study that called for a self-sustaining real estate development, with which he was comfortable, as this was his life profession. After numerous announced plans, Kevin

Adams settled on a "real estate" solution—purchase 608 South Kent Street and turn it into a Patsy Cline Museum.

But this idea proved impossible to execute. Hilda Hensley would not even answer the door to meet with him. Any effort, Adams reasoned, needed Hilda's help, but she and Adams had two had different agendas. Hilda was writing stories for her book *From the Cradle to the Grave,* which she planned to publish to finance her museum. She handwrote anecdotes on legal yellow tablets as she remembered past events. Hilda would fill one tablet, and then start another. About this time, Hilda bought her daughter Sylvia a personal computer so that Sylvia could transcribe the stories. Meanwhile, Kevin Adams waited as Hilda unrealistically held onto her dream. She believed that she needed one million dollars.

In 1997, Hilda Hensley even began to generate cash by renting some of her items to Opryland Attractions, Inc., operator of the Opry Land Museum. With no legal advisor or agent, all Hilda got was two payments of $3,000 each. The items included a royal blue and white western suit with six inches of white fringe; one red two-piece, wool gabardine western suit with four inches of fringe and rhinestone notes; one pair of white leather size 8 western boots; a brown wig, used by Patsy Cline to cover her facial scars after her June 1961 auto accident; and assorted other memorabilia. All this, Kevin Adams was willing to purchase, but Hilda Hensley refused to deal with a wealthy Winchester. These items stood as the core of Hilda's museum.[2]

Thus, any local action to honor Patsy Cline moved at a slow pace. On the front page of the February 14, 1997, the *Winchester Star* headlined, "A Welcome Entrance Sign's Construction Signals 5-Year Project Is Almost Done." It had taken three mayors, five years, and miles of red tape after working-class Winchesterite Hunter Hurt began his quest to erect a more attractive "welcome sign" at the entrance to Winchester; controversy swirled as he wanted to include most prominently "Home of Patsy Cline." Finally, crews assembled the fifteen-by-eighteen-foot wooden sign just off Interstate 81.

In 1997, as Patsy Cline's iconic status swept the United States, the Winchester-Frederick County Chamber of Commerce joined forces with Hurt to have the sign erected to increase tourist dollars. But the social powers of Winchester, as they had ten years earlier with their reluctance to rename Pleasant Valley Road, Patsy Cline Boulevard, objected to the "Home of Patsy Cline" portion of the welcome sign, and the city denied Hunt's request to erect the sign. The Winchester City Council would not allocate any monies for the construction of the sign, so Hurt and the Chamber of Commerce had to solicit the materials for its construction and the labor to create the sign from a half-dozen companies as in-kind donations. Shenandoah University provided the land. The City Council finally relented—but only after five years. On one level, this request seemed like a small matter; to natives, however, it was an admission that Winchester was embracing Patsy.[3]

By August 27, 1997, the *Winchester Star* reported on Kevin Adams' mission and quoted him as stating, "The CPC is raising money to fund a museum in honor of Cline and hopes to fuel that effort in coming years with funds from the weekend. [Indeed] the primary purpose of the weekend has been to raise money," said Adams. CPC Chairman Richard Dick (no relation to Charles Dick) said he hoped to make big plans for the 1998 event to jump-start the smoldering effort to establish a museum as "[past events] have been a lot of work and haven't always been so successful financially." Richard Dick had been a local politician and hoped to convince those who voted for him to help fund the museum effort. Dick had no luck in his struggle.[4]

Over the Labor Day 1997 weekend, the museum issue hovered over the several hundreds who had journeyed to the Patsy Cline Fan Club meeting, and attended the CPC events. These attendees were working-class folks. One fan, a warehouse manager for an electrical sales firm, reported that he had sold all his Beatles recordings to pay for the trip to Winchester. Newspaper report after newspaper report noted that CPC could not fill the 1,300 seats of Handley High's auditorium for its special events, and thus the money the organization raised measured only several thousand dollars. Simply put, unless Kevin Adams stepped forward, there seemed little chance that a museum would open anytime soon.[5]

That September weekend, the Sunday night before Labor Day, Hilda Hensley's Patsy Cline Memorial Foundation met, as well, but also raised little money. Attendance was about one hundred, mostly made up of relatives, close and distant, of Hilda's. Her Patsy Cline Memorial Foundation did not openly prospect for money, but it auctioned off items that Hilda had made, such as items she knitted as she watched TV. Hilda put her big hopes on her autobiography. At that point, in September 1997, Hilda seemed a healthy older woman. No one suspected—not even her family—that she would be dead in a year and three months.

On September 2, 1997, the *Winchester Star*'s Adrian O'Connor, in his "Valley Pike" column, argued that Winchester had a museum—as he openly praised the efforts of the one man: "Doc and His Customers Keep Patsy's Flame Alive at Gaunt's." Harold "Doc" Madagan, who started working at Gaunt's in June 1958, six years after Virginia Hensley left, was a rare independent druggist in an age of chain drug stores. To draw more customers, he exploited the fact that Patsy Cline had worked there. Madagan maintained an ever growing Patsy Cline display, and when Labor Day weekend attendees and year-round fans pulled up for a visit, Madagan picked up extra business. Visitors who looked for a museum only found his display of a dozen photographs, a crude booth Madagan maintained had been served by Patsy Cline, and tales of glories past. The *Winchester Star* seemed happy that Doc was the primary keeper of the Patsy Cline legacy. He was a "townie."[6]

Kevin Adams sponsored CPC's hiring of consultant after consultant to lay out elaborate plans and propose solutions to its fundraising challenges. So for example, on March 5, 1998, CPC met with Cultural Communications, a local professional museum-planning company, to develop a "vision statement" to plan for the development of a Patsy Cline Museum. But this came to nothing, as the consultants laid out an elaborate museum, but offered no realistic way to raise the money to pay for it.

For Labor Day 1998, fan and Patsy Cline Web site master, Bill Cox, posted his observations from his first visit to Winchester for the Labor Day festivities. Cox lived in Knoxville, Tennessee, and confessed, "As the time for the [Labor Day] 1998 Festival drew near, it appeared that, once again, I wouldn't be able to [afford] the trip." Cox was another working-class Patsy Cline fan. While he skillfully spread the word about the glories of Patsy Cline to anyone who could access the Internet, Cox did not have any means to pay for a museum.

Cox reported that, during his September 1998, visit the CPC had announced the target for the opening date of the Patsy Cline Museum in Winchester as September 8, 2001. The envisioned complex, to be located downtown, also included a performing arts center, a Patsy Cline–themed café, and an office for the fan club. But Cox noted, "One idea for the project that didn't meet with the fans' approval [was] a sixty foot high neon sign, a winking Patsy (I shudder to think of it)." Offended, Cox turned his Web site into a fan forum for how properly to honor Patsy Cline in Winchester.

On Sunday, August 31, 1998Cox attended the annual graveside memorial service, conducted by Patsy's cousin, Patricia Brannon, as Hilda Hensley was not up to it. Cox did get to attend the Patsy Cline Memorial Foundation dinner and briefly met Hilda Hensley. "I wanted to get a picture of Mrs. Hensley, but she declined." (Hilda Hensley declined all requests for photographs at this point in her life.) Cox accurately described the Patsy Cline Foundation event: "There was a table full of bonnets, dolls, vests, afghans and aprons (handcrafted by Mrs. Hensley over the previous year) that were being sold, along with photos of Patsy, as fund raisers for the Foundation." One of the dresses that Hilda had made for Patsy (gold and black) was on display, along with a pair of shoes, Patsy's handwritten "idiot notes" (as she called them) of the first draft of the "invite" list to her wedding with Charles Dick, her bible from the 1940s, a scrapbook she kept as a teenager, and her Lifetime Achievement Grammy. Later, online, Cox mused that he been lucky to meet Hilda as this had been a once-in-a-lifetime opportunity. Hilda died three months later.

On September 3, 1998, Cox learned that at present, there were no cost or size estimates for the museum. Kevin Adams had paid for the "vision statement," and promised: "It will be a Disney World for Patsy Cline." (Adams seemed unaware of the Disney America theme park that had failed in Northern Virginia four years earlier.) Adams stated that the project would cost between three and ten million dollars would be needed: "Frankly, I think we need to go outside the community, as generous as our community is, to raise the full amount of money." That would prove to be an understatement.[7]

The December 10, 1998, death of Hilda Hensley—and the ensuing legal struggle between her daughter and son—called a halt to the creation of any museum. As part of the settling of the estate of Hilda Hensley, on February 3, 2001, Kevin Adams finally was able to purchase 608 South Kent Street, as well as 605 South Kent Street, where Hilda had lived for nearly 40 years. But the items to fill any museum were still in court, as Samuel L. Hensley, Jr., age fifty-nine, and Sylvia Hensley Wilt, age fifty-five, disputed their ownership. Both were poor and saw their mother's estate as a big payday, only they had polar opposite views on how each should and would collect that windfall. Sam, Jr., wanted to sell the materials for the money; he attached no sentimental value to any of them. In contrast, his sister had invested much of her identity in being "Patsy Cline's sister," and wished to keep all items "in the family."[8]

At age eighty-two, Hilda Hensley lost her battle cancer after a long life of poverty and bitterness as a woman who never prospered, despite the success of her world-famous daughter. Hilda died at the Winchester Medical Center, now located on the west side of town, not the same facility where she had delivered her famous daughter sixty-six years and three months earlier. Hilda's funeral proved a subdued Monday afternoon affair, held on December 14, and handled by the Jones Funeral Home, the same one that had handled Patsy's funeral thirty-five years earlier. Patsy's cousin Patricia Brannon handled the Hilda's arrangements. At the time, no one knew that, on March 26, 1988, Hilda had written her will on a yellow tablet at her dining room table in 605 South Kent: "In case of my death I leave all my furniture, clothes, real estate, and assets to my children, Sam and Sylvia to share equally in all things. It is my wish they will share this in friendship. They have only one another now. Please keep the family ties." Looking back, it seems as if Hilda feared that Sam and Sylvia would be incapable of sharing. Her motherly instinct proved correct.

Hilda's obituary, despite all attempts at avoiding publicity, graced the front page of the *Winchester Star* on Friday, December 11, 1998. Inside, the paper noted that "the family will receive friends from 7-9pm Sunday at the Jones Funeral Home." That is when Hilda's two surviving children started what would become a six-year battle over their mother's estate. As witnessed by Daniel K. Jones, then manager of the funeral home, the Rev. George Nickels, Rebecca "Becky" Williams (Sam Hensley, Jr.'s, fiancée), Patricia Brannon, and Christine Cole, Sylvia's eldest daughter, Sam and Sylvia publically argued over the details of the funeral. Sam protested the eulogy his sister had written, and they disagreed on the wording of the official obituary to appear in the *Winchester Star*. Sam wanted a closed casket; Sylvia wanted to give friends an opportunity for two viewings. As they screamed at each other, neither Sylvia nor her brother cared to mask their animosity. The only thing that they agreed on was that Hilda Hensley would be buried, at government expense, in a space she had reserved at Winchester's National Cemetery, next to Sam Hensley, Sr.[9]

The major wire service in the United States, the Associated Press, picked up the story of Hilda's death, and in 187 words, summarized the fact that Patsy Cline's mother had died. It never became a national story. But the real news was sitting in the Winchester Judicial Center, across the street from the *Winchester Star*, in the form of Hilda's handwritten will awaiting probation. Hilda had *not* named an executor for her estate. The Commonwealth of Virginia required a legally appointed executor before any division of assets could start. A few days after the funeral, Sam, Jr., advised his sister that he had contacted an attorney, and so on December 22, Sam, Jr., and Sylvia Hensley Wilt met with attorney Charles Alton for a consultation on probate procedure. This meeting was, as with all matters between brother and sister, heated, to say the least. Alton interceded, stating that he would have to acquire copies of all the pertinent documents, and scheduled a second meeting for December 28.

Meanwhile, on 23 December, Sylvia wrote a letter, and sent it to anyone who had ever supported the Patsy Cline Memorial Foundation. "Mother had been ill for some time, but in her usual way did not like to complain and was always concerned about being a 'bother' to anyone, not just family. After a steady weight loss of about four months [during fall 1998], she contracted the flu, which after about three weeks, seemed to be on the mend." Things came to a head, according to Sylvia, on Monday, December 7, 1998, at two p.m., when she took her mother to the emergency room of the Winchester Memorial Hospital. By Wednesday evening, December 9, 1998, the attending physician told Sylvia that test results had revealed that her mother had advanced cancer. "By the next afternoon, December 10, at 3:13 p.m., Mother softly closed her eyes and gently drifted away from us into a world free of pain, infirmity, or hardship." Hilda had suffered for four decades in Winchester; her living offspring were now poised to inflict as much suffering on each other as they legally could.

Sylvia stated idealistically in the letter to the supporters of the Patsy Cline Foundation: "From the affluent doctors and businessmen for whom she babysat and sewed, to those who felt themselves somehow not so worthy, Mom never took note of their station in life and treated everyone the same." Hilda's status as a poor woman remained to the end of her life, and even as the mother of Patsy Cline, she still lived in a rundown section of town. Hilda had struggled to make a life as a single woman, and had set an example for her elder daughter. But her younger daughter, then living close to the poverty line despite her graduation from high school, reminded all of the class distinction her mother never escaped as long as she remained in Winchester.[10]

If Winchester's class-consciousness defined Sylvia's bitterness, her brother's attitude proved far less complexly drawn. Sam, Jr., wanted to retire. With his identity less wrapped up in being Patsy Cline's brother, he saw his mother's death as an inheritance. He quickly learned that the value of her two South Kent Street houses stood at nearly $125,000, and that Kevin Adams had been seeking to buy them for years. So he pushed to sell both. It took his sister about a year of accumulating legal fees to agree to sell the houses to Adams. Sam had no interest in passing his mother's work on to his children, but wanted an annuity to guarantee that he and Becky Williams (eight years younger) could retire comfortably. This clashed with his sister's view; she clung to the idea that her mother's possessions should be preserved for a museum. Simply put, Sam wanted money, and Sylvia wanted the role of guardian of the Patsy Cline memorabilia. This eventually brought brother and sister into court with legal wrangling that lasted until 2004, six years after their mother's death.

To start the process of probating the Estate of Hilda Hensley, then Winchester City Clerk Michael M. Foremen recorded the will, noting the assessed value of the houses: 608 S. Kent at $51,800 and 605 S. Kent at $71,300. To avoid taxes, as advised by Charles Alton, Sam and Sylvia agreed to place an initial estimate of Hilda's personal property at $4,000. Brother and sister learned all this from the December 28 meeting with the lawyer. They also learned that, before they could sell the houses, an executor had to be named. Both wanted the job.

On January 8, 1999, Sylvia Hensley Wilt initiated her quest and made a video tape of the contents of 605 South Kent Street. Even Sylvia did not know about all the Patsy Cline related materials Hilda Hensley had possessed. Watching the video tape she made and later placed in the official record, we see Sylvia and her daughter peeking into one closet after another as Sylvia tries to remember the source of each object. Sylvia seems to be surprised at the dozens of Patsy's high heeled shoes that Hilda had stuffed into the depths of one of her upstairs closets. Then, in another closet, there were so many dresses that it proved difficult for the two women to wrestle them out and look at them. On tape, Sylvia remarked casually, "Mom never threw anything away."

Sylvia's daughter even found an old plow that Hilda used to plant her garden in the backyard. Until her death, Hilda Hensley proved to be a Great Depression subsistence farmwoman. Somewhat surprisingly, given the prevailing mythology, there was no evidence that Hilda Hensley had had any interest in music, other than the framed Patsy Cline Gold Records.

Under the laws of the Commonwealth of Virginia, any executor would get 5 percent of the value of the estate, plus expenses, but that required the beneficiaries, Sam, Jr., and Sylvia, to agree on an executor. This took a year. From the start, the process was acrimonious. For example, Sylvia accused her brother of harassing her and stormed out of one meeting, leaving a handwritten note that became part of the court record: "Think it over. You have nothing to lose but a sister."

Sam took this threat seriously. He knew his sister had worked as a paralegal and would take him to court. Previously, Sylvia had indicated she would sue anyone who mistreated her. One local who had graduated with her and was trying to help with the museum efforts wrote to Sylvia and she countered: "Not only do you have no right to intrude into my personal life, but you do <u>NOT</u> have permission to use my name or any information about me for any material, written, video, or otherwise, for your use, commercial use, or personal gain, and if you do or persist in that manner, I WILL SUE THE HELL OUT OF YOU!" She reiterated, "Almost everything that's been written has been full of misrepresentations and/or distortions of the truth." She then expressed that she was the proper heir to "Patsy Cline," and this would remain Sylvia's professed assertion all through the legal proceedings.[11]

On January 12, 1999, according to the legal records, Sam Hensley hired an attorney who advised Sylvia that, unless she responded by January 28, her brother would begin administration of the estate—alone. This prompted Sylvia to get her own lawyer that very same day. On February 2, Sam proposed to divide the clothing and costumes once belonging to Patsy Cline "50-50." Sylvia immediately turned down the offer. She did not wish to divide the estate "into bits and pieces," and her attorney argued that legal procedures, such as an inventory, still needed to be completed. Sylvia delayed. In one meeting, for example, Sam screamed at his sister that she stole a trunk from their mother's home, and Sylvia screamed back that the trunk belonged to her. This initiated a spate of accusations by Sam that Sylvia was robbing the estate. The animosity grew so heated, according to testimony at a later trial, that after a meeting on February 19, Sylvia went home and burned the approximately ten legal tablets on which Hilda had written her stories of her life with Patsy Cline. This invaluable manuscript was permanently lost.

On February 27, Sam formally proposed, through his attorney, "to divide the clothing and costumes once belonging to Patsy Cline," and ignored the question of an executor. That might have been a simpler and cheaper process, but the legal process demanded an executor. Sam and Sylvia looked for help and met with Winchester Clerk of the Court

Michael Foreman, who remembered later, "I told them a basic premise of probate law is that you 'cannot control beyond the grave.' So let's say she leaves her things to her children on the condition they never sell them. And let's say that 10 years after her death, one of the children does sell what she received. Who would know?" Foreman explained the basics of the law to both parties, and he thought that he had negotiated a solution, as he knew both from his days as a teacher. Foreman told them that, the longer they postponed agreeing on an Executor, the more the legal costs would accumulate, and their half-share of a small estate would shrink.

All Michael Foreman, with all his goodwill, accomplished was to inspire Sam and Sylvia to change attorneys. In an attempt to start a formal inventory, Sylvia arrived at her mother's house and found her brother, Becky Williams, and a new attorney, Stephen Pettler, already there. This session went no better than prior meetings, and another screaming match ensued.

Finally, on May 7, 1999, Pettler filed suit against Sylvia to force her to sell the two homes on South Kent Street and then split the cash equally with her brother. Pettler knew that Kevin Adams was still willing to pay top dollar. On June 1, Phillip Griffin, II, Sylvia's attorney, stalled. But the legal expenses accumulated, and on December 15, 1999, Judge John E. Wetsel, Jr., ruled that the two homes on South Kent Street be sold. Judge Wetsel's ruling brought a dose of reality to the brother–sister struggle, and they and their attorneys approached Charles Alton, who agreed to become the executor. On January 1, 2000, Kevin Adams sent Charles Alton an offer of $250,000 cash for both homes. Sylvia balked. On March 31 of that year, Judge Wetsel appointed Pettler and Griffin special commissioners to affect a sale. The properties had to be sold by October 2000, or would risk going to public auction.

"Charles Alton's Office with Patsy Cline Items"

On May 22, Kevin Adams wrote a check for $1,000, as a down payment. Sylvia protested, stating that, as "a single person, with only one income, and a mortgage on my present home, it was not possible for me to negotiate a loan sufficient to buy another house." She continued to stall but on August 23, Kevin Adams came to an agreement with Sam for both homes for $127,000 cash. By this time Adams knew of the legal struggle and was no longer willing to pay $250,000. On August 31, Judge John Wetsel ordered the sale to Kevin Adams for both 605 and 608 South Kent Street properties. Still, it was not until the end of the year 2000 that Sylvia formally agreed, and in early 2001, Kevin Adams finally took possession of the homes; their contents were transferred to Estate executor, Charles Alton's, office. Had this struggle gone on any longer, a public auction would have taken place, since six weeks after Kevin Adams purchased Hilda's two homes on South Kent Street, on February 19, 2001, he died at age forty-three, of a heart attack while playing tennis. At least CPC got 608 South Kent Street for use as a possible museum.[12]

The next set of necessary decisions revolved around legally dividing the contents of 605 South Kent Street—that is, the "Patsy Cline items," as they were called in the legal proceedings. So starting on October 16, 2000, Sam and Sylvia, their attorneys, and executor Charles Alton met six times before the end of the calendar year to first divide anything *not* related to Patsy Cline. Sylvia would not even consent to this proposed division of the non-Patsy Cline items.. Knowing her brother's desire for cashing out, an infuriated Sylvia stalled on *any* division of property. So, on January 10, 2001, Stephen Pettler filed a suit against Sylvia Hensley Wilt for the theft of "17 missing items" belonging to the Hilda Hensley estate. Thus began the legal process that led to a civil trial of Sam Hensley, Jr., and executor Charles Alton (represented by Stephen Pettler) versus Sylvia Hensley Wilt (as represented by Phillip Griffin, II), a civil matter regarding the theft from the estate of Hilda Hensley. The actual trial was not held until February 28, 2002 and March 1, 2002.

Through most of 2001, legal documents flew back and forth, delaying the inevitable trial, and only adding to attorney and executor's expenses. On April 9, 2001, with Sylvia failing to produce the manuscript her mother had written, estate executor Charles Alton tallied up an estimate of the most valuable of the estate of Hilda Hensley: (1) a brown fur wrap, $50,000; (2) a brown two-piece suede skirt and vest with long leather fringe, $50,000; (3) a white chiffon dress, $50,000; (4) a light-weight red wool fringed western shirt and skirt, $50,000; (5) a red gabardine fringed western outfit, $50,000; (6) a blue rhinestone and fringed western outfit, $50,000; (7) a black and gold two-piece shirt and skirt outfit, $50,000; (8) a black gabardine two-piece fringed western pants outfit with embroidered white roses,

$50,000; (9) a black gabardine western pants outfit with white piping, $50,000; (10) a white fringed outfit with horse print and white and gold boots, $50,000; (11) a fringed denim vest and skirt with powder blue boots, $50,000; and (12) a full-skirted white dress with feathers around bottom, $50,000. These twelve items came to $600,000—well in excess of the valuation first placed by Sam and Sylvia, $4,000. Then adding in the still unseen manuscript, executor Charles Alton doubled the estimate, bringing his total to over $1.2 million. With more than a million dollars at stake, a trial was inevitable.

Through his depositions, Sam revealed his life history for the first time for the public record. After he dropped out of Handley High School, he had moved to Silver Spring, Maryland, a suburb of Washington, DC, to live and work. He returned to Frederick County, Virginia, in 1969, divorced, and then in 1985, moved to Bunker Hill, West Virginia, and shared a home with his fiancée, Becky Williams. He used his mother's address as home address so that he could retain his Virginia Master Plumber's License, confirmed that for *Sweet Dreams,* the movie, his mother got $100,000 and shared it equally with her two children. Sam had gotten a check for $33,000, but had netted $23,000 after taxes. As for the manuscript, he stated that Patricia Brannon and Becky Williams had read it. Becky said, "It was a beautiful piece."

By September 4, 2001, Judge John Wetsel, Jr., had had enough delays, and he ordered a trial for February 28 and March 1, 2002. On January 15, 2002, Charles Alton as the Hilda Hensley estate executor filed his first bill for $9,421 for expenses. As requested, on February 8, Alton filed with the court a plan to sell some items to pay his bill. Sam and Stephen Pettler proposed selling four items. This infuriated Sylvia. The stakes were growing, and the family squabble was about to turn into the most sensational local story of the year.

On February 28, 2002, at nine a.m., the civil trial—formally titled *Hensley and Alton v. Wilt*—began. At issue were the contents of a trunk, two dresses, and the still unseen Hilda Hensley-penned manuscript as Judge Wetsel trimmed the original list of 17 missing items to these four issues.. Sam and Charles Alton claimed that Sylvia had taken these items from the estate of Hilda Hensley. Charles Alton's estimate that these four Patsy Cline items were worth well in excess of $600,000 came mostly from a guess at the value of the manuscript Alton had not seen. (Indeed during trial testimony, one expert estimated the value of the missing manuscript at $700,000). At the center was John E. Wetsel, Jr., fifty-three, circuit court judge in Winchester. He had graduated from Washington & Lee. He had been appointed by the Virginia General Assembly to the Winchester Circuit Court in 1991, and this was his highest profile case in more than a decade on the bench.[13]

The March 1, 2001, *Winchester Star* headlined on its front page: "Who Owns Patsy Cline's Clothes?" The local press played this as a hillbilly family dispute. In Winchester the elite now had another reason to shun anything associated with Patsy Cline. With the manuscript as the most valued Patsy Cline item, Hensley and Alton argued that Hilda Hensley had given the handwritten tablets to her daughter to edit. Before a seven-member jury, Wilt's attorney, Phillip S. Griffin, II, argued that the manuscript belonged to Wilt, not the Hilda Hensley estate.

In the course of the trial, Sam had testified regarding what he knew of the manuscript.

Question: Mr. Hensley, when did you first learn about the existence of that manuscript?

Answer: I am not sure of the year. It was either somewhere around 1993, '94, '95, along in there. I went by mom's house one day and she went to fix me a cup of coffee. There was two or three legal pads laying there on the table. She said: "I want you to take a look at this."

Question: Mr. Hensley, did your mother tell you what her plans were for that manuscript?

Answer: Yes, sir. She said that she was going to have my sister type it up in page form. And that she was going to try to have it published.

Two witnesses, Becky Williams, and Hilda Hensley's "niece," Patricia Brannon, testified that Hilda would write three- to five-page stories in draft form on yellow legal tablets.

Becky Williams stated she had read the whole manuscript:

Question: Could you please characterize your relationship for the jury?

Answer: She was kind of like a mother. I mean, we were really close.

Question: How often did you visit Hilda Hensley?

Answer: Two or three times a week. I called her every day.

Question: Could you please describe what the manuscript looked like?

Answer: It was like nine legal pads, crammed full of her writings.

Question: Did you read the whole thing as it was presented to you?

Answer: Yes.

Question: And, what was the book about?

Answer: It was Hilda Hensley's life with Patsy Cline, from her birth until she died in the plane crash.

Question: Did it have a title to it?

Answer: I think she told me she was going to title it, "From the Cradle to the Grave."

Then Becky Williams told the jury about Hilda's lifelong obsession with fishing. She had started fishing when she lived on the Hensley farm in 1932, and then, later, when she could buy fish at the grocery store, she still like to "go fishin'" to relax. Becky Williams often joined her.

Hilda Hensley's "niece" Patricia Brannon also testified regarding her knowledge of the manuscript:

Question: And, were you close to your aunt?

Answer: Yes. Very.

Question: And, how often did you use to visit Ms. Hensley?

Answer: Sometimes once a week, and if I was in [Winchester] more. I would go by there every time I was in town. And, the last three or four years, at least three or four times a week.

Question: Now, during the time you knew Aunt Hilda, did you come to learn about a book she was writing?

Answer: Yes.

Question: Could you describe the book?

Answer: Well, she called it her "pages," and she would chuckle to herself and say she was writing a manuscript. She was writing down things about her life with Ginny from the time she was born up until the time she got killed in that plane wreck.

Question: And, what format or style was the book written in?

Answer: She wrote it in her own hand.

Question: Did you ever have an occasion to read the entire manuscript?

Answer: I read eight and a half, almost nine full legal pads, and she said she was not quite done.

Question: And, did Hilda Hensley ever tell you what she planned to do with the book? *Answer:* Yes.

Patricia Brannon then told the jury of Hilda Hensley's idea of using the royalties to finance a museum.

———————————

The March 2 headline that dominated the front page of the *Winchester Star* read: "Jury Believes Sister's Explanation Over Brother's Story." The jury ruled her not guilty of theft from her mother's estate. After a two-day trial, it took the jury but two hours of deliberation to decide. Sylvia swore under oath that she had destroyed the manuscript, and she stated that her mother had "washed her hands" of the manuscript after Sylvia revealed a childhood secret to her mother. Sylvia implied that this was abuse at the hands of an unstated family member. Although the jury of four men and three women exonerated Sylvia, in the long run, she lost the war because, as she had testified, she had burned the manuscript.

While Patsy Cline's bother and sister were battling in court, Patsy Cline was named by the Virginia Foundation for Women as one of outstanding women in Commonwealth history and forty-eight hours before the March 3 telecast of a local PBS television special "Patsy Cline: The Lady Behind the Legend." To those who lived outside Winchester, a museum seemed logical. But few in Winchester would give money to a museum that could easily have been financed by a brother and sister if they had worked together? Judge John E. Wetzel, Jr., had warned Sylvia that she had legally relinquished all rights to the manuscript and that he would hold her in contempt of court if she had lied. (As of 2011, the manuscript had not surfaced.)

With the trial resolved and Sylvia acquitted of any wrongdoing, and the estate halved in value, on March 21, 2002, Judge Wetsel reminded both parties that they would have to pay Charles Alton. Wetsel told them that he had ordered the houses to be sold and he would force another sale if necessary. He pushed both to compromise. On April 18, 2002, Alton pressed Sam and Sylvia to pay him. Frustrated, Judge Wetsel stated: "Choose three things to sell—if you all cannot do it, I will." Sylvia's lawyer, Phillip Griffin, II, proposed to sell a turquoise vest & shift, a pair of white western boots, and lavender vest with rhinestones. Sam readily agreed. Executor Charles Alton contacted Profiles in History, a broker of items associated with historical figures, and then Judge Wetsel warned them all of the possibility of a second round of sales, as he was leery of appraisals, which always seemed to become overestimates. He asked both parties "to grip reality; or more things will be sold." Wetsel wisely warned, "You all risk getting nothing. This is a family struggle and there is nothing more than a death struggle." On November 23, Wetsel ordered the brother and sister to have Profiles in History, of Beverly Hills, California, auction three of the items the following month. More bad press for the Hensley family.

"Profiles in History Catalog"

On January 24, 2003, Profiles in History reported to the court:

Item	Lot No.	DESCRIPTION	NET PROCEEDS
01	377	Patsy Cline cowgirl blue western outfit	$3,400
02	378	Patsy Cline stage outfit lame ensemble	$3,400
03	383	Patsy Cline white Western boots	$3,187.50

The total net amount added to only $9,987.50—and by then, Alton's fees exceeded $23,000, and were still climbing, as he charged to negotiate the public auction. Wetsel's warning had come to pass. A second sale would be required. Virginia Commonwealth law required that the executor be fully paid before the estate could be legally settled. So on April 14, 2003, Alton was back in court, wanting to be paid. Judge Wetsel pushed Sam and Sylvia to settle, rather than run up more legal fees. But Sylvia would not give up. On August 21, Sylvia stated, "This has been a conspiracy of five years to decimate the estate. They (her brother, Sam's lawyer, and Judge Wetsel) thought I'd not fight, and I fought. My brother stated he would keep me in court for twenty years and cost me everything. And it has."

On that same day, Judge Wetsel issued a court order for another auction to pay Charles Alton's fees. On November 18, 2003, the auction house, Christie's of New York City, sold sixteen "Patsy Cline items," for a net of $123,919. Wetsel concluded that the controversial sale had come about because of "the bitter fruit of internecine conflict," which bore not a feast but "a time of famine and anguish." Wetsel went on:

"I say, sell it all (and) wind this case up at the end of the year. I'm sorry this case has come to this." Sylvia openly wept in court.

Christie's put far more effort into this sale than had Profiles in History. Indeed, for this second forced auction, the auction's highest winning bid for a single item—$20,000 for "Patsy Cline Red Skirt and Top with Wagon Wheel/Steer Head Motif," made by Hilda Hensley, exceeded the whole of the proceeds of the first auction. On December 19, 2003, Christie's made its sales records part of the ongoing legal record:

Sale: 1307 DATE OF AUCTION = 18 NOV 20003 Entertainment Memorabilia

Lot#	Description	Hammer Price	Commission/ Rate	Insurance	NET SUM
70	Sold	$4,500	-360.00 8.00%	-67.50 1.50%	$4,072.50
Patsy Cline Royal Blue Western Skirt and Top with Star Motif					
71	Sold	$20,000	-1,600.00 8.00%	-300.00 1.50%	$18,100.00
Patsy Cline Red Skirt and Top with Wagon Wheel/Steer Head Motif					
72	Sold	$6,500	-520.00 8.00%	-97.50 1.50%	$5,882.50
Patsy Cline Lavender Dress with Mauve High Heels					
73	Sold	$4,000	-320.00 8.00%	-60.00 1.50%	$3,620.00
Patsy Cline Navy Skirt and Blouse with Gold Trim					
74	Sold	$4,000	-320.00 8.00%	-60.00 1.50%	$3,620.00
Patsy Cline Blue Linen Dress					
75	Sold	$12,000	-960.00 8.00%	-180.00 1.50%	$10,860.00
Patsy Cline Pink Pants and Shirt with Black Record Design					
76	Sold	$8,500	-680.00 8.00%	-127.50 1.50%	$7,692.50

Patsy Cline Green Skirt and Shirt with White Fringe and Musical Notes

| 77 | Sold | $9,500 | -760.00 8.00% | -142.50 1.50% | $8,597.50 |

Patsy Cline Red Western Skirt and Top with Musical Note Motif

| 78 | Sold | $3,800 | -304.00 8.00% | -57.00 1.50% | $3,439.00 |

Patsy Cline White Skirt and Blouse with Silver Trim

| 79 | Sold | $4,800 | -384.00 8.00% | -72.00 1.50% | $4,344.00 |

Patsy Cline Leather Jacket and Stole

| 80 | Sold | $2,800 | -224.00 8.00% | -42.00 1.50% | $2,534.00 |

Patsy Cline Gold Lame Pants and Matching Shoes

| 81 | Sold | $10,000 | -800.00 8.00% | -150.00 1.50% | $9,050.00 |

Patsy Cline Cowboy Boots—Tooled with 'Patsy'

| 82 | Sold | $3,200 | -256.00 8.00% | -48.00 1.50% | $2,896.00 |

Patsy Cline Red Cowboy Boots

| 83 | Sold | $3,000 | -240.00 8.00% | -45.00 1.50% | $2,715.00 |

Patsy Cline White Cowboy Hat

| 84 | Sold | $1,100 | -100.00 Min | -16.50 1.50% | $983.50 |

Patsy Cline Belts (Two)

| 85 | Sold | $6,000 | -480.00 8.00% | -90.00 1.50% | $5,430.00 |

Patsy Cline Accessories: Knit Top, Black Hat, Wigs, Gold Heels, 2 Purses & Petticoat.

As before, what came to the Court proved far less than the "almost $124,000" reported in the press since Christie's sent Charles Alton a check for $93,836.50, the net. This settled Charles Alton's fees as executor. But this scattered the contents of a museum to all parts of the world. The "Patsy Cline items" that had been resting in 605 South Kent Street had gone off to the highest bidders. To potential backers of a museum to be located in Winchester, the question loomed large: What would it display? The press implied that there was little to show to the public. But there was much more in the estate.

Away from press coverage, on January 22, March 18, April 22, and May 20 of 2004, Judge Wetsel held open court sessions to distribute the remaining items. On May 20, Wetsel issued a court order calling for the parties to distribute all known assets by July 16, 2004. On June 7 and 8, the remaining items were divided, with Becky Williams and Stephen Pettler standing in for an ailing Sam and Sylvia, assisted by her attorney Philip Griffin, II, alternating in selecting items from the piles located in the office of Charles Alton. Each party had one minute to choose and all personal property items were finally disbursed.

They were distributed the following way: Sam got some clothing (a black and silver Mexican-style crepe dress, a gray leather colt skin long coat, red chiffon skirt, green and white gingham dress, silver lamé pants, royal blue rhinestone spaghetti-strap dress, spaghetti-strap cotton dress, among other items), a white "hoedown" cowboy hat, the cream colored hat identifiable from her wedding, assorted slacks, and dozens of shoes. Mixed in were photographs, belts, costume jewelry, gloves and scarves, necklaces and earrings, and Hilda Hensley's sewing machine. (In time these would make their way to the museum planned by CPC.)

Sylvia selected what she deemed to be valuable family heirlooms. She chose a brown fur coat, a Navy blue taffeta dress, a pink sun dress with gold leaf design strap over the left shoulder; a silver lamé-topped dress with a chiffon bottom, and a dress made of black chiffon. Indeed most of what Sylvia chose was clothing, mainly dresses, purchased from stores. If there was a theme for Sylvia's selections, it seemed to be clothing: turquoise blue Bermuda shorts, pink Capri pants, gold slippers, multicolored high heels, black zebra-stripe shoes, brown alligator high heels, and high-heeled black shoes with "see through" lace. Surprisingly, Sylvia selected only one outfit sewn by her mother, and passed on her mother's sewing machine. It seemed that Sylvia was creating her own ideal Patsy Cline fashion museum.

By August 19, 2004, the legal battles seemed to be over—almost six years after Hilda Hensley's death. Then executor Charles Alton found even more items to distribute. In open court on December 22, Judge Wetsel had the parties alternate choosing items until he was satisfied that the Estate had been fully distributed. Each party had spent at least $60,000 on legal fees. And they never realized any of the monies from the anticipated publication of the manuscript.[14]

In the end while Sam paid his legal bills, Sylvia ended up owing her lawyer $47,307.45, which she never paid. By November 2004, Sam was dead, and Sylvia was working as a receptionist at the Winchester Medical Center, the very place her mother had died six years earlier. But the headlines from the ongoing legal battle made raising money for a proposed museum very difficult. The trial only convinced Winchester's elite that the family was still "hillbilly trash," and the court battles reminded the town's upper classes of the Hatfields and the McCoys. Sylvia and Sam gave the already biased elite of Winchester a reason *not* to donate to a museum for Patsy Cline.

On March 23, 2005, a new president of CPC invited me to lunch, knowing of the days I spent in the Winchester Clerk's Office, taking notes and copying legal documents from the brother and sister's legal wrangling. Asking for suggestions about first steps, the new head of CPC bit at my final pitch: Apply for a Virginia State Highway Marker to be placed in front of 608 South Kent. It turned out that he was a historical marker buff, and he loved that this could happen for only twelve hundred dollars. After contacting the authorities and verifying my information, the new CPC president asked me to help write the sign. The state regulations stated, one hundred words! But the new head of CPC brushed aside the rules, and wanted to send in three hundred.

On April 5, 2005, Scott Arnold, manager of the Commonwealth of Virginia's Historical Marker Program, sent me the following e-mail: "Thanks for providing me [the required 100 words]. This is exactly what I needed. Scott (Scott Arnold, Manager of the Historical Highway Marker Program, Department of Historic Resources, 2801 Kensington Avenue, Richmond, VA 23221)"

On May 12, CPC's board approved the text, and so did Scott Arnold's advisory board. The official unveiling ceremony was scheduled for Saturday afternoon, September 3, 2005.

On June 2, Arnold sent me another e-mail:
Subject: RE: Patsy Cline Virginia Historical Marker

Good day, the approved text (same as the one I sent to you earlier this week) states: "PATSY CLINE: COUNTRY MUSIC SINGER—Patsy Cline (Virginia Patterson Hensley), world-famous singer, lived in this house. She was born in Winchester Memorial Hospital on 8 Sept. 1932. On 21 Jan. 1957 she won Arthur Godfrey's Talent Scouts national television show's competition singing 'Walkin' After Midnight.' In 1961

'I Fall to Pieces' became a hit. Her iconic 'Crazy' was released a year later. Her haunting voice took her to the top of the charts, and her style and popularity have never waned. She died in an airplane crash on 5 Mar. 1963 in Camden, Tennessee. In 1973, she was inducted into the Country Music Hall of Fame. Cline is interred at nearby Shenandoah Memorial Park." I have placed order for the sign in preparation for the dedication on September 3, 2005. Sincerely, Scott Arnold

On August 21, the head of CPC e-mailed me, "Re: Historical Marker Ceremony Douglas: Yes, it does seem a bit unreal to think back on our introductory lunch [and] your suggestion for the Historical Marker . . . thank you."

On September 3, 2005, the historical marker was dedicated, and Charles Dick and Patsy's Julie Fudge journeyed Winchester for the ceremony. At last fans had an official, permanent recognition of Patsy Cline in Winchester, no museum but a symbol to visit—which they did by the thousands in the following years.

The Commonwealth of Virginia had finally approved a local marker recognizing Patsy Cline's iconic status of an icon. The Commonwealth Marker Program recognized her greatness as a singer and her transformation of country music into the pop genre it had become by 2005. Winchesterites seemed puzzled. Why would this Handley High School dropout deserve to be ranked with great Virginians, like Civil War General Stonewall Jackson and the first president of the United States, George Washington, both of whom had museums in town? The historic marker represented a step toward local recognition, but only a small one.

It would take five more years for CPC to open 608 South Kent Street as a historic house, complete with tours and displays of rare Patsy Cline memorabilia. Responsible for this was Judy Sue Huyett-Kempf, who reconstituted the CPC board, and worked to raise the necessary money. Finally, in 2011, fans had a central place to find Patsy Cline in Winchester.

N O T E S

Chapter 10

[1] WS, May 6, 2009: B1.

[2] WS, February 15, 1997: A8; TRIAL.

[3] WS, February 14, 1997: A1, A8.

[4] WS, August 27, 1997: B1; WS, August 28, 1997: B1.

[5]   NVD, August 30, 1997:1.

[6] WS, September 2, 1997: B1.

[7] NVD, January 23, 1999: 1.

[8] WS, August 30, 1999: B1; WS, September 3, 1999: B1; WS, September 4, 1999: B1: WS, September 7, 1999: B1; NVD, November 11, 1999: WS, February 3, 2001: B1.

[9] WS, December 11, 1998:A1; WS, December 12, 1998, A1.

[10] Patricia Brannon Collection.

[11] Letter in CPC Collection.

[12] WS, February 21, 2001: A1.

[13] WS, March 16, 2002: B1.

[14] Notes taken by the author.

Chapter 11

The World Embraces Patsy Cline

Patsy's music has never stopped selling. At the end of the first decade of the twenty-first century, any serious list of the top one hundred worldwide best-selling musical artists of all time included Patsy Cline. The measure was the total number of singles and albums sold worldwide, in any form, including paid digital downloads. Statisticians estimate that Patsy Cline has sold in well in excess of one hundred million singles, LPs, eight-track tapes, audio cassettes, CDs, and downloads.

But this figure is undoubtedly conservative. No one could fairly or accurately estimate all the bootleg audio cassettes and all the independent, cheap LPs that fans have bought. And for international sales, estimates are crude; for example, I personally found in a visit to Amsterdam's open market that I was able to purchase a dozen CDs without any copyright labels.

Nevertheless, Patsy Cline's sales stand at an astonishing number. Record companies can make only so many compilations from her 102 recorded songs and two dozen live performances. The corporate behavior of music company executives suggests that they understood this fact. For example, in May 1997, RCA Records, by then owned by Bertelsmann AG of Germany, released a CD called *The Essential Patsy*

Cline. How could RCA release this CD when Patsy Cline had never recorded for that label? RCA simply licensed some of her 4-Star material from Sony Music, which owned the legal rights to those recordings, because RCA officials figured that the CD would sell—and it did.

So would "new" Patsy Cline sell? Yes. On June 28, 1997, *Billboard* announced that a forthcoming CD of a Patsy Cline live performance would be issued by MCA on the thirty-sixth anniversary of its recording. *Live at the Cimarron Ballroom* became headline news, as there existed no album of any live recording of Patsy not created for broadcast. On 29 July 1961, Patsy Cline had appeared with Leon McAuliff and the Cimarron Boys in Tulsa, Oklahoma. Somehow, someone had made a tape, and more than thirty years it was found at a yard sale. MCA bought exclusive rights from the parties it would not name, had its engineers clean the tape and released it as a CD. Fans brought the CD to hear Patsy Cline "perform live." MCA promoted that this CD contained three songs that Patsy had never recorded in a studio: "Shake, Rattle and Roll," "When My Dreamboat Comes Home," and "Stupid Cupid." With these songs as hooks, since they were pop and rock classics, MCA reasoned that it could easily sell this crossover. MCA Nashville chairman, Bruce Hinton, explained that he had heard the tape in 1995, it was of poor quality but Hinton approved MCA invest the necessary funds to make it sound like a "live" appearance—which it did because of its very flaws. Hinton explained: "Patsy Cline ranks up there among the other big musical influences in America in the last half century. They always say the Beatles, Frank Sinatra, and Elvis Presley, but to me there's a fourth, and it's Patsy Cline." Hinton even agreed to include her banter between songs.[1]

Patsy Cline's iconic status guaranteed wide praise—and made this CD a necessary purchase for any collector of popular music. In 1997 *Country Weekly* applauded *Live at the Cimarron Ballroom* as defining "country sophistication for the ages as authoritatively as Aretha Franklin defines soul." In short, the Cimarron Ballroom CD humanized an icon, and demonstrated her versatility—her ability to sing pop, country, and rock. To all commentators, this live performance showed Patsy Cline as a hard-headed genre buster with the will to perform sitting on a stool six weeks after she had almost died in a car crash. No longer was she just a country singer; the critics heralded Patsy Cline as simply a great singer.[2]

As the twentieth century neared an end, on March 20, 1999, *Billboard* noted, "Patsy's Popularity Won't De-Cline." Even though she had died in a plane crash two generations earlier, Patsy Cline lived on through her recordings. *Billboard* noted that her *12 Greatest Hits* set a record of 624 weeks on its charts, first on Top Country Albums (1987–91), and then, after the advent of SoundScan, on the catalog country charts (1991–99).[3]

On October 27, 1999, Rhino records released a five-CD box set called *R-E-S-P-E-C-T: A Century of Women in Music*. This was the first of the box set surveying the history of female singers in popular recorded music. Rhino selected only those women whose status demanded entry and would generate sales. Its selection crossed all popular genres and included signature tracks by 114 singers. Disk 1 offered Mamie Smith's 1920 "Crazy Blues," the first blues recording, male or female. Disk 2, *Torch, Twang and Swing,* covered the era from the mid-1930s through the mid-1950s, the rise of jazz (Ella Fitzgerald, Billie Holiday, Anita O'Day), and country (Patsy Cline's "Walkin' After Midnight"). Here Rhino settled for the original 4-Star recording because rights were cheap.

Rhino had asked for "Crazy," but balked at paying MCA's price. The five-CD box set also included an eighty-page book of essays and history, photos, and sound bites from such icons as Eleanor

Roosevelt, Shirley Chisholm, Rachel Carson, Margaret Sanger, and Gloria Steinem. Four years earlier these were the very women who had joined Patsy Cline on the "Heroine Worship" cover of the November 24, 1996, *New York Times Magazine.*

―――――――――

Honors abounded. In 1999, in Virginia Beach, part of the Hampton Roads urban complex, city officials voted Patsy Cline as a member of the first class of "Virginia Legends," for the city's version of a "Hollywood Walk of Fame." The Virginia Beach community leaders selected Patsy Cline to be honored along with the likes of George Washington, Thomas Jefferson, Ella Fitzgerald, Arthur Ashe, Robert E. Lee, Patrick Henry, Edgar Allan Poe, Woodrow Wilson, James Madison, James Monroe, Pearl Bailey, and Bill "Bojangles" Robinson, to become part of the city's "Legends Walk." The city had called for nominations, and required that the person be a legend "in politics, sports, music, science, or other field, had to either have been born in Virginia or lived in Virginia during a time in their lives, and had to have a national or global significance.

After the nominations closed, Virginia Beach city employees compiled short biographies and sent them to the presidents of every college and university in Virginia, the heads of all county and city historical societies, the heads of all public and college libraries throughout Virginia, the managing editors of every daily newspaper in Virginia, and the news directors of every television station in the Commonwealth. Each of the judge chose twenty-four potential legends in rank order. Then Virginia Beach city employees tabulated the votes and Patsy Cline other historic Virginia figures.[4]

On March 1, 2002, the city of Richmond—the former capital of the Confederacy, famous for its Monument Avenue to the heroes of the "Lost Cause"—recognized eight of Virginia's most notable women, past and present, during a kickoff event of Women's History Month. The Virginia Foundation for Women selected the notable women on the basis of their social and cultural contributions. The honorees included Hannah Lee Corbin, of Westmoreland County, who was Virginia's earliest known proponent of voting rights for women; Janie Porter Barrett, of Hanover County, who built a school for African-American girls; Jessie Menifield Rattley, of Newport News, the first black woman on the Newport News City Council; and Patsy Cline, of Winchester, "who became a world-famous and often-emulated singer."[5]

In March 2004, a national honor came when the Library of Congress added Patsy Cline's "Crazy" to the National Recording Registry; This list included "the most important recorded sounds—spoken, sung and instrumental music"—and Patsy Cline's "Crazy" was among the first chosen. In announcing her selection, the Librarian of Congress included in his formal statement, "Patsy Cline is considered one of the greatest country music singers and an inspiration to many contemporary female vocalists." Recommended by a board of experts, after nominations from across the United States, the selectees also included Judy Garland's Live Concert at Carnegie Hall, Otis Redding's soul classic "I've Been Loving You Too Long (to Stop Now)," and the Beatles' album Sgt. Pepper's Lonely Hearts Club Band. This meant that the Library of Congress, the largest library in the world, would preserve a copy of "Crazy" in its mammoth storage facilities. Patsy Cline had been declared an example of selected great recorded sounds.[6]

In the United States, Patsy was everywhere on TV. For example, starting in March 1997, AT&T began running a television advertising campaign featuring two teenagers coming home after a date, then sending each other love notes (via AT&T Internet service). Over this narrative-pitch came Patsy Cline singing "Walkin' After Midnight." On March 30, 1997, in an Internet post, a teenager went on a mission to find out what that song was. She asked her mother, who suggested Patsy Cline. The teen then posted, "What a great song! I managed to capture the commercial on tape the other day when I was taping a TV show that I wanted to watch. I've run that tape over and over again!" The process of youthful discovery of Patsy Cline continued.[7]

On October 25, 2000, the CBS television network broadcast a made-for-TV movie called "One True Love," about a firefighter and a kennel owner who are engaged to others, but meet when they have an auto accident. In a flashback, we learn that both, while driving toward the place where they would collide, were searching for something to listen to on the radio and ended up on the same station, which was playing "Crazy." This lasted a few seconds as both were mesmerized by Patsy Cline -- and then they crashed. The rest of the movie shows them getting together and finally marrying—a classic romance. Here "Crazy" was used by a new generation of TV professionals to symbolize the mythic romance of the right person for everyone for all the wrong (crazy) reasons Young people who had grown up during the 1980s, when Patsy Cline was becoming an icon, were beginning to use her recording of "Crazy," with its complexity and appeal as popular music, in new and different ways.

On May 24, 2003, Willie Nelson and his TV Birthday Bash graced the cover of *TV Guide,* then still one of the top-selling publications in the United States, with a circulation in excess of twenty million. The *TV Guide* article burst a bubble for some, as it revealed that Nelson had written "Crazy." By this point, a whole new generation solely associated "Crazy" with Patsy Cline. Nelson even took advantage of Patsy Cline's iconic status as he plugged his "new" CD called *Willie Nelson—Crazy—The Demo Sessions.* Patsy Cline's iconography was so strong that any rediscovered "new" material sold. Yet as Nelson plugged the CD on this TV special, all it did was remind TV viewers that the song had become Patsy Cline's, even if Nelson was the composer.

Popular TV shows have regularly used Patsy Cline. For example, the creators of the hit show *Lost* (2004–10, on ABC) employed Patsy Cline's hits as a narrative motif. In this serial narrative, which that followed the lives of plane crash survivors on a mysterious tropical island somewhere in the South Pacific, each episode featured a flashback to another point in a character's life, and this was where Patsy Cline songs defined the mood. Key were the memories of Kate, who in a first season's flashback remembered Patsy Cline's "Leaving on My Mind" as an Australian farmer gave her a ride in his car. In the second season's "What Kate Did" and the third season's "Left Behind," Kate remembered Cline singing "Walkin' After Midnight," on a record player, and later as a tow truck helped her. Patsy Cline's songs were so familiar and so suggestive of mood that a mass TV audience easily understood their use in the ongoing story line.

Hollywood feature films played over and over again on cable TV's multitude of movie channels. For example, Howard Deutch's comedy *The Whole Ten Yards* (2004) used "I Don't Wanna," from Patsy Cline's 4-Star period, as part of its comic story. In contrast, Martin Scorsese's *The Departed* (2006) was a crime thriller, staring Leonardo DiCaprio, Jack Nicholson, and Matt Damon. To represent a less complicated past, Scorsese used Patsy Cline's "Sweet Dreams" five times in that movie.

In the early days of the Web, on June 27, 1996, Per Jonsson, in Sweden, started an international Patsy Cline Web site and enabled Patsy Cline fans from around the world to share their love of Patsy. On March 5, 1998, from Michigan, Lisa Flood launched a second important new site called Patsified.com. Flood posted, "I hope you enjoy [my Web site], and that it spurs you to read more about her fascinating life. If it does, then my job is done."

Flood coined a word for an obsessed fan: *Patsified*. She wrote, "I myself was Patsified, in spite of all of my resistance over the years. All I have to do is look at a picture of [Patsy], and she seems to just smile out at us as if to say she knows we're all a buncha damn fools, but she loves us anyway." Flood was a new fan, as she was born in 1960, and never experienced Patsy Cline's initial popularity. She had earned a Bachelor of Fine Arts, and was a typical Baby Boomer fan of Patsy Cline. Her musical tastes ran a wide spectrum: classical, pop, country, world music, jazz, soul, and R&B. Her favorite singers, apart from Patsy Cline, were Edith Piaf, Jerry Jeff Walker, the Beatles, Roberta Flack, Jimmy Buffett, Gordon Lightfoot, The Killers, and Johnny Mathis. Along with the rest of the movie-going world, Flood discovered Patsy Cline in the 1980s. In October 1996, she switched on her local cable system and found *Sweet Dreams* playing on HBO. Her life changed.

Not to embarrass herself, as a college-educated middle-class American, Flood secretly bought a *12 Greatest Hits* tape. "I didn't want to spend money on a CD." She anticipated that once she tired of the tape, she would throw it away. But she was hooked, so she spent sixty dollars for *The Patsy Cline Collection* box set. Flood confessed, "Against my will, against my better sense, against all logic [I was Patsified]."

So this thirty-six-year-old mother learned the proper computer skills and created an important Web site. In her most important contribution, she took out a notebook, and while listening to her box set, noted every word Patsy Cline sang in every song. What she found was that the recordings were the definitive versions, as sheet music proved misleading.

In April 2004 came the third major Web site—www.patsycline.info—from Bill Cox of Knoxville, Tennessee. He had regularly logged onto and posted on Per Jonsson's and Lisa Flood's Web sites. Cox described his own Patsification and noted the insanity and hard work of maintaining a Web site: "Bill, What Were You Thinking? Over the past year, I've asked myself that question on many occasions." But when Lisa Flood complained that she needed help maintaining her own site, Cox started of Knoxville, Tennessee volunteered to help Flood. He first posted an invaluable Patsy Cline discography, and then, in August 2002, agreed to assist Flood with her "Patsy Cline" news section. By April 2003, Cox took the complete plunge, and registered www.patsycline.info—and added more pages.

Cox then launched officially on March 5, 2004, the forty-first anniversary Patsy Cline's airplane crash. At least a dozen other Web sites have come and gone, but Bill Cox and Per Jonsson continue as the standard-bearers.

Other technological changes in the first decade of the twenty-first century helped spread the iconic fame of Patsy Cline. In February 2005, YouTube began hosting its video-sharing

Web site, where users could upload, view, and share video clips. This site quickly became a repository of bootleg videos of Patsy Cline clips, posted by fans. In July 2006, the company revealed that people were watching more than 100 million videos every day. As the first decade of the twenty-first century ended, nearly five thousand Patsy Cline–related videos are available on YouTube.

Over Labor Day weekend of 2005, Patsy fans journeyed to Winchester to witness the unveiling of the historic marker (noted at the close of the previous chapter) and they could also purchase the DVD *Patsy Cline: Sweet Dreams Still*. Most had seen a version on public television but wanted to purchase their own copy. Charles Dick made that possible. *Patsy Cline: Sweet Dreams Still* offered the first legal compilation of uninterrupted DVD copies of films Patsy Cline had made.

The DVD starts with Patsy Cline singing "A Church, a Courtroom and Goodbye," filmed at a Grand Ole Opry show in 1955. Thereafter fans could see and hear her sing "Come On In" (in two different versions), "Walkin' After Midnight" (in two different versions), "I Fall to Pieces," her magnificent "Crazy," and her final hit, "She's Got You." There was a Grand Ole Opry cast (including Patsy) performance of "I Saw the Light," and a duet with Ferlin Husky, "Let It Snow," which neither Cline nor Husky had ever recorded for an LP. In all, this remarkable video contained fourteen songs, plus commentary by journalist Robert Oermann, and it ended with a "conversation with Charlie Dick."

Charles Dick had made a deal with American Public Television (hereafter APT), based in Boston, to premiere the video in June 2005 on public television in the United States. In its publicity, APT announced that it was celebrating the "Timeless Sound of Patsy Cline in a New Public Television Program." Its PR showed the change that iconization had made: "Patsy Cline had a hypnotic, seductive sound capable of luring your ears and absorbing your senses. Set against the jazzy rhythms of her band, Cline's smoky voice loomed over the music with the perfect mix of country charm and pop appeal." While the quality of the filmed material varied, Charles Dick had compiled the best of her filmed shows. On June 28, 2006, Bill Cox wrote on his web site, "This is the DVD Patsy Cline fans have been waiting for. ALL of the performance clips are shown in their entirety with no voiceovers or commentary." Cox noted that the last two clips came from Patsy's final TV appearance, filmed on Tuesday, February 26, 1963; she would be in Kansas City the following Sunday—and would then die the following Tuesday.

In the United States, no week went past without some venue presenting a Patsy Cline tribute show. *Always . . . Patsy Cline* was even mounted Off-Broadway. On June 26, 1997, *Always . . . Patsy Cline* premiered for a six-month run, and while the *New York Times* panned the production because it was not a big-time musical, on June 25, the *New York Post*'s Clive Barnes explained what he had seen and heard: "Ever since the premature but romantic deaths of Shelly and Keats, it has been evident to the cynically inclined that, for an artist, an early demise can prove a shrewd career move. There is little more poignant or tantalizing than the specter of lost promise." This was, for Barnes, the basic appeal of the play. He went on to explain that he was touched by the "odd but effective tribute to the Cline mystique," and stated, "Against all my expectations, I thoroughly enjoyed it. (I saw a quite different Patsy Cline show in London a few years back.)" He liked the tribute singer, Toni Lynn Palazola, but qualified his praise: "Like James Cagney, [Patsy Cline] is easy to imitate, impossible to capture." Barnes, known for his stuffy put-downs for the *New York Times* (1965–78), explained that he had spent an evening of good-natured, sentimental, down-home nostalgia, full of torch songs for betrayed love. He judged the work for what it was—a tribute to Patsy Cline, and he ended by reminding readers how great a singer Patsy was.[8]

Outside New York City, *Always . . . Patsy Cline* continually found devoted audiences. Often productions would feature former TV stars in the Louise Seger role. For example, in Las Vegas, on August 3, 2000, *Always . . . Patsy Cline* opened with Sally Struthers, star of the number one TV show in the United States from 1972 to 1974, *All in the Family,* in the Louise Seger part. Business was good, as tourists embraced the tribute. And the Baby Boomers who could afford Las Vegas remembered Sally Struthers from the hit TV comedy. By this point, everyone who journeyed to Las Vegas knew the iconic Patsy Cline songs and so Struthers served to differentiate this production.[9]

All over the United States, this two-woman play did well in smaller community theaters; it sold out—even in university towns. Consider the case of Eugene, Oregon, home of the University of Oregon. On September 5, 2004, the *Eugene Register-Guard* titled its Fall Arts Preview "From Ballet to Flamenco, from Chopin to Patsy Cline." And so, on November 24, 2005, the local repertory theater featured *Always . . . Patsy Cline,* and packed the house. That same week, members of the University of Oregon community could also have attended a chamber music series at the University of Oregon; *The Real Inspector Hound,* a whodunit parody by Tom Stoppard; *Lysistrata,* Aristophanes' bawdy satire; or the Eugene Symphony Orchestra. But *Always . . . Patsy Cline* drew the biggest crowds. Patsy Cline had crossed over to appeal even to an academic audience.[10]

The Dean Regan tribute, *A Closer Walk with Patsy Cline,* never tried Off-Broadway, but it played throughout the United States, even at the Wayside Theater, in Middletown, Virginia, in 2006—sixty years after Patsy had lived a mile from the theater. The *Winchester Star* printed a glowing review by Frances Lowe, who had grew up listening to Patsy Cline: "Boy, was I surprised." Morgan Duke, as Patsy Cline, impressed Lowe with her singing, as did the band, which was positioned in the center of the stage. For an added touch, the Wayside Theater projected images of Patsy Cline on the wall above the band through most of the show, adding a multimedia component.[11]

While the two key tribute plays could be found all across the United States, by May 15, 2003, Patsy Cline's music was inspiring "serious art"—in this case a ballet. The Ballet Tennessee spring production of 2003 was entitled *Ballet Goes Country . . . and More*. It contained three parts, including a tribute to Patsy Cline. Choreographed by Van Cura, of the Ballet Tennessee, at the University of Tennessee-Chattanooga, this effort took a chance based on Patsy's crossover appeal. It worked.[12]

———————————

Contemporary stars celebrated Patsy's work and covered "her" songs. So for example, in 1997, driving south on I-81 following a concert, the *Cat in the Hat* tour, then country music sensation Terri Clark emerged from the stateroom on her tour bus yelling: "Stop the bus!" The driver obeyed, and she directed him off I-81 to Shenandoah Memorial Park, where Patsy Cline is buried. So, a little after two a.m., Clark led her bus to the cemetery, where they put pennies on Patsy's grave, and then sat quietly for twenty minutes. As they left, no one spoke.

"Fans at Patsy Cline's Grave"

Clark was hardly alone in her admiration. From 1997 to 2004, as far as it can be determined, the following musical artists covered "Crazy:" Moe Bandy (1997), Mandy Fox (1997), Rosie Flores & Ray Campi (1997), Four Bitchin' Babes (1997), Don McLean (1997), Palolo (1997), Yami Bolo (1998), Johnny Cash & Willie Nelson (1998), Renee Geyer (1998), Kidney Thieves (1998), Kukuruza (1998), Marisela (1998), David Osborne (1998), LeAnn Rimes (1999), James Galway (1999), Marc Jordan (1999), Dobie Gray (2000), Hot Club de Norvege (2000), Lori Johnson (2000), the Motels (2000), Jimmy Rosenberg & Ola Kvernberg (2000), Colleen Sexton (2000), Timi Yuro (2000), Hawk Arps Jazz Band (2000), Michele Anastasio (2001), Sue Keller (2001), David McLeod (2001), David Acker (2002), Blue Sandcastle (2002), Tierney Sutton (2002), All-Star Girls of Country (2003), Stephen Collins (2003), Diana Krall (2003), J. C. Lodge (2003), Frank Lowe (2003), Norah Jones (2003), and Chaka Khan (2004)—with more covers to come from 2004-2011. If one added in other Patsy Cline covers, the list grew to nearly one thousand.

In 1999 came a new generation of digitally created electronic "duets" with Patsy Cline—now far easier to fashion than the Patsy Cline and Jim Reeves duets of 1981. For example, on October 2, 1999, a whole CD called simply *Duets* went to country number 70 on the *Billboard* charts. These had been mixed in Nashville, Los Angeles, and Hollywood. Released by Mercury Records, all were overdubs of Sony-owned 4-Star songs: John Berry and "There He Goes," Bob Carlisle and "That Wonderful Someone," Beth Nielsen Chapman and "If I Could Only Stay Asleep," Glen Campbell and "Too Many Secrets," Mila Mason and "Crazy Dreams," Willie Nelson and "Life's Railway To Heaven," Waylon Jennings and "Just Out of Reach," Crystal Gayle and "I Can't Forget You," and Michelle Wright and "Walkin' After Midnight." All these duets helped new fans discover Patsy Cline.

In September 2003, MCA released *Remembering Patsy,* a collection of Cline's hits, as performed to new arrangements by various current stars from the country, pop, and jazz worlds. Country star Terri Clark did her version of "Walkin' After Midnight." Contemporary Christian singer Amy Grant recorded "Back in Baby's Arms." Jazz artist Diana Krall transformed "Crazy" into a lazy lounge ballad, while pop superstar Norah Jones covered "Why Can't He Be You." And Nat King Cole's daughter, Natalie Cole, took on "I Fall to Pieces," with twice as many strings as Owen Bradley had originally hired. Finally, k.d. lang offered a rendering of "Leavin' on Your Mind," bluer than the original. But with the Internet surging, fans turned to downloading Patsy Cline as originally recorded.

The biggest name in total music sales at the end of the first decade of the twenty-first century was nineteen-year-old Taylor Swift. In article after article, Swift told interviewers how much she loved Patsy Cline. Swift was born in Pennsylvania in 1989, three years after the bio-pic *Sweet Dreams* had come out. She saw it on television, and begged her mother and grandmother to play Patsy Cline for her. Swift who turned eight on December 13, 1997, was as struck by Cline's voice as the eight-year-old Virginia Hensley had been by Big Band singers in 1940. Swift was a product of the iconization of Patsy Cline.

By 2009, the nineteen-year-old Swift ranked as the largest selling singer in the United States, yet she was harangued as not being country enough—or not country at all. Like her idol, Patsy Cline, who was labeled a pop singer in the 1960s, the genre of country music was again changing. Cline and Swift broke with the confines of the genre. For example, the Taylor Swift and T-Pain duet of "Thug Story" proved a very funny and lighthearted mash-up of country and rap. The enormous popularity of Taylor Swift—and her continual references to Patsy Cline—simply reminded music lovers that labels like "country music" invited a process of cross-fertilization.

In 2009, Rosanne Cash again brought back her connection to Patsy Cline—thirteen years after the influential article in the *New York Times Magazine*. It turned out that, in 1973, when Rosanne Cash was eighteen years old and traveling with her father, Johnny Cash grew disturbed about his daughter's musical knowledge. So Johnny Cash put together a list of what he called "100 essential country songs." Rosanne Cash saved the list, and in 2009 turned it into a widely praised CD called "The List," featuring her versions of the songs her father championed. One was Patsy's "She's Got You." Thus Rosanne Cash added to the iconic image of Patsy Cline not only with words, as in 1996, but with a popular, praised CD in 2009.

No analysis of Patsy Cline's continuing influence could even be complete. As the first decade of the twenty-first century ended, references to her steadily flooded the new and old media. As fans throughout the world embraced her iconic status, they added new meanings to her as a symbol. Consider that in 2002, on a cable TV special cablecast in the United States, noted poet and intellectual Maya Angelou said of Patsy Cline, "It's wonderful that whenever her name is mentioned, people's voices fall and they become right sentimental. And, rightly so."[13]

NOTES

Chapter 11

[1] Billboard, June 28, 1997: 67.

[2] CW, August 5, 1997:31-32.

[3] Billboard, March 20, 1999: 35.

[4] WS, July 20, 1999: B1.

[5] The Richmond Times-Dispatch, March 2, 2002: B4.

[6] Variety, March 21, 2004: 45.

[7] Posted on Per Jonsson's website by Ellen Tunstall of Chonshohocken, Pennsylvania, United States (a suburb of Philadelphia) on 30 March 1997.

[8] web site www.tg4.ie/bearla/corp; WS, July 29, 2009, B1.

[9] The Las Vegas Review-Journal, August 4, 2002: E1.

[10] The Eugene (OR) Register-Guard, September 5, 2004: C1.

[11] WS, February 6, 2006: B1.

[12] The Chattanoogan [newspaper], May 15, 2003: C1.

[13] Country Music Television cable television's "Countdown of the 40 Greatest Women in Country Music," shown repeatedly during December, 2002.

INDEX

Fredericksburg, 115

Gore, 33, 36-38, 58, 74-76, 78

Lexington, 43

Middletown, 70, 383

Portsmouth, 57

Round Hill, 72

Virginia Foundation for Women, 359, 375

Virginia Legends, 374

Virginia Military Institute (VMI), 45

W

"Walkin' After Midnight" (Cline), 17, 121, 124-27, 136, 143, 145, 151-52, 155, 157-63, 168-69, 172, 176, 180, 296, 376-77, 385

Washington and Lee College, 50, 356

"Washington and Lee Swing, The," 46

Wasserman, Lew, 2, 53, 295, 309

Webb, Del, 233-34

Wells, Kitty, 122, 127, 130, 222, 264, 300

West, Dottie, 279, 282

Wetsel, John, 352, 356

Whitacre, Frank, 78, 109

Whiteman, Paul, 49, 51

Williams, Hank, 125, 180-81, 260

Williams, Rebecca "Becky," 347

Wilt, Sylvia Hensley, 317, 322, 326, 346-47, 350, 354

WINC, 89, 230, 327, 333

Winchester Memorial Hospital, 34, 174-75, 348

Windle, Ken, 87, 89, 94, 100

WMAL-TV, 128, 143

WSM, 126, 181, 209-11, 215, 218-19, 231, 284

WTTG-TV, 175, 179

Wynette, Tammy, 22, 214, 298

Y

"You Belong to Me" (Cline), 24

"Your Cheatin' Heart" (Cline), 98

Z

Zuckerman, Charles, 318, 321